Proactive Recruiting

In A War For Talent Economy

By Paul Siker

First published in 2007 by:
Advanced Recruiting Trends, LLC (USA)
15636 Britenbush Court, Suite 200
Waterford VA 20197
(540) 882-9077
www.artofrecruiting.com

10 9 8 7 6 5 4 3 2 1

ISBN 978-0-9788674-0-9

Printed in the United States of America

To Joni,
For Your Love, For Your Laughter

Acknowledgements

So many people have played an instrumental role in my recruiting career that it would be impossible to thank them all, or thank them enough. That said, I offer special thanks to the following: My brother, David Siker, MD for recruiting me into recruiting, and for projecting an infectious entrepreneurial spirit; Mike Kohonoski and Bill Joyce for not only being great business partners and friends, but also for personifying integrity in action and deed; Don Evans for his friendship, all his efforts with ART, and hours of spirited debate about virtually every facet of the recruitment lifecycle.

I would be remiss if I didn't pause to recognize the entire cast of characters at The Guild Corporation, truly one of the finest (and funniest) recruiting teams ever assembled: Danielle LaCharite, Kelly Edens, Heather Young, Jeanne Hickox, Tracy Ferry, Pam Berg, Laura Poisson, Jenn McCormick, Angela Harrell, Julie Vogt, Bill Boczany, Sam Russell, Mark Spanninger, Dave Grant, Dave Martin, Stephen McCarthy, Rob Todas, Brian Sarman, and Jeremy Bennett. Whether you were aware of it at the time or not, each of you taught me something of consequence.

I also have to thank Patrick Marshall and Rob Patten, both for their years of friendship, but especially for their willingness to critically read initial drafts of this book. I also extend my gratitude to others in the recruiting landscape who have been helpful at various junctures: Rob Caulfield, Bob Corlett, Andy Misovec, John Rudder, and John West.

Also, I want to thank the many client organizations I have come to know and the countless recruiters with whom I have had the privilege to work. There are too many names to cite here, but I trust that you will know who you are and will accept my heartfelt thanks.

Your excitement and passion for recruiting is an ongoing inspiration to me.

I must extend a special note of thanks to Brenda Sargent for her editorial diligence and devotion, and especially for her efforts to keep this project moving forward. Thanks also to Noemi Arthur for her periodic editorial input, and to Debbie Ranson for her ongoing graphic design support.

Finally, when I set out to write this book, I'm sure that I wasn't truly cognizant of what I was getting myself into. Between search projects, training engagements, and various other commitments my greatest frustration on this journey has been finding the time to write. With this in mind I gratefully acknowledge my wife, Joni, and my sons, Steven and Scott for allowing me to steal time that undoubtedly belonged to them.

Table Of Contents

Preface

Like so many people within the recruiting landscape, some twenty years ago I found myself entering a profession for which I was admittedly ill-equipped. Unlike most other vocations, one truth about recruiting is the frequency with which people simply fall into the role of "recruiter."

As a colleague of mine has aptly remarked on various occasions, *"Paul, no one at the age of 12 says, 'When I grow up, I want to be a recruiter'."* And this assessment is correct; at the point when kids consider future careers they tend to think about becoming Doctors, Scientists, Police Officers, Athletes, etc. But I have yet to meet anyone who, at a very young age, has said that they envisioned themselves becoming a recruiter or sales professional.

When I got into the business of recruiting, I joined a small start-up firm called The Guild Corporation that had been started by my older brother, David, and a friend of his, Mike Kohonoski. Both had graduated from Carnegie Mellon University with degrees in Electrical Engineering, and after working in the trenches as engineers, and briefly for a national recruiting firm, elected to create their own technical search firm in McLean, VA outside of Washington, D.C.

In joining The Guild Corporation, I found myself within a fledgling business. I don't use the term "fledgling" lightly. This was truly a start-up entity, comprised of two guys and a Macintosh computer with an external floppy drive. We had a reception area that was outfitted with a desk, on which sat a broken CRT monitor, and a phone that didn't work. A sweater was permanently draped over the receptionist's chair, and we would rotate various pieces of fruit on the reception area desk to lend the appearance that we *actually had* a receptionist.

At this time, there was no Internet, email, or voicemail, and fax machines were a rarity. My formal training commenced and ended in my first week on the job, and was largely comprised of situational role-plays that were designed to expose me to some of the selling scenarios I would likely encounter.

It immediately became evident that my deficiencies as a recruiter were as vast as they were profound. While theoretically I had a degree in science, my degree was in Political Science (ah yes, the default college major!!), which hardly equipped me to interact with Engineers and software professionals. In truth – I knew nothing. I knew nothing about recruiting, nothing about working with candidates (let alone interviewing them), nothing about the technology domain, and perhaps most significantly, nothing about sales.

In my first year in the business I worked extremely hard and muddled through. Actually, I did okay, primarily because I had two people monitoring my every move.

But in my second year, I hit the proverbial sophomore slump. I officially knew enough to be dangerous -- mostly to myself. Deals that I worked on seemed to regularly find the most innovative ways of blowing up at the most inopportune times and in the most elaborate manner.

It got to the point where I likened the business as being similar to walking through a mine-field – the days you got through unscathed were the days you made money. But most of my days weren't complete without a couple of significant explosions. During this timeframe I continually reminded myself that "adversity builds character", and became convinced that if this were true, I was rapidly becoming one of the biggest characters in the metropolitan Washington area.

During my teenage years, my father, E.S. Siker, MD, offered timeless advice in saying, *"Son, always consider the consequences of your actions."* These words had always served as a guiding light, prompting me to consciously and thoughtfully consider important decisions in my life. As I confronted my inadequacies as a recruiter, I couldn't help but wonder if I had disregarded my father's advice by entering a profession without fully understanding what I was getting myself into.

As the months unfolded, I started to seriously question whether or not I was in the right business. One day, I met a friend for lunch who shared a simple observation when he said, *"Paul – it's like chess – to be successful in this business, you have to think strategically, execute tactically, and work doable deals."* Sometimes it's the seemingly simple pieces of advice that can cause an epiphany, and for me these words were catalytic.

It was as though someone clicked a switch. As I really became cognizant about the assignments I was working on, and began taking the time to bring a value-add to candidate and client relationships, I started realizing greater levels of success. As I began to meaningfully appreciate and understand candidate motivators, and the subtleties of relation-based selling, most of my deals started closing themselves. My management and utilization of time improved dramatically. As the recession of the early 1990's unfolded, I pursued understanding my client's business mission with greater interest and intensity, and despite the recession, repeat business opportunities presented themselves with increasing frequency.

While my brother had since departed the firm to go to medical school, we began adding staff and brought in a third partner, Bill Joyce. Over the next 7 years we grew net revenues by over 25% annually and typically achieved a 95% annual repeat-business ratio with our clients. At the point where we sold the firm, we had 18 tenured recruiters and less than a 5% annual attrition. We had built an extremely service oriented, boutique search firm, and had crafted a brand identity that was synonymous with quality.

In my own experience as a recruiter, I have endured a great deal of what I refer to as "experiential learning." As my father-in-law, Julius Nemeth once advised me: *"Good judgment comes from experience....and experience, well that comes from poor judgment."*

To his point, some of the lessons that I have learned over the years have been extremely painful, costing me a significant amount of time and money. Other lessons were true revelations, where something really wonderful happened because I had the good fortune to effect a creative solution or approach that meaningfully addressed an aspect of the recruiting sales puzzle.

Barring an unforeseen economic collapse, we are poised to be in a candidate-driven marketplace for the foreseeable future. The demand for talent will continue to increase, which means that organizations and recruiters will face a significantly greater degree of competition in engaging, securing, and winning the best possible talent for existing openings.

In the training programs that I conduct, I regularly cite my belief that the recruitment sales process is among the most complex selling cycles within the business world, principally because many aspects of the recruitment sales process are not particularly or naturally intuitive. In recognition of this, I have devoted a tremendous amount of time and energy to exploring how recruiters can optimize their performance, while minimizing the amount of negative experiential learning that they must incur; and this is ultimately the underlying premise of this book, *Proactive Recruiting in a War for Talent Economy.*

In this initial edition of the book, I have tried to address what I perceive to be fundamental truths about various aspects of the recruitment sales cycle. I have also highlighted specific approaches and techniques that will positively impact the performance of all recruiters, regardless of whether they work within an in-house corporate recruitment function, or work within a staffing agency or search firm. Furthermore, I have addressed subject matter in a manner that doesn't merely consider the theoretical, but that presents tested, real-world, tactical approaches that fundamentally work.

Whether you have been performing as a recruiter for ten years or ten weeks, and regardless of whether you are an agency or corporate recruiter, I'm confident that as you read this book, you'll uncover a host of useful information and ideas that favorably impact your own efforts in recruiting. To this end, I wish you all the best.

Paul Siker
Waterford, Virginia

Chapter 1: Passive Vs. Proactive Recruiting

For many organizations, both large and small, key talent acquisition and general staff recruitment are a fundamentally passive affair. This chapter compares and contrasts passive and proactive recruiting methodologies and highlights the importance of implementing proactive recruiting tactics in a tightening employment marketplace.

In most corporate environments, the principal external recruitment approaches are:

- Corporate Website Employment Listings
- Print Recruitment Advertising (Newspapers/Journals)
- Internet Job Board Postings
- External Career Fairs
- Internal Referral Programs
- Mining Internal Candidate Databases

In the overall recruitment matrix, each of these approaches has its place and will yield some measure of success in identifying talent. With the exception of Internal Referral Programs and mining archived candidate data, all of these approaches are passive in nature. The relative success or failure of each approach depends upon whether or not prospective candidates respond to the particular recruitment method being utilized.

For a newspaper ad to be successful, a prospective candidate must read the ad and elect to respond. Similarly, with an internet job board posting, a prospective candidate must invoke a search and then transmit a resume to the postings that are of interest. For a Career Fair to be successful, a candidate must first know about the event and then elect to attend.

Passive recruitment approaches can work very well when an organization is looking to staff a role that doesn't demand significant experience or a highly specific skills inventory. Passive recruitment methods can also be very effective when used in an industry area where a robust applicant pool exists or in a geographic area where labor is plentiful.

However, when utilized to recruit highly specialized talent or within a highly competitive industry sector where the demand for talent outstrips the available supply, passive recruitment approaches can become inefficient and waste considerable resources (notably time, energy, money). Let's address the positives and negatives associated with each of these recruitment modes.

Corporate Website Career Listings

It makes perfect sense for an organization to post employment openings on its website. But the overall effectiveness of these postings is ultimately dependent upon an organization's ability to attract applicable candidates to its web site. If an organization enjoys some measure of name recognition or brand identity or is regarded as a leader in a particular industry, the likelihood of securing qualified unsolicited candidates for employment openings is reasonably good. Success in garnering candidates via a corporate website will also vary widely dependent upon an organization's business, location, and the nature of its employment opportunities. If an organization has been able to generate a public relations buzz that highlights accomplishments, growth, new project/product initiatives, etc., a steady flow of quality candidates may well come knocking at its door. But for most organizations, website employment listings will only supplement or compliment external recruitment advertising or Internal Referral Program activities.

Internal Referral Programs

Of all the approaches highlighted above, Internal Referral Programs are probably the most effective. Not surprisingly, Internal

Referral Programs are the only active recruiting method on this list. Internal Referral Programs are great because: A) the individual making the referral in all likelihood has prior work history with the candidate who is being referred; and B) some genuine consideration has been given to the abilities and personality of the candidate being referred. In many respects a referral candidate has been pre-qualified and is perceived to be a fit for the organization and the work at hand.

However, the actual effectiveness of Internal Referral Programs ends up being a mixed bag. Some programs provide nominal incentives to existing employees to provide referrals, implying a philosophic belief that it is simply incumbent upon every employee to help the organization identify and secure talent. More progressive organizations offer substantial incentives to employees who provide referrals that result in a hire.

Interestingly, offering a sizeable bounty for internal referrals is not a guarantee that the program will yield favorable results. I recall speaking with a Recruiting Manager from a rapidly growing consulting firm who lamented that despite having an Internal Referral Program with awards up to a $5,000.00 bonus for providing a lead that resulted in a hire, the organization had failed to bring in a single recruit. Not one. Despite regularly promoting the referral program in staff and management meetings, the Recruiting Manager confided that his firm's Internal Referral Program was an abject failure. Individuals within the organization simply didn't feel passionate about the growth of the firm or were too preoccupied with their own work to invest the time and energy necessary to bring other qualified professionals to the firm's attention.

During the employment boom of the late 1990's, some Internal Referral Programs offered significant employee incentives (trips, cars, cash, you name it), but many of these programs were ultimately deemed to be too expensive. Also, some employers had difficulty ascertaining whether employees were making referrals because they truly believed in the individual's ability or because they were more interested in the prospect of getting a fat referral bonus.

More recently, some organizations have adopted pro-rated referral bonus programs. In these programs, the referral bonus is spread out over a period of three to five years and is predicated on the new hire sticking around and becoming a tenured employee.

Regardless of the degree to which existing employees are offered an incentive, an Internal Referral Program's ultimate success is directly tied to how effectively it is promoted to existing employees. For the purposes of this discussion, let's assume that Internal Referral Programs are a viable recruitment tool if implemented properly.

Print Advertising/ Internet Job Boards & Job Postings

Help wanted newspaper ads and job board advertising generate an estimated $10 billion - $20 billion in revenue. That's a lot of recruitment advertising.

As newspaper subscriptions nationwide have diminished over the past few years, employers have increasingly steered an escalating portion of their recruitment advertising dollars towards online job boards such as Monster.com, CareerBuilder, and HotJobs. Additionally, niche job boards can be found for virtually every industry and employment discipline, with more on the way.

The vast majority of employers utilize both print and online recruitment advertising as a principal means of attracting prospective candidates. Many organizations also allocate some portion of their recruitment budget to industry trade publications that reach specific target audiences, and employers are increasingly utilizing niche job boards oriented to distinct industry sectors.

While still passive in nature, Industry Trade Publications and niche Internet Job Boards channel recruitment advertising dollars in a more targeted fashion. By advertising job openings in these forums, an organization can theoretically promote its available positions to a fairly specific and therefore more qualified audience. But, as is the case with any passive recruitment channel, these methods only work when individuals actually see and subsequently elect to respond to the advertisement.

It cannot be denied that newspaper and trade publication ads, and online job boards yield candidates. And there is anecdotal evidence to support the fact that better written ads (more detailed/more descriptive) will produce better response rates. As a component of an overall recruiting matrix, it makes tremendous sense to utilize these advertising channels. However, as a primary mechanism for securing talent, especially highly skilled individuals, these approaches have distinct limitations and inefficiencies.

Any experienced recruiter can readily describe an occasion (or perhaps many occasions) when they ran a newspaper ad or job board posting that yielded either no responses, or even worse, numerous responses from people who were absolutely unqualified for the position at hand.

In my experience, the degree of complexity associated with a position directly correlates to a recruiter's likely success in attracting qualified candidates via a newspaper ad or job board posting. As a rule, the more complex the position, the less likely a recruiter will find applicable candidates by running a newspaper want ad or job board posting. But in the present market climate, job complexity is not the only factor that dictates whether an ad or posting will be successful. Another issue is the relative demand for talent in a particular market job niche or market sector. The trucking industry, for example, cannot staff available openings. There simply aren't enough drivers to go around.

Career Fairs Or Job Fairs

Like newspaper or job board advertising, Job Fairs are essentially a passive means of securing talent. While they can offer an employer the opportunity to gain exposure to numerous prospective candidates in a short timeframe, there is little guarantee that highly qualified professionals will attend these functions. Also, because multiple employers participate in a typical Job Fair, highly talented professionals who do elect to attend often end up being courted by multiple suitors. No single employer has exclusivity with respect to an attractive prospect, so competition for the best people is particularly keen.

Furthermore, some professionals will never attend a Job Fair. They see Job Fairs as nothing more than "Cattle Calls." Finally, some professionals, especially those who are gainfully employed, have to wonder who else they might encounter at a Job Fair; and heaven help them if they encounter a colleague, or worse yet their boss. While convenient for the employer, numerous job seekers who have attended these functions report that they were not impressed by the process of standing in a line of people waiting for their opportunity to briefly interact with an employer.

Some Job Fairs are free and are sponsored by Chambers of Commerce, local governments, or Economic Development Agencies. Colleges and Universities also host Job Fairs, albeit on a more limited basis. But, free doesn't necessarily translate to productive.

Most Job Fairs require employers to pay a fee that can run anywhere from $1,000.00 to $5,000.00 or more, depending on the event, the anticipated attendance, and the target audience. For an organization seeking to make a number of basic hires quickly, participating in a Job Fair may yield results. But again, for organizations seeking to identify highly skilled professionals, particularly in a functional niche or discipline where demand outstrips supply, Job Fairs are not necessarily a great investment.

Internal Corporate Candidate Databases

Many organizations have invested in the creation of proprietary candidate databases, while many others have purchased off-the-shelf Applicant Tracking System (ATS) software or Recruiting Information Management Systems (RIMS) to archive and manage job requisitions, candidate data, and resumes. Internal Corporate Candidate Databases can be very useful. A candidate deemed too inexperienced for a particular role might be well worth contacting again in a year or two. An individual with a solid background who is not quite aligned with a current opportunity is certainly someone an organization should make note of and consider for future opportunities.

At the end of the day, candidate databases are only as good as the data they contain, and many of them are rife with data integrity issues. The reason for this is that people are incredibly dynamic creatures. They move geographically. Phone numbers change. Skill sets change. If an individual submitted a resume to an organization a year ago, chances are very high that he or she ultimately made a job move and probably is not interested or poised to consider making another move. Furthermore, if an organization uses a distributed database solution, there is no assurance that individuals using the tool are consistently entering data in a uniform manner. While many organizations have candidate databases that contain a great deal of information on individuals who previously submitted resumes, the actual value of this data and the degree to which it is utilized for new recruiting initiatives is difficult to assess.

Passive Recruiting In A War For Talent Economy

The problem with passive recruitment techniques, especially newspaper ads and job board postings, is that their relative effectiveness is predicated entirely upon whether or not qualified potential applicants actually even see the advertisement. While many individuals utilize newspaper want ads or job board postings as a primary means of executing a job search, just as many opt to utilize their own network of contacts to secure a new opportunity. Because newspaper ads, job boards, trade publications, and corporate websites have no ability to proactively engage a prospective candidate, they have an undeniably limited potential audience.

Increasingly, I am encountering organizations that regard passive recruiting channels as being entirely ineffective, especially with respect to helping them obtain mission critical or highly specialized talent. In various instances, despite having spent thousands of dollars to run numerous postings on a plethora of different job boards, these same organizations were forced to bring in outside search firms to address their openings. These scenarios are not an anomaly.

Passive recruitment is not terribly different from casting a big net into the ocean, pulling it in, and hoping for a great catch. Depending on the type of talent being sought, an employer may ultimately get what they're looking for, but chances are just as good that they won't. Additionally, recruiters all too often become mired in sorting through a sea of unqualified candidate responses with the hope of finding one or more truly viable prospects. In summary, passive recruitment techniques can be a real "crapshoot" and are dependent upon a recruiter being fortunate enough to put forth the right ad at the right time via the right medium to attract the "right" candidate.

Further complicating the effective utilization of passive recruitment methods is the reality that demographic and other employment data suggests that the battle for skilled talent will grow increasingly more competitive. According to Bureau of Labor Statistics data, 46 percent of our collective workforce is comprised of Baby Boomers, individuals who were born from 1946 – 1964. This group of individuals consists of 76 million people.

Generation X consists of individuals born from 1965 – 1981. In contrast, this cohort is made up of 45 million people and accounts for 29 percent of the overall workforce. The size and potential impact of Generation Y (1982 – 2000) is more complicated to assess, because consensus has not entirely solidified among statisticians regarding the birth years that should be used in the demarcation of this population cohort.

If we merely consider the Baby Boomer Generation, the reality is that individuals born in 1946 will hit retirement (age 65) in 2011, or several years from now. Many Boomers aren't necessarily waiting until they are 65 to retire. Some unknown number will exit the workforce sooner.

Much debate has ensued regarding how the workforce will be impacted by the loss of these older workers. Some experts contend that the departure of Boomers from the workforce will result not only in the loss of substantial industry domain knowledge, but will also create an even more dramatic demand for workers that could result in millions of unfilled jobs.

This view is not universally shared or accepted. The U.S. Bureau of Labor Statistics has expressed concern regarding predictions that have been made using BLS data to support the concept of a looming labor shortage. While the BLS doesn't deny the reality of a demographic shift or an aging workforce, they have argued that studies promoting the idea of a significant labor shortage fail to consider that a portion of the Boomer Generation may delay retirement or re-enter the workforce on a part-time basis.

Currently, the U.S. Unemployment Rate is hovering near historic lows. While no one definitively knows what the employment landscape will look like in the coming years, it seems obvious that in the absence of a significantly negative economic event, unemployment will remain incredibly low. Increasingly organizations will be required to invest not only in the retention of existing talent, but also in the proactive acquisition of new talent.

Passive recruitment channels can and have limited many a recruiter's effectiveness by creating a "path of least resistance." For example, if a steady stream of resumes flows into an organization in response to an Internet job posting, a recruiter is much more likely to devote the bulk of his or her time to addressing this pool of applicants, as opposed to pursuing proactive approaches that require a greater degree of strategy and direct action. To use a simple analogy, it is far easier to pick the low hanging fruit from a tree than it is to devise a strategy and put forth the effort required to pick the fruit that is seemingly out of reach. As I will explain in Chapter Three - Proactive Sourcing, organizations that are wholly reliant upon passive recruitment channels are likely to encounter a greater degree of competition for talent, because the professionals they are pursuing are equally accessible to a spectrum of other talent-hungry organizations.

Regrettably, many recruiters are fundamentally uncomfortable with proactive recruitment measures for several reasons:

> 1) They don't understand the strategic or tactical aspects of accessing prospective candidates who aren't necessarily in the job market;

> 2) They don't see themselves as front-line sales professionals charged with reaching out and engaging talented individuals to consider new opportunities;

> 3) They are hopelessly trapped in a transaction-based recruitment model that assigns greater value to the frequency of specific recruitment activities than to the quality of specific recruitment activities (i.e., the number of interviews conducted in a month versus the relative caliber of individuals interviewed in a month).

In order to meaningfully secure a competitive recruiting advantage, organizations are going to have to recognize the need to distinguish themselves as an employer of choice. They are going to have to deploy a candidate-centric approach that regards talent as an asset, not as a commodity. They are going to have to implement sales continuity throughout the hiring lifecycle, where all participants in the hiring process understand that they must sell the virtues of affiliating with the organization. Finally, they are going to have to adopt a recruitment model that balances the need for quality prospective candidates with the need to meaningfully measure activities throughout the recruitment lifecycle.

As a means of assessing yourself or your organization relative to proactive recruitment, consider your responses to the following statements and assign a value of 1 – 5 based on the degree to which the statement applies to you (with 1 representing strongly disagree and 5 representing strongly agree). See how you score.

1. I actively source passive candidates as a component of my recruiting approach. _____

2. I am experienced at devising and deploying proactive search strategies that identify target environments from which to recruit. _____

3. My company assigns great value to the quality of prospective candidates in consideration for given openings and is less concerned with the quantity. _____

4. I am comfortable and experienced at engaging passive prospective candidates (people I have never talked to and for whom I don't have a resume) in a career-related discussion. _____

5. I am confident in my ability to effectively execute a compelling and engaging cold call. _____

6. I am adept at securing prospective candidate referrals from outside sources. _____

7. I do an excellent job of meaningfully conveying my employer's (or client's) compelling story to prospective candidates and generating candidate enthusiasm and excitement. _____

8. I actively utilize a consultative selling style in my communications with prospective candidates. _____

9.   I know how to engage and work effectively with internal hiring managers, relative to fully understanding how and why a given position supports the organization's overall business mission.

    _____

10. I am someone who has not succumbed to the "path of least resistance." I actively work outside the parameters of an established, entrenched, and typically passive recruitment process. _____

11. I regularly get unsolicited referrals from applicants with whom I have worked previously. _____

In considering the above statements, you probably recognized areas of strength and perhaps areas of weakness. If you scored 50 – 55 you should write a book on recruiting! If you scored 35 – 50, you are likely a very effective recruiter who is biased towards proactive recruiting, but who can likely improve certain aspects of your role. If you scored 20 – 34, you have a real opportunity to bolster performance across the board. If you scored under 20, you are probably in a highly transactional, passive recruiting environment, and you have a substantial opportunity to employ an array of techniques that will help optimize your performance.

In subsequent chapters of this book, I will highlight the net benefits of proactive recruitment, as well as the benefits of adopting a consultative approach in all facets of the recruiting sales cycle. Additionally, I will share a variety of tactical approaches that any recruiter can implement to elevate his or her performance.

The employment marketplace has changed, and we are collectively in a War For Talent economy for the foreseeable future. Recruiters must embrace the reality that true success is now dependent upon their ability to become talent scouts who play a pivotal role in building the companies they support. As a result, recruiters must reduce their reliance on traditional, passive, shot-gun approaches to recruiting. Instead of reactively casting a net into the employment marketplace and hoping for the best, recruiters must proactively engage and interact with the right people who possess the right skills and who presently work within the right target environments consistent with available openings.

While leveraging technology will continue to be essential to effective recruiting, long-term recruiting success will also be directly tied to the proactive acquisition of passive candidates, (individuals who are not actively looking for a new role), but who would consider select opportunities if approached in a compelling and engaging manner. Cultivating and utilizing proactive recruiting approaches will provide recruiters with the very best opportunity to implement an efficient and replicable candidate acquisition methodology that will yield optimal results.

Chapter 2: Consultative Selling In Recruitment

Developing and optimizing strong selling skills is of critical importance to recruiters who are interested in maximizing their long-term success. Recruiting is selling. That's the bottom line. Regardless of whether a recruiter works within a corporate setting or is affiliated with a staffing agency or search firm, he or she is a front-line sales professional, a corporate evangelist if you will, engaged in what I regard to be one of the most complex sales cycles in business.

This chapter addresses qualities and attributes inherent to the recruiting sales process. It also highlights the significance of incorporating consultative selling approaches within all facets of the recruiting lifecycle and how utilizing a consultative approach can enable a recruiter to consistently realize greater levels of overall success.

Selling In Recruitment

As I referenced above, recruiting is absolutely a sales process, and the role of "recruiter" is a front-line sales vocation. Recruiters are in the business of selling opportunity.

On the candidate side of the equation, recruiters sell select employment opportunities that exist within a particular market niche or company. On the employer side of the equation, recruiters sell their ability to help a hiring authority acquire the specific talent that is critical to the success of an organization's mission.

The recruiting lifecycle also includes a host of situational selling scenarios that go far beyond the notion of simply selling opportunity or the ability to acquire talent. A recruiter is fundamentally responsible for creating meaningful introductions between a candidate and an employer, stewarding the overall hiring process, and facilitating a candidate and organization's mutual understanding and appreciation for one another. It is incumbent upon a recruiter to provide information and insight to hiring authorities and candidates so that they can make an informed decision about the merits of moving forward together. And, when they do elect to move forward together, a recruiter realizes success.

From a sales perspective, I have often been asked: Why are some recruiters far more successful than other recruiters? Why are some recruiters more apt to secure unsolicited referrals, while others seem to languish in this area? Is the success of a recruiter tied to the mechanics of how they approach the business, or does success somehow directly correlate to basic salesmanship?

Attributes Of The Recruiting Sales Process

The reality that recruiting is a sales profession is a fact that many people entering the industry often fail to fully understand, let alone embrace. Any experienced recruiter can probably cite a time when they encountered someone with a very naïve view of the recruiting function. As a case in point, I can remember getting a call from a former candidate who was interested in becoming a recruiter and wanted to know more about what being a recruiter entailed.

His perception of the recruiting function was rather simplistic. From where he sat, recruiting was nothing more than a process in which one evaluated the skills of prospective candidates and then matched them up with corresponding jobs. He reasoned that if an individual had effective people skills and a reasonable knowledge of the relevant subject matter, then the job would be easy.

I asked him whether or not he felt that he had a strong sales aptitude. *"Sales?"* he questioned, *"What do you mean by sales?"* I spent a few moments explaining that recruiting was fundamentally a sales profession. I advised him that having good people skills and an understanding of the subject matter or industry domain were certainly important attributes, but that without a solid sales aptitude or tangible selling experience, it would be difficult at best to become a successful recruiter.

I suggested that he read a couple of books about selling. A week later he called me up, and said: *"I took your advice and did some reading. I think you're right - I really don't see myself being able to make the types of sales calls that recruiting would require."*

Over the years, I have known of other individuals who asked for similar advice, but who ultimately discounted the sales component of the recruiting profession. They got into the business, rapidly became frustrated, and got out of the business - end of story.

To be effective at recruiting, you must understand that the recruiting sales cycle is both a complex sale and a strategic sale. Recruiting is a complex sale for several reasons. A recruiter's "products" are people and the inherent skills and abilities they possess. Human beings are unique in that they are the only product that has the ability to terminate the sales process at any juncture by saying "No." In virtually every other type of sale, tangible or intangible, the product doesn't have this capability. Appliances can't say no; cars can't say no; insurance policies, stocks & bonds, furnishings, and clothing can't say no (although we can all think of instances and people where perhaps clothing would be doing us a big favor by saying, "No").

Regrettably, people can and do say "No" to new career opportunities. As a result, the human dynamic adds a great deal of complexity to the recruiting sales process. This point also highlights the fact that the recruiting sale has a two-sided close. In order for a deal to get done, both the hiring authority and the candidate must agree that it is in their respective best interests to move forward together. As a recruiter, you are effectively acting as a broker attempting to bring two parties with different priorities and objectives to a point of resolution, ideally one where an offer is extended and accepted.

In addition to functioning as brokers in a sales process with a two-sided close, recruiting professionals must also conduct themselves in a manner that is extremely sensitive to the wants, needs, and desires of both hiring authorities and candidates. The recruiting sales process can be highly emotional and stressful for all participants in the process *including the recruiter*. Making a job change is unquestionably a stressful life event. While a job change may not rank as highly as other stressful life events such as the loss of a loved one, birth of a child, or geographic move, it is nonetheless an anxiety laden event and with good reason.

Making a job change is more than just electing to go to work for a different employer at a new job site. Work is where we spend a significant portion of each day striving to make a living. Work is also the place where we formulate professional and personal relationships. Where we work, the mentoring we receive, and our ability to grow are all things that impact us significantly. The work that we do has great bearing on our overall satisfaction with our lives. Therefore, changing jobs is a big deal, and, as a result, is often a process accompanied by a lot of emotion.

The hiring process can be just as emotional on the employer side of the equation. Many hiring managers are emotionally attached to the recruiting process. They accurately perceive that their own ability to hit goals and enjoy career advancement is directly tied to selecting the right employees. Given this emotional element, it is imperative that recruiters be capable of expressing and demonstrating real empathy to candidates and to hiring authorities, with one caveat. While being empathetic they also must be pragmatic, so as not to get sucked into an emotional abyss with each and every deal.

Another element of complexity in the recruiting sale is that recruiters must have both a detailed and flexible base of knowledge. By a detailed base of knowledge, I mean that a recruiter must possess a solid grasp of industry or domain knowledge specific to the market sector in which they recruit. In other words, if you work as a physician recruiter, you must know the difference between family practitioners, pediatricians, obstetricians, surgeons, and so on. And, within each of these specialties, you must be cognizant of and have some appreciation for relevant sub-specialties. If you are a Physician Recruiter, I am not suggesting that you need to know how to deliver an anesthetic or perform surgery in order to perform your job. But regardless of your recruiting focus, you must know enough to convey some measure of knowledge and credibility with respect to the market niche you serve.

In addition to understanding the nuances that differentiate one position from another, you must stay on top of changes or advances within your market sector if you expect to be successful. Your ability to project contemporary knowledge of innovations, advancements or other trends within your marketplace will unquestionably enhance your overall credibility in the eyes of prospective candidates.

Flexible knowledge simply implies that the market sectors you serve, the individual candidates you meet, and the hiring situations you encounter are unlikely to be static. Unless you only recruit for one extremely specific skill set that is immune to change, you must have the ability to know what information matters and how to use this information in your discussions with prospective candidates and hiring authorities. Ideally, over time, you will inevitably add both depth and breadth to this base of knowledge and cultivate true marketplace expertise.

Finally, you must recognize that in the recruiting sales cycle, no two situations are going to be exactly alike. This truth is one of the most intriguing and potentially troubling aspects of recruiting. Whenever you work with a hiring manager, you get to learn about their business, what makes their organization and opportunities compelling, and their near-term business issues and challenges. With candidates, you get the opportunity to work closely with individuals attempting to make career enhancing and often life-changing moves. Developing an effective and proficient recruitment practice that helps both sides proceed with clarity is very rewarding and seeing a deal progress to completion provides a great sense of accomplishment.

The fact that every candidate and employment situation are unique unto themselves means that you will perpetually be dealing with hiring authorities and candidates whose attributes, issues, and buying motivations are dynamic. Because recruiters work within a business where things are rarely black and white, the recruiting sales process can be fraught with ambiguity and competing interests. This poses an interesting challenge for recruiters, particularly for individuals new to the function, of where, how, and with whom to invest their valuable time. Because a spectrum of variables and factors can influence the employer and candidate's respective buying motivations, it is imperative that a recruiter be able to effectively qualify the extent and degree to which these motivations are "real."

This last point can't be overstated. It underscores the simple fact that good recruiters must be *especially good* at qualifying and understanding the realities associated with the wants, needs, and desires of everyone who has a stake in the recruitment process (candidates & hiring authorities). As I will state again and again throughout this book, a recruiter's most precious resource is time; and how a recruiter elects to spend his or her time has a significant and logical impact on the likelihood for success.

Top performing recruiters recognize that even with the best presentation and communication skills, they must commit and adhere to both a strategic and a tactical sales plan in order to maximize their utilization of time and optimize their potential for success. For example, a recruiter who spends no time on the phone is unlikely to have much success. Likewise, a recruiter who doesn't allocate an appropriate amount of time to carefully qualifying the needs of hiring managers or candidates is unlikely to realize success. I address time management and daily planning comprehensively in Chapter Twelve.

Going From A Transactional To Consultative Approach

When I started in recruiting some 20 years ago, my sales approach was absolutely of a transactional nature. I subscribed to the notion that my ultimate success or failure as a recruiter would in many respects be tied entirely to the number of people I was able to contact and incorporate into my candidate network.

By my way of thinking, the more "transactions" that I could affect, the more success I would realize. If I communicated with a large number of prospects, I would inevitably have more candidates. With more candidates, I would theoretically be better poised to make more placements. And, talk to prospective candidates I did; lots and lots of prospects.

But, like many people new to the recruiting profession, my selling approach wasn't particularly sophisticated. Nor was it especially oriented to the wants, needs, and desires of the people that I was contacting.

Instead, my selling approach was more about "me." I was apt to lead off an initial discussion with a potential candidate by characterizing the fact that *"I"* had a job that might be of interest, or *"I"* was working with a client that needed a specific type of professional. Over time, I came to realize that what *I believed* might be a great employment situation, or what *I thought* would potentially be in the best interests of a prospective candidate was of little consequence to the people I was attempting to recruit. It was of little consequence because I had fundamentally failed to take the time to understand or appreciate whether or not these individuals possessed the requisite motivations for entertaining the possibility of making a career change, let alone considering the specific opportunities that I was representing. In other words, I was putting "the cart before the horse."

Furthermore, my approach was more oriented to *telling* than to *selling*. In speaking with prospective candidates about a particular opportunity, I was great at pointing out what I thought were the highlights of an organization or role (telling), but wasn't adept at helping prospects appreciate how the attributes of a particular role substantially aligned with their career objectives and life goals (selling).

I was eagerly talking to prospects about what I perceived to be great opportunities without having qualified where these individuals were in their respective careers and lives, or learning what, if anything, might compel them to consider making a move. I had failed to understand the most basic rule of human behavior; namely that people will typically do only what they perceive to be in their own best interests.

I realized that by not making it about "them" and what they were trying to achieve in life, I came across as being a very self-serving salesperson. I also came to recognize that I needed to utilize a more consultative approach, one that would allow me to better appreciate what was important to the prospects with whom I was speaking, as well as equip me with the ability to engage all candidates in a manner that would engender goodwill.

I also concluded that I had to reassess my own definition of what constituted a "qualified candidate." In assessing my performance and candidate interactions, I determined that if I treated everyone well and invested a bit more time towards establishing rapport and understanding each prospect's long-term personal and career goals, then I would have the ability to begin forging high quality, multi-dimensional relationships that could progress in a number of interesting directions. In essence, I realized that I could be far more successful if I aspired to progress beyond simply being a transactional salesperson.

Obviously in order to be an effective recruiter, one must have the ability to handle many transactions in the course of a business day. So, I am not suggesting that incorporating consultative selling within recruiting mitigates the need to reach out and contact a lot of people on a regular basis. If you aren't communicating with a host of prospective or active candidates each day, you will not realize success.

But, by the same token, if you conduct yourself in a purely transactional manner, pausing only to engage the prospects that you think you can work with today, you will be missing out on a phenomenal opportunity to nurture many extremely worthwhile relationships that will, over the long-term, bear an incredible quantity of fruit.

Consultative Selling in Recruitment

In order to be most effective in today's fast paced and talent constrained employment marketplace, it is critical for recruiters to adopt a consultative selling style. But what exactly does this mean? In my view the process of being consultative is really relatively simple. Consultative selling, as it relates to recruiting candidates, is grounded in the notion that an initial discussion with a prospective candidate *should not* necessarily be about a specific employment opportunity, but rather it *should be* about understanding a particular candidate's current situation and whether or not he or she is poised and appropriately motivated to entertain potentially career enhancing opportunities.

In short, consultative selling in recruitment is about building relationships that are grounded in a genuine desire to understand the needs and motivations of the individuals you are trying to recruit. Furthermore, the consultative approach is about recognizing and accepting that there is still great value in pursuing relationships with candidate prospects even if they are not at a point in their lives where making a career change makes sense or are not well aligned with a particular job.

The ultimate goal of implementing a consultative approach is to build long-term, *actionable relationships* with highly skilled professionals who align well with your particular industry or market niche. By 'actionable relationship,' I mean that recruiters must create high quality business associations that are of a long-term nature and that can be '*acted upon*' to serve multiple purposes. I have absolutely no doubt that you will be well rewarded if you concentrate on building a spectrum of actionable relationships with talented professionals in your market sector.

Actionable candidate relationships are created as a result of forging long-term associations with professionals in your market sector or industry, regardless of whether or not they are poised to make a job change today. Too often recruiters harbor a short-term view that is focused exclusively on the here and now, as in, "I have a position *here*, and I want to fill it *now*." In many respects, whether or not a prospective candidate is poised to make a job change at the time of your initial call is immaterial.

As a rule, consultative selling in recruitment means that we are actively and appropriately listening to what a prospect tells us and that we acknowledge by action and deed that we respect them, whether they are open to considering a new situation or not. For example, if my initial discussion with a prospective candidate reveals that she just recently moved into her present job and is extremely happy, it wouldn't be particularly consultative of me to reply by saying, *"Hey, that's really wonderful that you are happy. Now let me tell you about this other job and why you would be crazy not to consider it."*

If a prospect says, *"Hey, I really appreciate your call, but honestly I am very happy in my current role,"* who are we to suggest that they are not happy? Any pressure that we apply is likely to diminish the prospect's potential interest in speaking with us in the future and will almost certainly destroy the opportunity to build a relationship grounded in trust.

I vividly recall a recent marketing call that I received from an individual in the financial services industry who gave new meaning to the term, "transactional salesperson." Within the first 15 seconds of his pitch about why I needed to invest in an energy stock, I interjected to say that I had a long-standing relationship with another broker, and that I simply wasn't at a point where I could make an investment. Undeterred, the broker continued to hammer away on why I needed to take a $5K - $10K position in the particular stock he was promoting.

Finally, after repeatedly reiterating that I wasn't in a position to invest, the call came to an abrupt end – he had hung up the phone!

As I thought about what had just taken place, it struck me that he really hadn't listened to anything that I was saying. His way of responding to my objections was to simply plow forward with his pitch. Yet it could have played out very differently. Had he been even modestly respectful of my situation and what I was trying to convey, he could have easily transitioned the discussion into a mode where he learned a little about me and secured the right to contact me in the future. Would he have walked away with a sale that day? No. But as he grew to know me and adapted his selling style, he might have been able to secure a sale at some point in the future. Instead, he utilized a classical transactional approach that screamed out, *"I need to close a deal.....now."*

This story underscores another truth, namely that consultative selling in recruitment mandates some degree of patience. Several years ago, I read a tremendous article in "Sports Illustrated" that described a Tarpon fishing tournament where anglers tested their skill by using ultra-light line and tackle. Tarpon is widely regarded as one of the strongest and most superior fighting fish. By using ultra-light tackle, the challenge for the angler is to never apply too much pressure. If the angler exerts too much pressure or jerks the rod while playing the fish, the line will become fatigued, the monofilament will snap, and the fish will be gone. If the angler is cautious and patient, he or she has a good chance of landing a trophy fish, although it may take hours to accomplish this task.

A consultative selling approach in recruiting is not about applying pressure; it's about eloquently asking questions that help you to understand whether an individual is open to discussing how, when, and whether they might advance their career. While it is gratifying when prospects are interested in considering new opportunities, a negative response from a prospect doesn't have to be a terrible thing at all. As recruiters we need to recognize that while we are unlikely to obtain immediate gratification from every individual we attempt to recruit, by treating people respectfully and actively listening to what they are saying, we are sowing seeds of goodwill that will more often than not yield real dividends.

While an individual's disposition to making a move is a significant consideration, it should not be the sole consideration. It is equally important to assess whether a prospect has the capacity to bring value to your network. If you determine that a prospective candidate's background has merit and wish to incorporate them into your professional network, then you must be willing to allocate the time and energy necessary to nurture the relationship so that it has the ability to bear fruit over the long-term.

Will you successfully place this individual into a job at some point down the road? Maybe you will, or maybe you won't. But, having a great relationship in place with a talented prospective candidate greatly increases the likelihood that they will seek you out first when they are ready to consider new situations.

Regardless of whether or not you ultimately recruit a talented prospect for an immediate opening, by crafting a high quality relationship, you are also creating a tremendous potential source of referrals. Over the years, I have built countless professional relationships that have yielded a steady stream of both solicited and unsolicited referrals. These relationships typically began as nothing more than an introductory cold call to a very content prospect with little desire to make a move.

As I mentioned earlier, too many recruiters focus solely on determining whether or not a prospect is open to entertaining a specific career opportunity _today_. And, if the individual expresses that he or she is content, the recruiter's immediate response is, *"Do you know anyone else who's looking?"* or *"Can you recommend anyone else for this position?"*

Don't get me wrong – seeking referrals is a very productive thing to do. But, if you seek referrals without having learned much about the prospect on the other end of the phone, without having taken the time to appreciate the prospect's near term goals and objectives, or without having humanized yourself as more than a recruiter "banging out cold calls," your odds of securing quality referrals aren't very good.

Some recruiters mistakenly conduct themselves with a degree of assumed familiarity that neither engenders trust nor goodwill. If a prospect doesn't trust you or feels that they are being used, they are unlikely to help you. Period.

In deploying a consultative approach, it is just as important to work diligently on having high quality interactions with all prospective candidates as it is to 'touch' as many people as possible. In my experience, by outwardly expressing a desire to learn about an individual first, and by communicating in a direct, honest, and non-threatening manner, prospects have tended to open up. And, as the discussion has progressed, they have also gotten the chance to get to know me as a person with whom they may have many things in common, and not simply as just another recruiter trolling for talent. As a result, despite being happy in their current roles or simply not at a point where considering a job change made sense, many individuals have nonetheless proven to be an invaluable resource.

For example, on a recent executive search assignment, I cold called a woman whose background I suspected would be a good match for my client. After introducing myself and inquiring about her background and experience, I learned a great deal about this individual including the fact that she was six months pregnant and simply not in a position to move. I invested about 15 minutes getting to know her and had a very nice conversation about the excitement that she was feeling at the prospect of having children. Before our conversation terminated, I was the recipient of three quality referrals, and I had also secured the right to contact her in the future.

On a subsequent assignment about eight months later, I again reached out to this individual, who was now at home enjoying being a mom. We simply picked up our conversation where we had left off, but this time she offered five quality referrals at the conclusion of our discussion.

In retrospect, I didn't have to spend ten seconds speaking with this individual about her pregnancy. I could have simply said, *"Hey, you're pregnant, have fun changing diapers for the next two years,"* and quickly terminated the discussion. But, I absolutely believe that my genuine interest in her as a person changed the complexion of our relationship and made her inclined to help me by offering referrals.

I highlight this story because it conveys the importance of making recruiting calls that are not solely and exclusively about filling positions today. If you determine that a prospect is not willing to consider a move, you are still well-advised to invest in constructing a relationship that can yield future value.

On another project, I contacted a well-qualified individual regarding a great sales leadership position that mandated a fairly significant amount of travel. It became readily apparent to me that he was eminently qualified, but was at a point in his life where reducing travel was taking on a greater degree of urgency. He had kids and really wanted to be in a position to spend more time with them. He was very open to the prospect of making a move, especially one that would allow him to spend more time at home.

After we discussed his background and priorities, we began to discuss the role that I was representing at which point I said, *"Tom, there's no question that your background aligns well with this job, but I don't think it's the right role for you at this time."* I went on to explain that I fully respected his desire to have more quality time with his kids and explained that as much as I would enjoy representing him to my client, I was concerned that this position might not be in his best interests given the travel demands.

After a long pause, he said, *"Paul, I don't know many recruiters who would attempt to talk me out of considering a job, but as a sales professional myself, I really appreciate your candor, and more importantly, that you actually took the time to listen to me."* He then offered background information on three referrals, one of which I placed into the position a month later.

This scenario underscores another significant attribute of consultative recruiting. A recruiter's charter is not only to assess whether a prospective candidate is willing and able to meaningfully entertain a given opportunity, but is also to help a prospective candidate opt out of the process when the parameters of a particular position are not aligned with what the prospect is attempting to accomplish.

In the situation above, I could have sugar-coated the travel element or encouraged the candidate to take the interview anyway. I could have hoped that the interview would have resulted in a love-fest between him and the hiring authority, one so powerful that any perceived negatives regarding travel would magically disappear. I could have done many things, but long ago I learned that a recruiter's responsibility is to: A) make meaningful introductions between talented individuals and employers and B) help all participants make informed decisions.

In working as a professional recruiter, I have always believed that at the end of the day all we have is our integrity and our reputation; if you sacrifice the former, you destroy the latter. In my mind, it is far better to help someone opt out of consideration for an opportunity that may not align with their goals than it is to talk them into doing something that may lead to significant long-term regrets.

Neither of the above scenarios is an isolated event. I could share countless stories about individuals who have said, *"I have never worked with a recruiter like you."* I don't share this to bolster my own ego, but as a way of highlighting the value of getting to know prospects as people, not just candidates, and to reiterate that you should make your discussions with every prospect about more than a particular job requirement at hand.

Consultative selling in recruitment is really about following the "Golden Rule" – *"Do unto others as you would have them do unto you."* By actively utilizing a consultative selling approach, you will ultimately engender a tremendous amount of candidate goodwill.

This goodwill becomes the foundation for the "actionable relationships" that I characterized earlier, and the basis for significantly better results in all facets of the recruiting lifecycle.

In subsequent chapters on Proactive Sourcing and Advanced Introductory Calls, I specifically address tactical scripts that embody the consultative approach and that can be used to engage prospective candidates in a meaningful career dialogue. Also, Chapter Seven addresses various qualifying and questioning techniques that can be utilized to meaningfully obtain and assess candidate motivators, while additionally establishing solid candidate rapport.

Chapter 3: Partnering With Hiring Authorities

In conducting in-house training programs, I am increasingly asked to address how recruiters can cultivate more effective working relationships with the hiring managers that they support. This issue is cropping up with greater regularity, because the difficulty associated with identifying and recruiting talent has begun to tangibly (and negatively) impact many organizations. The ability to maintain the status quo let alone realize growth objectives has become increasingly difficult. As a result, hiring managers and recruiters alike are feeling an escalating sense of pressure.

While recently preparing to address a group regarding this topic, I decided it might be interesting to define this issue with imagery. I created a series of slides that incorporated photos of stressed out corporate professionals expressing the following sentiments:

- *"We need more candidates!"*
- *"We need better candidates!"*
- *"We need to find candidates faster!"*
- *"Why can't we get candidates for these openings?"*
- *"WHERE ARE MY PEOPLE?"*

As the slides scrolled by in sequence, the groans from the audience became progressively louder. I had not simply touched upon a source of ongoing frustration, but I had struck a nerve and a raw one at that.

I asked the program attendees to share their perceptions of how their hiring authorities regarded recruiters and the recruiting process. I also asked them to share their sentiments about the effectiveness of hiring authorities as business partners in the recruiting process.

After a slow start, where it was apparent that some individuals within this group privately wondered whether it was heresy to openly criticize a hiring authority, a couple of recruiters spoke up to share their feelings. A few moments later the responses flowed in rapid succession. It was as though I had released the air from a balloon.

Once this group got going, they rattled off a number of revealing observations. *They don't understand what we do,"* one person commented. *"They think that the people they are looking for are growing on trees,"* someone else suggested. *"They keep on changing their minds about what they want,"* another person offered. *"They tell me that they need to make a key hire ASAP, but when I press them for feedback on a candidate, there doesn't seem to be a sense of urgency at all,"* yet another person summarized.

When all was said and done, I had documented a range of different perceptions that highlighted a fundamental disconnect between this group of recruiters and the hiring managers they supported. One could argue that this scenario resulted from a dysfunction within this particular organization or that this kind of situation is primarily endemic to in-house recruiters. I don't agree with either of these assessments. I have completed similar exercises with recruiters of just about every persuasion and across various industries with the same results.

A recurring theme has been that when it comes to fully appreciating everything that is involved in the recruiting lifecycle, many hiring managers have expectations that are simply unrealistic. In short, *"They just don't get it."*

This chapter addresses communication strategies that recruiters can utilize to construct more productive working relationships with hiring authorities. I also discuss key considerations associated with defining job requisitions or formulating position requirements that can help to eliminate ambiguity and enable hiring managers and recruiters to work together with greater synergy.

"They just don't get it." While not necessarily an inaccurate observation regarding the depth of knowledge that many hiring managers possess relative to the subject of recruitment, I believe that the more important underlying question to ask is, *"Why should they get it?"*

As reflected in Figure 3.0, for most hiring authorities, recruitment is an important yet peripheral function of their job. Business development, budgeting, project oversight, staff management and mentoring, customer and vendor relations, and goal acquisition and planning are often more typical, day-to-day focal points. Additionally, for many hiring authorities recruitment is largely handled outside their immediate domain and is not directly under their control.

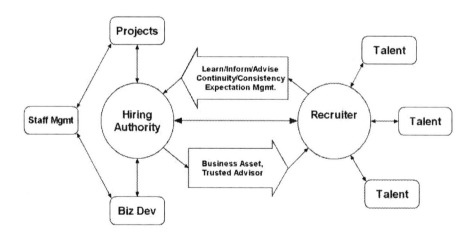

Figure 3.0

Usually a hiring manager's involvement in recruiting is comprised of drafting and communicating information about jobs that need to be filled, ensuring that open positions can be funded, interviewing prospective candidates, and making final hiring decisions. In fairness, many hiring managers have a skewed or inadequate perspective regarding the intricacies and nuances of talent acquisition. Sometimes this lack of knowledge may be by choice, but I believe that just as often it is because no one has taken the time to educate them. As a result, they are left to formulate their own expectations about how recruiting works or should work; expectations that may or may not be grounded in reality.

What's a recruiter to do? After all, a hiring authority is effectively a client or customer. Some recruiters may not see hiring authorities in this light and regard the terms 'client' or 'customer' as placing them in a subservient role. But I regard these terms to be perfectly appropriate descriptions. Regardless of the label that is used, these people are relying on you to help them address and solve a near-term or immediate business problem.

Communicate, Communicate, Communicate

I believe that there is a direct correlation between the quality of a recruiter's working relationship with hiring managers and the overall recruiting results that can be achieved. In order to effectively help a hiring authority, it is extremely important that you have the ability and wherewithal to construct a high quality working relationship. At its core, any good working relationship is grounded in effective communications, and communicating effectively is the hallmark of what good recruiters do. Figure 3.0 highlights several basic communication objectives that are worth considering. These objectives include the following:

- Communicate Proactively

- Communicate to Learn

- Communicate to Advise

- Keep Communications Timely

Communicate Proactively

Provided that you have something of substance to share, you can rarely over-communicate with hiring managers. From the vantage point of many hiring managers, once a position has been defined and transmitted to a recruiter, it might just as easily be broadcast into a massive black hole. Maybe, at some juncture, candidate resumes will magically appear – or maybe they won't. Managers may have some intuitive understanding for certain facets of the process, but they don't understand the day-in, day-out responsibilities of a recruiter or the time that is expended in different phases of the recruitment lifecycle.

This limited appreciation for the recruiting process means that part of the communications charter with hiring managers must be oriented to helping them understand the overall recruiting function. I am not suggesting that hiring managers should be given a crash course in recruiting (although, in a perfect world this wouldn't necessarily be a bad thing). Over time, in all stages of working through an assignment, especially a difficult one, a wise recruiter will help the hiring manager understand recruiting activities that are being pursued as well as issues, challenges, or problems that are being encountered.

In fairness many recruiters have an impressive ability to communicate proactively with hiring authorities. They go to great lengths to communicate regularly and consistently with hiring managers out of recognition of the fact that many hiring managers are either too busy or too detached to possess a comprehensive and real-time appreciation for recruiting.

Good recruiters recognize that communicating proactively is the only way to manage a hiring authority's expectations regarding the complexities that may be associated with recruiting for a particular role. Additionally, good recruiters know that there are various types of communications inherent to a successful relationship with a hiring manager.

Communicate to Learn

A recurring criticism of many human resources representatives and recruiters is that they *don't understand* a hiring manager's business objectives or functional area. The only way to establish long-term credibility with a hiring manager is to obtain and convey a comprehensive appreciation for their business and the issues that are of consequence to them. This means that you must not only acquire some measure of domain knowledge about the business or functional area for which you are recruiting, but must also make the hiring authority aware that getting and expanding this knowledge base is personally important and will enable you to recruit more effectively on their behalf. As the saying goes, *"Knowledge is power."*

With respect to talent acquisition, a recruiter is essentially functioning as a hiring manager's eyes and ears on the marketplace. Again, the ability to successfully perform in this capacity is predicated on having an appreciation for not only *what* is important to the hiring authorities you support, but *why* it is important. Learning about a department or functional area within an organization is rarely a one-time proposition, but something that occurs incrementally over time.

Communicate to Advise

There are significant peripheral benefits associated with understanding and appreciating the business areas and activities of the hiring managers you support. First, the best way in which to acquire a hiring authority's trust and respect is by cultivating and projecting true business acumen. Second, knowing important attributes and key priorities of a business unit or departmental function will enable you to communicate with conviction about candidates that you regard to be qualified for specific opportunities.

This knowledge is important because in reviewing the resumes of prospective candidates, many hiring managers are predisposed to immediately look for what's missing or lacking in an individual's background. Hiring managers really want to identify individuals who will hit the ground running, will not require a great deal of hand-holding, and as a former colleague liked to say, *"Will play nicely with others."* At the risk of making a sweeping generalization, many hiring managers believe that the best conceivable recruiting outcome is to hire candidates who are as close an approximation of themselves as possible.

A recruiter's job is not only to identify relevant prospects, but also to help hiring authorities make informed decisions about talent. You need to be able to leverage your knowledge and market expertise in a manner that helps your hiring managers to see all candidates in their entirety, not just as they may be reflected within a resume. This is the alchemy of recruiting – being able to make educated and knowledgeable judgments about how and whether people fit into opportunities, and then making it easy for the hiring authority to not only see what you see, but to also assign immense value to your perspective.

In Chapter Seven, Reaping Reference Check Rewards, I recount a Software Development Manager search that underscores this point. The ability to understand the hiring authority's environment and communicate with conviction played significant roles in persuading the hiring authority to consider a prospective candidate that he would have otherwise been predisposed to regard as being unqualified.

Keep Communications Timely

We live in the information age. Fueled by an array of technologies that have increased our productivity and access to data (Internet, email, voicemail, mobile phones, PDAs, etc.), our society seemingly has an insatiable appetite for timely information. The speed with which we are now able to acquire or convey information has directly contributed to a business climate whose pace only seems to accelerate. We have been progressively conditioned to expect and anticipate that our needs will be met sooner, better, and more efficiently.

Today, consumers have the ability to purchase just about anything online – pizza, clothing, and even automobiles. And they can reasonably expect that these goods will be delivered within a day or so (except for pizza, which gets delivered within the hour).

If you think of hiring managers as consumers, it's easy to appreciate why they might view recruiting as a service whose deliverables should be available on demand. After all, just about every other process in the business world has a finite beginning and ending. The distinction, of course, is that the delivery of talent (people) is quite different than the delivery of any other service or product. Recruiting is by no means finite; there are spectrums of variables that impact how long it takes to staff an opening.

With the pace of business moving ever faster, providing regular status updates to hiring authorities should not be regarded as a mere courtesy. Communicating in a timely manner with hiring managers is probably one of the most critical things a recruiter can do, both as a means of managing expectations and enhancing working relationships. In the eyes of many hiring managers, <u>a recruiter who fails to communicate has effectively communicated failure</u>.

Determining the appropriate frequency with which to communicate to a hiring authority is up to you, but if you're in the initial stages of forging a working relationship or are recruiting on a mission critical role, it pays to over-communicate versus under-communicate. Put yourself in the shoes of a hiring manager: your positions are important, and the rate at which they are staffed tangibly impacts you in all respects. As a result, it is important that hiring managers are made to feel as though they have their finger on the pulse of what is happening relative to their outstanding openings.

I recommend formally communicating with hiring authority's at least once a week, and for critical roles it may be more appropriate to communicate twice weekly. For certain requirements, it may behoove you to communicate daily. These communications should include a synopsis of exactly what has transpired since the last contact – candidate prospects that have been identified, the disposition of candidates who have been screened or interviewed, issues or challenges that you are encountering – anything that helps the hiring manager understand what's happening relative to his or her opening. The ability to meaningfully quantify and qualify the status of your activities on a particular opening can't be overstated. This information will directly affect a hiring authority's overall judgments about your performance on their behalf.

Some recruiters may wonder if providing frequent status updates to hiring managers regarding outstanding openings is overkill. Ultimately this is your judgment call to make. If you haven't been proactively communicating with hiring managers to advise them of what you have been doing on their behalf, however, I highly recommend that you consider doing so.

The vast majority of hiring managers regard their open positions to be incredibly important – don't underestimate this. Don't assume that a hiring manager automatically knows that you are actively working on his or her openings. And don't assume that they will conclude that not hearing from you regularly should be translated to mean that you are diligently working on their behalf. Unless you have had the opportunity to forge a very close working relationship with a hiring manager, failing to communicate regularly is a huge mistake. In short, if you want to be regarded as a key part of the recruiting solution as opposed to being regarded as part of the recruiting problem, again, it's always best to over-communicate.

The worst thing that can happen when you over-communicate is that the hiring authority will ultimately say, *"Okay, I get it – you're working on it!"* Or *"Please, you're killing me with information. Don't feel the need to status me as frequently!"* This is not negative feedback at all. Negative feedback from a hiring authority is apt to sound more like, *"Geez, I have no way of knowing where things stand* *on my openings. The only way I can find out whether we are making progress on my openings is <u>when I call</u> the recruiter."*

If you receive an email or voicemail from a hiring manager, be timely in your response – even if you have to say, *"Jane – I am totally wrapped up today, but wanted to let you know that I got your (email or voicemail) and will ring you in the morning to provide a complete status update.*

Also, it pays to ask hiring managers if you are communicating frequently enough and in a manner or mode that works for them. Remember, that although hiring authorities are your partners, the recruiting process will largely remain a peripheral responsibility for them.

Engage Hiring Authorities Consultatively

Cultivating true business acumen relative to the areas you support, and communicating proactively with hiring authorities will give greater credibility to your recommendations regarding talent and will enhance your ability to provide meaningful input as to how positions are drafted and defined. This latter point is extremely important because how a position or job is constructed will have a direct bearing on the degree of difficulty associated with finding qualified candidates.

To operate consultatively you must have the ability to ask thoughtful questions as a means of distinguishing and determining the critical success factors associated with a particular role. In other words, you must have the capacity to help a hiring manager *help you* to differentiate between which skills and abilities inherent to a position are "must haves" versus "nice to haves."

It is the rare occasion when a hiring manager says, *"I have gone to great lengths to define this position as broadly and open-mindedly as possible – specific skills and experience don't matter – just get me a great person and I will do the rest."* In fact, job requisitions are far more likely to be biased towards the hiring authority's perception of the perfect or ideal candidate. Again, you're unlikely to hear a hiring manager say, *"You know, for this role I'd really like to see a few candidates who only have 50 percent of the skills required for this position."*

Over the years I have occasionally read job descriptions produced by hiring managers that left me wondering why they didn't include a preference for a candidate's hair color or zodiac sign. All joking aside, it is far more preferable to work with hiring managers who possess a clear vision for the kind of individual they want for a given job – provided that this vision is grounded in reality. In the long run, you're much better off working on behalf of someone who knows what they want as opposed to someone who projects ambivalence.

When discussing job opening particulars with a hiring manager, it is extremely productive to validate that requirements they deem as being important are *indeed* important. This is not to say that you should attempt to challenge a hiring manager on every attribute of significance noted within the job requisition or position description. If you are given a "needle in the haystack" job requisition that lists 87 essential attributes, however, you must be able to discern what is truly of significance (must haves) from what is of lesser significance (nice-to-haves). In these instances, your best approach is simply to ask the following questions:

"Jeff, I want to do my best to show you great candidates....can you help me understand the significance of why XYZ skill is important to this position?"

Or:

"Kathy, I know that you are seeking a number of key attributes for this position. Can we walk through the job criteria and rank your priorities so that I know what qualities are of greatest significance?"

Or:

"Mark, you have shared your priorities relative to this position, which I really appreciate. If I see someone who only possesses your top three criteria for this position but lacks other desired experience, how should I proceed?"

The objective of asking any of the above questions is to get at the true essence of the role on which you will be recruiting. If you perceive that a role will be difficult to fill, it is highly productive to validate what constitutes the most important criteria for evaluating prospects. It also pays to stretch the hiring manager's expectations towards considering those prospects who possess many, but not all, of the desired qualities.

Get Them To Help You "Sell" The Job

Another important step to pursue at the onset of any recruiting initiative is to ask the hiring authority to articulate what he or she perceives to be the relevant "selling messages" associated with a given role. In order to do the best possible job in presenting an opportunity to a prospective candidate, you should ask the hiring manager to answer the following questions:

- What makes the role compelling?
- What are unique features, attributes or factors associated with this role that a candidate should consider or value?
- What should a new hire expect relative to career or skill development?
- What should a new hire anticipate working on in the first year?
- What is a new hire's likely growth trajectory moving forward? How will performance be measured?

In short, you want the hiring manager to explain why someone would want this job. The answers to each of the questions above will provide you with important insights that will not only enhance your own understanding of the opportunity at hand, but also will give you valuable information to share with prospective candidates.

Hiring managers may not be accustomed to expressing what they perceive to be the selling features associated with their jobs. Therefore, this exercise may prompt them to think about the roles within their department or organization in a new light – one that is candidate-centric. This exercise alone is no guarantee that a hiring manager will suddenly or automatically go into selling mode during candidate interviews, but it certainly can't hurt.

Some managers naturally seem to understand that they must allocate time during an interview to sell a candidate on the opportunity at hand, while other managers may seem completely oblivious. A third group of hiring authorities operates from the perspective that candidates should be thrilled that the organization is deigning to consider them in the first place.

If nothing else, being equipped with the hiring manager's own interpretation of what makes a job in his or her organization compelling may present you with the opportunity to offer gentle reminders about the importance of selling the opportunity during candidate interviews. This notion goes back to the idea that you are not only a recruiter, you are also an advisor. Part of being an advisor is helping your customer to present themselves in the optimal light. To accomplish this you might say, *"Judy, when we spoke several weeks ago regarding the ABC Analyst position, you shared some really great insights about why you felt the role was so compelling. As you know, Hector Morales is coming to interview tomorrow. I know that he is considering several firms right now, and I believe that it would really make a difference if you could highlight some of the key features of the role. I think it would mean a lot to him to hear it from you directly."*

Present Candidates With Conviction

Earlier, I highlighted the importance of getting hiring managers to see candidates in totality – not just the individual as they may appear on paper. Part of being an effective recruiter is to verify and validate that a candidate possesses the skills and experience that are essential to a particular job. An equally important aspect of being an effective recruiter, however, is having the perceptive skills and intuition to recognize when there may be more to a candidate's background than meets the eye.

When presenting a candidate's background to a hiring authority, it is essential to highlight the parallels that exist between the candidate's background, experience and abilities and the job at hand. I have seen candidate introductions from recruiters to hiring managers that project the same level of enthusiasm that a teenager might reflect when going to the orthodontist to get braces. These memorandums of introduction often go like this:

"Hi John – Attached is the resume of Stacy Collins. I thought she might be right for the XYZ opening you have. Let me know what you think. Thanks, Steve."

Or:

"Jack – When you get a moment please review the attached resume of Rich Brown. He has several years of ABC experience, but I'm uncertain as to whether he has the level of depth you need for the XYZ role in your department. Please advise – Roger."

Or:

"Alan, the attached resume came in a few days ago. Seems that this person has some of the departmental oversight experience you're seeking. I spoke with her earlier today, but can't tell if other aspects of her background totally align with what you are looking for – when you get a chance, let me know.

The above introductory notes do absolutely nothing to tell the hiring manager why he or she should be interested in opening the candidate's resume let alone be excited at the prospect of a potential interview. In each of the above examples, the recruiter has, for the most part, done a disservice to the hiring manager and to the candidate whose background is being presented. The first example conveys no information about the candidate, and the second and third examples are loaded with doubt.

In contrast, effective candidate introductions to hiring managers attempt to draw clear connections between a candidate's experience and the hiring manager's opening. These communications also seek to impart intangible information about the candidate to the hiring authority. Finally, effective introductions seek definitive action from the hiring manager. These communications might sound like this:

"Kim – Attached for your review and consideration is the resume of Scott Williams, who I believe warrants serious consideration for your Marketing Communications Manager role – let me explain. Scott has:

- *Four years of progressive experience in overseeing the development of all external and internal marketing collateral for a $200 MM firm.*
- *Direct oversight of a team of six individuals responsible for Public Relations (including Media Relations and Consumer Relations), Website initiatives, and Special Communications (promotions). Also has responsibility for a $2 MM annual budget.*
- *Exceptional presentation/communication skills with specific experience handling crisis communications (his firm had to manage a major consumer product recall).*
- *Won his firm's Outstanding Associate Award for three consecutive years – this is given out to individuals who comprise the top 5 percent of all performers in his firm.*

- *Noted expertise in the area of creating and leveraging corporate brand identity via email marketing channels (while not reflected on his resume, he has given four presentations on this topic at industry trade shows this year).*

Scott and I have discussed your opportunity at length, and he is extremely interested in the possibility of meeting you. Let me know what your schedule will accommodate, and I can work on getting Scott set up to come in for a meeting. Also, I have done preliminary reference checks, all of which were outstanding. Look forward to your reply – Tony"

In the above communication, the recruiter highlights specific aspects of the candidate's experience that correlate with the hiring manager's job opening. Also, the recruiter brings additional value by highlighting aspects of the candidate's experience that aren't reflected within the resume. The communication notes that references have been checked and further support the recruiter's contention that this is a candidate that the hiring manager should meet. In fact, the recruiter uses an assumptive close by saying, *"Let me know what your schedule will accommodate and I can work on getting Scott set up to come in for a meeting."* Now that's speaking with conviction!

Does every note of introduction need to be as detailed as the example above? No, but any introduction, oral or written, must connect the dots between the candidate's background and the hiring manager's needs. Enough relevant information must be conveyed to enable the hiring manager to see what you see.

It should go without saying that if you are going to make a bold statement about a particular candidate or some aspect of his or her experience, you better believe in the validity of what you are communicating. Nothing is worse than promoting a candidate to a hiring manager and subsequently learning that your representation of the candidate was completely off target. If you are perceived as being prone to overstating or embellishing the ability levels of the candidates you present to hiring managers, your long-term credibility will be at risk. If you don't possess a reasonable degree of domain knowledge, it pays to exercise some measure of caution in how you characterize a candidate's background.

Building cohesive, long-term working relationships with hiring authorities is critically important if you want to maximize your recruiting proficiency. Obtaining relevant marketplace and functional knowledge, fully understanding a hiring manager's priorities relative to talent acquisition, and working to build a respectful and honest relationship that is grounded in trust does not happen overnight. Like any worthwhile relationship, it will require time, energy and patience.

Deploying a timely and effective communications strategy, one that is grounded in candor and oriented to realistically managing expectations is critical if you hope to forge a recruiting partnership that will yield tangible dividends over time. In the long-run, recruiters who build this type of working relationship with hiring managers will not only be regarded as business assets, but ultimately as trusted advisors.

Chapter 4: Proactive Sourcing Techniques

As any successful recruiter can tell you, to be effective in today's fast-paced marketplace you must consistently invest time into proactively identifying and recruiting talented candidates. While the advent of the internet and job posting boards has certainly enhanced our ability to rapidly identify potential candidates, many recruiters now define candidate acquisition as the process of going online to a job board, performing a keyword search, and then contacting those individuals whose resumes seem to be a match.

While I won't dispute that a recruiter may find qualified candidates via website postings, newspapers, or job boards, a recruiter who relies too heavily on these passive techniques will ultimately be far inferior to the recruiter who makes proactive candidate acquisition a part of each recruiting day. The simple truth is that Internet job boards, like other passive recruiting methods, are diminished by the fact that they can only consider a candidate population comprised of those individuals who are or were _actively_ looking for a new opportunity (i.e. job board archives).

A recruiter who exclusively performs searches via job boards ultimately dismisses as much as two-thirds or more of the total candidate universe. Furthermore, in contrast to his or her counterparts who regularly utilize proactive recruiting strategies, a recruiter who is wed to passive recruiting techniques is far more likely to end up directly competing with other companies and recruiters for talent. Finally, candidate prospects who post resumes to job boards don't necessarily begin to qualify as "best in breed." There are many talented individuals who will never post a resume online, feeling that there is a stigma associated with doing so.

As I stated in Chapter One, job boards often represent the path of least resistance for some recruiters with respect to locating potential candidates. Again, it makes perfect sense to use job boards as a channel within a broader recruiting matrix, but to rely on them exclusively is short-sighted.

For example, if I want to become a good golfer, I will need to gain some degree of proficiency with all the clubs in my bag: driver and woods, irons, wedges and putter. If I go to a practice range and flail away at a couple of hundred balls with my driver, will that make me a better overall golfer? Maybe I will become more effective with my driver, but I won't have worked on the other aspects of the game that are inherent to scoring and ultimately to success.

Fundamentals of Sourcing

Sourcing is the process of proactively and methodically identifying prospective candidates within the market sector you serve. Note that the key word here is *proactive* and *not* passive. Passive recruiting and candidate identification methods (i.e. Internet job boards, career sections of corporate websites, and classified newspaper ads, etc.) can only work when a prospective candidate actually reads the advertisement or posting and is actually compelled to respond.

To ensure that I don't come across as being overtly opposed to passive recruiting approaches, let me reiterate that these techniques have a place within any organization's recruiting matrix. In fact, according to a report released by The Conference Board in December 2005, three out of four job seekers still utilize newspapers to look for a new position, and three out of five job seekers utilize the internet to find new opportunities. These modes of recruiting virtually assure that an organization will communicate with individuals who are actively looking to make a job change, but they are unable to engage passive prospects who might elect to activate themselves as candidates if presented with a great opportunity.

In August 2006, the Computing Technology Industry Association (CTIA) surveyed roughly 1,000 IT professionals about their careers. Over 48 percent of respondents indicated that they were seeking an opportunity with a new employer (an additional nine percent said they were seeking new opportunities but only with their current employer).

In considering the responses more closely, however, little more than 15 percent of the total survey audience regarded their job search as being "very active," while the majority of respondents acknowledged that their job search was either "somewhat active" or "not very active." In other words, these last two groups of individuals effectively acknowledged that while they were open to the prospect of making a move, they had not actively pursued this goal.

The survey didn't attempt to qualify respondents on the basis of who posted their resumes online, regularly reviewed online or newspaper job postings, or proactively submitted resumes. Nor did the survey assess the actual job search channels being utilized by respondents who indicated they were "actively" or "somewhat actively" looking for new opportunities.

For the purposes of discussion, let's apply The Conference Board's conclusions regarding individuals who utilize the Internet and/or newspaper as a means of identifying a new job to the CTIA respondents who expressed a desire to find an opportunity with a new employer. We could then conclude that 32 percent of those surveyed might respond to passive recruiting channels as part of their job search. (Rather than bore you to death with the statistics behind the above percentages, I will ask that you simply trust me to have crunched the numbers correctly!)

While this analysis is largely hypothetical and doesn't consider every variable as relates to this specific survey audience, my point is that a recruiter or organization that relies exclusively on passive recruiting channels (newspapers/Internet job boards) will access only a small portion of the total workforce. Furthermore, there is no assurance of actually securing the "best" person for the job at hand. This is where proactive sourcing comes into play.

Proactive Sourcing

Proactive sourcing entails identifying and communicating with prospective candidates who are not necessarily engaged in a job search. Your objective in cold calling these individuals is to determine whether they possess the skills, characteristics, and other attributes that align with your openings, as well as a legitimate interest in considering a job change.

I will readily acknowledge that some portion of the prospects that you contact will not be interested in considering a near-term job change, but neither should you be overly preoccupied by this reality. As I highlighted in Chapter Two, your long-term objective is to forge the basis of a relationship with all passive candidates, even those who are not poised to make a move today. As I will reiterate again, and again, you must adopt a long-term view towards passive candidates who may not want to entertain making a job change today. Remember, if engaged correctly, these individuals can become a valued component of your professional network, and you may have the ability to place them at some point in the future.

In contrast to identifying job board candidates, who typically have an interest in making a job change immediately, proactive sourcing is deliberately intended to provide us with the ability to access passive candidates who are not actively looking. Unlike the candidates who populate job boards, passive prospects are unlikely to: A) be working with multiple recruiters, B) have posted their resumes on the Internet, or C) be actively interviewing. One of the distinct advantages associated with proactive sourcing is that it dramatically reduces the extent to which you must overtly compete for talent with other recruiters and organizations.

In the training programs I conduct, I often ask participants to tell me what *they* perceive to be the percentage of individuals throughout the entire workforce (all industries and all functions) who are actively looking for a new job at any given time. Not surprisingly, the responses I receive cover the spectrum of possibilities: 10...15...30...50 percent, and so on.

The Computing Technology Industry Association survey referenced earlier suggested that 48 percent of information technology professionals envisioned finding a new job with a new employer, and concluded that perhaps 30 percent of all respondents were in some mode of seeking a new opportunity. Because we don't have trigger points that distinguish what differentiates "very actively looking" from "somewhat actively looking," the actual number of job seekers is hard to pin down.

In a broader context, while the Department of Labor tracks unemployment data, there is no absolute means of determining the overall number of people who are "actively" looking for a new job across the entire workforce. Nor is there a concrete way to assess the number of individuals who are actively looking for a new opportunity within a specific industry sector, market niche, or geographic area.

If you are an in-house recruiter, however, I would submit that your company's annual attrition rate is a reasonable indicator. If your company has an annual year-to-year attrition rate of 23 percent, and there have been no systemic changes to corporate operations or deployment of employee retention programs to mitigate attrition, it's reasonable to expect that 23 percent of the individuals within your firm are actively looking for a job <u>RIGHT NOW</u>! That's almost one fourth of your workforce. A little scary, isn't it?

Before I get too far off track, let me make my point. If your predominant mode of recruiting is built around job boards, it is not important whether the total number of people actively looking for a new job in your market sector is 23, 20, or 32 percent. What *is* important is the ratio between the number of individuals actively utilizing job boards to identify new opportunities and the relative number of organizations attempting to recruit these individuals.

In Figure 4.0 below, you will see a pie chart that addresses what I am trying to convey. The area shaded in black represents a theoretical population of candidates who are actively engaged in a job search, or in this example, 25 percent of the overall employment marketplace.

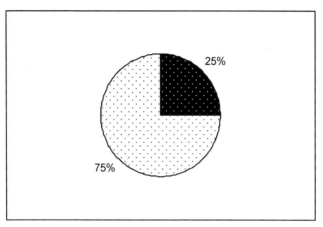

Figure 4.0

As part of their approach to finding a new job, these individuals are using an array of resources, including job boards, newspapers, recruiters, former peers and colleagues. If you utilize a passive recruitment channel and obtain the resumes of one or more qualified prospective candidates, naturally you're going to be delighted to speak with these individuals. In doing so, however, you must fully recognize that you are by no means communicating with a captive audience.

The people who comprise the shaded area of the pie chart must be regarded as individuals who are actively pursuing the market, and therefore are potentially communicating with a host of different recruiters and companies. As such, you must accept that if you bring these individuals into your recruitment lifecycle, your job or position is likely to be one of many potential opportunities they might consider. Yes, you have access to this segment of individuals who are actively seeking new positions, <u>but so does everyone else</u>.

You want to use proactive sourcing to reach out to the group of individuals who make up the other 75 percent of the pie chart reflected in Figure 4.0. These are passive prospects – individuals who are not actively seeking a new employment situation.

To realistically set your expectations regarding the long-term benefits of sourcing, you must remember the following:

A) In as much as you may hope to engage prospective candidates who are poised and interested in making a near-term job change, you must accept the fact that many of the candidates you contact via sourcing will not be prepared to make a move right now. If sourcing yields individuals who are indeed ready to consider new opportunities today, great. But you should be equally happy if you encounter individuals who may move in six months to a year, as this allows you to build future candidate inventory.

B) The overall intent of proactive sourcing is to diligently build and augment your candidate base, with an eye towards the future. Sourcing may not represent more placements immediately; but if you steadfastly make it an integral component of your recruiting process, sourcing will dramatically impact overall performance.

It makes sense to engage passive prospects via proactive sourcing for numerous reasons, and they are as follows:

1) Cultivating a pool of sourced candidates will ultimately result in an increased placement rate. By intentionally building an industry or market-specific inventory, a recruiter is poised to be more responsive to new job openings as they come online. Many recruiters don't necessarily enjoy proactive sourcing or cold calling. But

by investing time in sourcing, a proactive recruiter can consistently introduce quality prospects into an ever growing candidate network that can be leveraged at any time. In contrast, recruiters who don't engage in proactive sourcing operate in more of a one-dimensional mode, relying primarily on passive or reactive recruiting techniques (boards, newspapers, etc.).

2) Building quality relationships with sourced passive candidates can engender a greater degree of loyalty. By establishing rapport with a prospect early, you are able to lay the groundwork for a quality relationship well prior to the time when the prospect may actually consider making a job change. A candidate who is ready to make a move is much more likely to contact you than another recruiter with whom they have no relationship, provided that you have done a good job keeping in touch. Ideally, if you have worked hard to create meaningful rapport, prospective candidates will view you as not just a conduit to a potentially better opportunity, but also as a trusted confidante with whom they can discuss their career.

3) The sourcing process is comprised of highly targeted calls that can provide you not only with quality leads, but also with valuable market intelligence.

4) Proactive sourcing is timely. Simply put, you can initiate proactive sourcing on a new job requisition immediately after receiving it. If you only run an advertisement in a newspaper or on an Internet job board, you are adopting a passive approach that isn't necessarily going to deliver a timely response. People who elect to respond to your advertisement are doing so in accordance with *their* schedule and *their* perceived interests, not yours.

5) Proactive sourcing helps you become a "Marketplace Expert." If you are focused on a particular industry or niche, you will begin to amass an array of contacts exclusive to your marketplace and will truly become "plugged-in." Sourcing calls also force you to think on your feet, which will help you build your selling skills, presentation ability, and confidence.

I have discussed the many benefits associated with proactive sourcing. Now let's consider how to go about selecting the kinds of organizations from which you should source. The most obvious organizations to source from are companies that sit within the same vertical market sector. For example, if you recruit for a software company, it makes eminent sense that you consider sourcing from peer entities. If you recruit on behalf of financial services organizations, then it is likely that you will consider sourcing from other banking, insurance, or brokerage entities that align with your organization.

Many reference tools and directories can be utilized for sourcing. If you are looking for highly specialized experience that is specific to your organization's business or in support of a particular client company, you may want to investigate utilizing the North American Industry Classification System (NAICS) codes, which were formerly known as Standard Industry Classification (SIC) codes. These systems assign profiling codes to every business entity, and enable recruiters to quickly produce lists of businesses that are in the same or similar industries and within the same geographic area.

The reference section of any good library can provide access to NAICS sources, or you can simply go to the U.S. Census Bureau website (www.census.gov). Also, business intelligence firms like Dunn & Bradstreet and Hoovers (www.hoovers.com), among others, offer the ability to research companies in various industry sectors.

Alternatively, it may be productive to identify target source entities through trade association websites. As a rule, where there is an industry, there is a trade association. Where there is a sub-specialty within an industry, there is a trade association. Often trade association websites contain directories of companies or individual members, and/or publications that can be purchased and that are loaded with the names of industry or niche experts who can provide the basis for effective networking. Almost every trade association has an elected Board of Directors, and these individuals tend to possess outstanding professional networks. Chambers of Commerce or Economic Development Commissions can be another outstanding source of individuals who are "plugged in" with respect to the industries and companies that are based within their service area.

For skill-specific, individual contributor positions in areas like technology or accounting, it may be productive to utilize old resumes or reference check data to select source companies. You may also want to consider sourcing from companies with a negative reputation or that sit within a fundamentally uninteresting or stagnant market sector. Additionally, you may want to consider sourcing from organizations that are in a state of institutional distress (revenue losses, operating issues, attrition issues, cutbacks, etc.).

College and University Alumni Directories can be invaluable, particularly for locating and identifying individuals who possess specific degrees (Business/Accounting, Nursing, IT, Engineering, Pharmacy, etc.). Also, Alumni newsletters and/or the Class Notes component of an Alumni website can be an invaluable source of leads.

Beyond these basic approaches to identifying potential source entities, a host of other internet tools can be used to locate individuals or organizations that may be appropriate to source or contact. For the purposes of brevity and because new internet resources are emerging all the time, I will only mention a few of these resources. The most obvious tools are search engines such as Google (www.google.com), Yahoo! (www.yahoo.com), Altavista (www.altavista.com), and Ask.com (www.ask.com). LinkedIn (www.linkedin.com) is an excellent professional networking tool that enables you to build networks of contacts and subsequently leverage not only your own direct contacts, but the contacts of others.

Another interesting tool worth consideration is ZoomInfo (www.zoominfo.com) which captures a wealth of information on people and organizations via press releases, web sites, and other sources. This information can be searched and provides results that correlate people with the companies for whom they work. So, if I want to search on people who work at XYZ Corporation in Philadelphia, ZoomInfo allows me to construct a detailed query that usually produces a host of names.

Jigsaw (www.jigsaw.com) is an excellent tool that can enable you to quickly identify prospective leads or potential referral contacts. Jigsaw has created a company-specific nationwide leads database. Its subscriber community is charged with adding the names of employees that work at firms all over the country, as well as maintaining the accuracy and integrity of this information. Jigsaw allows you to either pay a monthly fee to access leads, or to enter new leads into the system in exchange for the ability to download leads that may be relevant to the searches you are executing. If you would like to try Jigsaw and take advantage of the opportunity to get 20 free contacts, go to:

http://jigsaw.com/company_information/slr-paulsiker.xhtml

If you seek marketing, sales, or IT professionals you may want to investigate using a tool called Cardbrowser.com (www.cardbrowser.com). Essentially, Cardbrowser.com captures business cards from attendees at major trade shows and conferences (mostly in the IT/Technology sector). These business cards are placed into a database that can be queried. So, if you are looking for a sales professional in a particular market sector, or with a particular firm, you can construct a simple query to identify prospects.

Numerous other sources can be accessed via the Internet as well: Weblogs, User Groups, Corporate Websites, etc. Again, the list of Internet-based tools is simply too long for me to address comprehensively here.

So now that I have briefly addressed the benefits of sourcing and touched upon source entities, let's discuss the theoretical mindset of the individuals you are likely to contact. Below, in Figure 4.1, you will see The Sourcing Graph.

Sourcing Curve

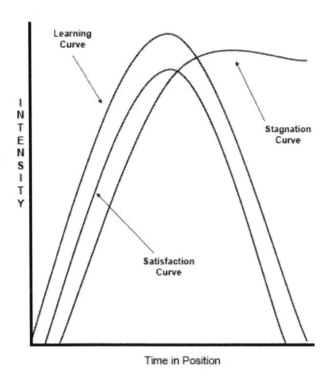

Figure 4.1

The X Axis on the graph is representative of Intensity, and the Y Axis is representative of Time. Specifically, the graph is intended to reflect the intensity of learning that occurs for a typical employee working in a particular role or job function. The graph also depicts how, over time, learning intensity levels change for reasons that will become readily apparent.

The first curve displayed on the graph is called the Learning Curve, a familiar term that characterizes the vast amount of information that just about any employee must obtain in beginning a new job. As is depicted in the graph, at the onset of a new job, individuals typically find their roles to be highly challenging because there is *so much* to learn. In addition to the fundamentals of performing in a particular job function, a new employee has to learn an array of other things, from where the water cooler is located to how best to communicate with new colleagues. Think of how steep your Learning Curve seemed when you first began to recruit. Eventually, as we begin to master our jobs, the Learning Curve diminishes.

The Job Satisfaction Curve closely parallels the Learning Curve simply because while an individual is gaining knowledge or obtaining new skills, he or she is most likely to derive a high degree of fulfillment and satisfaction with the role being performed. Typically speaking, while we are learning, we tend to be excited and engaged in our work. We are more apt to realize a sense of achievement, no matter how small, each day.

Ultimately, the Job Satisfaction Curve mirrors the Learning Curve because at the point where we are no longer learning or acquiring new skills, we begin to become dissatisfied with the role that we play. This reality is reflected by the Job Stagnation Curve, which intersects both the Learning Curve and the Job Satisfaction Curve shortly after they have hit their apex.

As the Learning and Job Satisfaction Curves begin a downward trend, Job Stagnation rises. As the opportunity to acquire new skills or tackle new challenges diminishes, our work inevitably becomes less exciting and less fulfilling. Boredom starts to creep in. As the Learning and Job Satisfaction Curves begin a downward trend,

Job Stagnation rises. And this reality, often in combination with other factors, is why most people will ultimately decide to explore new career challenges.

The amount of time that it takes for someone to become dissatisfied with a job will vary from person to person. Based on personal observation, however, it tends to range anywhere between 1.5 and 3.5 years, depending on the nature of the job and associated challenges. Unless an individual can secure new challenges via the acquisition of new responsibilities, job redefinition, or a promotion, career stagnation will occur and the desire to change will become intense.

Thus organizations that do not invest concerted energy in formulating career tracks for employees tend to experience a greater degree of attrition. Conversely, companies that offer merit-based career tracks and strive to continually offer new challenges to employees, are far more likely to retain employees for a longer period of time. Additionally, although the Sourcing Curve applies to a high percentage of employees, some individuals end up in positions or organizations in which they essentially perform the same role for extensive periods of time without ever feeling a sense of stagnation.

During my training programs, I often ask individuals to identify the point on the Sourcing Graph that represents the optimal time to initially communicate with a passive candidate. If you look at the graph for a moment or two, you can participate in this exercise. Simply note the optimal place on the graph where you might hope to connect with a prospective candidate to discuss new career opportunities.

Most recruiters respond by identifying a point somewhere to the right of where the Stagnation Curve intersects with the Job Satisfaction and Learning Curves. They identify this as the ideal point to call a prospect because they think the individual is more likely to respond, *"Boy, I'm glad that you called. I am completely ready to make a job change."*

Although you certainly will have a motivated candidate at this point, there are some potential negatives. Their resumes are probably on the internet. They're probably out interviewing. They're probably working with multiple recruiters. They may even have pending job offers. The main issue here is that once they pass the point where career stagnation has set in, you risk investing significant time and energy to work with a candidate whose search process is already well advanced.

I have periodically encountered individuals who upon getting my call have expressed, *"Wow, your timing is unbelievable. I was just dusting off my resume and in the preliminary phases of getting ready to make a move."* Does this happen often? No. Most talented professionals who have hit a point of ongoing stagnation within their job are not going to allow themselves to atrophy. More often than not, these individuals have taken a number of steps to activate their candidacy, which leads to my point.

In proactive recruiting, the ideal time to initiate a sourcing call occurs before a prospective candidate actively considers making a career move. With respect to the Sourcing Graph in Figure 4.1, you really want to be reaching out to prospects at some point prior to the apex of the Learning Curve and Job Satisfaction Curve, and certainly prior to the point where job stagnation sets in.

Remember, the intent here is to establish a relationship *prior* to the point where a candidate has conclusively decided to make a job change and to continue that relationship as they progress through the Curve. Again, we are not necessarily making sourcing calls to fill a job order this week. It may happen, and it's nice when it does, but ultimately this is not the prime intent of sourcing. The intent of sourcing is to regularly add 'clean' prospects to our inventory of marketable candidates. By 'clean' prospects, I am referring to individuals who haven't broadcast their resumes to 500 different recruiters.

Sourcing is most productive when conducted daily even if you don't necessarily have an open job order. By constantly augmenting your candidate base with sourced prospects you will ultimately construct an on-target network of warm candidate prospects. Furthermore, at some juncture, many of these prospects will be interested in making a job change.

If you effectively communicate with a sourced prospect over time, there is a reasonable likelihood that one day he or she will arrive at work and conclude, *"You know what? I think I need to make a change."* What will these individuals do? Will they post their resumes on the internet? Will they search the Yellow Pages for a recruiting firm? They may do these things, but in my experience, they are more likely to pull out the business card or email that you forwarded and initiate a call to you. Again, this scenario is predicated on having built some semblance of a relationship with the prospect and having stayed in periodic contact. If a recruiter has done these things, the individual is probably going to seek out a known and trusted career resource as opposed to going it alone.

Sourcing Calls

Sometimes, despite your best efforts to source prospects, you will run into the proverbial brick wall. When this happens you can still attempt to acquire the names of prospects directly from other organizations from which you may wish to recruit.

In initiating a sourcing call to a target organization, you will probably encounter a receptionist. Increasingly, you may encounter an auto-attendant, but even the auto-attendant function will usually allow you to speak with a receptionist.

The first thing that you want to do when initiating a sourcing call is to tell the person answering the phone at the source company who you are and why you are calling. Now, you could call a source company and say, *"Hi, my name is Tom Johnson, and I am a recruiter seeking to identify and recruit the most talented individuals in your firm."* This approach, while direct, is unlikely to aid you in securing the desired result.

Ideally, you want to start the call by saying something like:
Recruiter: *"Good afternoon, my name is Tom Johnson, and I am hoping that you can point me in the right direction?"*

Stating that you are, *"hoping to be pointed in the right direction,"* effectively says that you are seeking help. Next, you want to acquire the name of the receptionist or gatekeeper, which can be accomplished as follows:

Recruiter: *"Good afternoon, my name is Tom Johnson, and I am hoping that you can point me in the right direction?"*

Gatekeeper: *"I am happy to try..."*

Recruiter: *"Great...and, I'm sorry, your name is...?"*

Gatekeeper: *"Susan Petry...."*

Next, you want to explain the premise of your call. In this portion of the script, you can say:

Recruiter: *"Thanks, Susan. Again, my name is Tom Johnson and I am working on an organizational development project and I am attempting to network with people in the _____ Department. Who is the individual responsible for that Department/Area, please?"*

Note that the script factually states the purpose of your call. You *are* attempting to execute an organizational development project, by virtue of the fact that you want to complete a search for an internal hiring authority or external client. Furthermore, you *are* interested in networking with professionals in the specific departments that align with your search. Certainly the script should be tailored to optimize its effectiveness. For example, if I am conducting a search for a Tax Accountant, my script might sound like this:

<u>Recruiter:</u>   *"I am working on a tax project for a client and I am attempting to network with other corporate tax professionals who I presume would be situated within your Accounting or Finance Department. Who is the individual responsible for the Tax Audit function, please?"*

By volunteering who you are and suggesting the premise of your call, you increase your chances of being routed to individuals who are relevant to your job order. The only data that you haven't supplied is your firm's name, and often you can provide this information as well, with a couple of caveats.

Agencies that incorporate the terms "staffing," "recruiter," or "search" within their names are a dead giveaway, particularly to a seasoned gatekeeper. In these instances, if asked for the name of your firm, the truth is always your best bet, but be sure to answer the question and then restate your question. If the name of your firm is Technology Search Partners, for example, you can say, *"Sure, my firm is Technology Search Partners, and who would be the appropriate person to speak with in XYZ Department, please?"* Alternatively, if your firm regularly conducts business using an acronym, you may want to consider using the abbreviated name of the firm (i.e., TSP, Inc.) when making sourcing calls.

But there are also occasions when I have very specifically expressed the nature of my role to a gatekeeper by saying, *"I'm an Executive Recruiter (Search Consultant, Corporate Recruiter, etc.), and I am working on an accounting assignment. I was hoping to network with the individual who is responsible for the Tax Audit function. Who would that be, please?"*

Here are some additional guidelines that apply to the sourcing process:

1) Avoid Sounding Like A "Salesperson"

During sourcing calls, you should strive to speak using a deliberately slower pace with a lower inflection. It may seem awkward when you first attempt to communicate this way, but communicating in a calmer, slower manner will help to ensure that the gatekeeper listens to what you are saying, as opposed to how you are saying it. The object here is to avoid sounding like you are selling something, because most gatekeepers are adept at intercepting salespeople. Speaking rapidly or in an excited manner can often create undesired scrutiny.

One recruiter that I know was an absolute master at executing sourcing calls. He had a naturally slow, almost plodding rate of speech and low voice inflection. The last thing he sounded like was a salesperson, and as a result he was highly effective in getting past gatekeepers.

In contrast, another recruiter with whom I worked possessed one of the best sales voices imaginable. This woman's verbal presentation was incredibly crisp, but her speaking style also projected a great deal of energy and enthusiasm. Sourcing was a major weakness for her because she had a faster rate of speech and a higher degree of inflection. Gatekeepers would block her on virtually every sourcing call she made. Once she started slowing down her rate of speech, her sourcing calls became dramatically more effective.

If you find that you naturally have a higher inflection and faster rate, you'll need to consciously change your phone voice and concentrate on using a speech style more conducive to sourcing. You may want to practice making these calls and record your voice so that you can be more cognizant of exactly how you sound.

2) Convey That You Need Help

The approach should be that of "help me" versus "give me." Why? It may sound idealistic, but generally people like to assist others. The role of a receptionist, by definition, is to help people get to the appropriate parties within the organization. There is simply nothing to be gained by approaching a gatekeeper in a condescending or patronizing manner.

3) Be Prepared To Ask Follow-up Questions

You should consciously strive to ask questions. If the gatekeeper is asking all the questions, you're unlikely to get the information that you need; furthermore you are relinquishing control. Inevitably in the course of a conversation with any gatekeeper, you will have to answer some questions. Ideally, however, in answering questions you should attempt to ask follow-on questions at the conclusion of your response. This might flow as follows:

<u>Gatekeeper</u>: *".....And again, your name and the name of your company is...?"*

<u>Recruiter</u>: *"Sure, it's Scott Stevens with TechieTech Industries....and the best person for me to speak to in the Accounting function would be....?"*

<u>Gatekeeper</u>: *"Oh...yes, that would probably be Sarah Thomas."*

<u>Recruiter</u>: *"Great, and Sarah's title is...?"*

<u>Gatekeeper</u>: *"Um...the directory says that she is a Tax Auditor."*

If you answer the gatekeeper's question and conclude your response with a question of your own, you are in effect taking control of the conversation. By doing so, you are far more likely to obtain the information that you seek.

4) Remember, You Simply Want To Acquire Names

The purpose of your call is to get names. You want to get the gatekeeper's name, and you definitely want to get the name of any person to whom you are transferred. Also, remember that in making these calls, the more names you can drop, the greater the probability of being perceived as an "insider." Here's an example of what I mean:

Recruiter: *"Hi Debbie, this is Mark Rogers. We spoke briefly last week, and you suggested that I talk with Tom Baker or Boris Yeltsin about a Tax Audit project that I am working on. I tried to reach Tom and Boris, but gather that they are out of the office this week. Can you suggest a couple of other people in this area that I might be able to reach – any help you can give me would be greatly appreciated."*

After you obtain the targeted individuals' names, simply set them aside to call at another time. If possible, you don't want sourcing calls to turn into introductory or cold calls. Again, sourcing calls are intended to gather information (names). To maximize efficiency and assure some degree of "rhythm," I recommend that these calls be executed in dedicated time blocks.

5) *Get Away* From The Gatekeeper And *Get To* An Internal Support Function (ISF).

ISFs are essentially any corporate function or department that regularly handles incoming calls and is oriented to helping people secure information. If you find yourself blocked out by a specific gatekeeper, call back later and ask to be transferred to a functional department within the company, especially one that is accustomed to providing information. Examples of Internal Support Functional areas include: Sales, Marketing, Accounts Receivable, etcetera. The bottom line is that people who work within an organization's ISF departments aren't necessarily anticipating or screening out recruiter sourcing calls.

I can recall, for example, a search that I conducted several years ago where I was tasked to recruit a very specific type of Information Technology professional, one who worked within either the cable or network television industry. The desired professional had to have experience with media advertising sales processes, but from an IT perspective. Rather than calling into the IT departments of the media companies that I identified, I instinctively called into the Advertising Sales function. I made calls to the Advertising Sales departments of three television companies and in minutes had the names of six highly qualified individuals for my search.

6) Leverage Auto Attendant & Voice Mail Systems

Voicemail systems are often set up to provide a plethora of names. Many auto attendants will enable you to access departmental listings or employee name directories. For example: *"To access accounting, please press 8, to access engineering, please press 1."* The voice mail system may be configured to offer other options as well. Typically, you can quickly acquire a number of names by utilizing the auto-attendant feature.

I know various recruiters who are exceptionally successful at obtaining names by exploiting voicemail systems. Upon encountering voicemail at a source entity, they merely plug in common last names (Smith, Jones, Thomas, Allen, etc.) and begin retrieving leads. Also, for many of these systems, you do not need to enter the entire name; entering several letters and then pressing the * key will usually suffice.

Alternatively, while not always the case, if you know an accountant is at extension 108 of a target organization, other employees of the same skill set may be located at surrounding extensions (106-107-109, etc). When using the voicemail approach to acquire prospect names, your best bet is to call over lunchtime, before the work day starts, or after business hours.

7) Prepare To Answer, "What is this call in reference to?"

Several years ago, the television program "Saturday Night Live," featured an extremely funny sketch with David Spade functioning as Dick Clark's receptionist. Regardless of the individual or celebrity who arrived in the reception area (Roseanne Arnold, Dick Clark's mother, and even Jesus), Spade would ask each of them, *"And you are?"*, *"And you're with?"*, *"And this is in reference to?"* For recruiters who are executing sourcing calls, one of the most common questions from a gatekeeper is, *"What is this in reference to?"* The sourcing script that was introduced earlier attempted to anticipate and address this question. The scripted response is: *"I am working on an organizational development project."*

If you are pressed to provide additional details, you may need to get more specific. Usually the best approach for handling this request is to provide the Gatekeeper with more information than he or she may necessarily be seeking.

For example, if you are attempting to identify computer programmers, and are asked, *"What is this in reference to?"* you might reply by saying:

"I am supporting a project that ultimately involves the integration of XYZ software tools with ABC database products in a multi-tier, client-server environment. I'm trying to network with IT professionals or software developers who are familiar with these tools. Who would you recommend I speak to?"

This approach can be tailored to just about any profession and is intended to put the gatekeeper into a mode where he or she is simply unable to address your inquiry and now must pass your call on to someone else.

8) Before You Are Transferred – Get A Name

There is nothing worse than saying, *"I'd like to speak to the person that handles Bookkeeping,"* being asked to hold, and then being immediately transferred to someone else without knowing who that person is or the role that they perform. Always attempt to get the name and title of the person to whom you are being transferred. If the individual's title is Director or Manager, you can respond to the gatekeeper with something along the lines of:

"Tom Smith is the Manager of Development – that's great. In the event that Tom is not available, is there someone else you would recommend I speak to?"

Alternatively, you can also say:

"I appreciate your suggestion that I speak with Tom Smith, who manages Development, and I will give him a try. In that some of my questions are fairly technical, can you also suggest someone who holds the title of Software Engineer or Programmer/Analyst? They may be better positioned to help me."

9) Remember, Sourcing Is All About Getting Names

I want to reiterate that the object of any sourcing call is to secure names. If you get a name, you've had a productive call. Even if the person whose name you acquire is not necessarily aligned with the particular type of candidate that you are seeking, you have a name that you can use the next time you call into that particular organization.

None of these phone sourcing techniques will work 100 percent of the time. You will have to try various combinations of these methods to determine which ones work best for you. Your initial attempt to source from a particular organization may be unsuccessful. You may need to try different sourcing approaches over successive days. With each call that you initiate, however, you will get ever closer to your ultimate goal of uncovering high quality prospective candidates.

Sourcing is a bit like detective work. You know that a particular organization has individuals who possess experience that aligns with the openings on which you are working. The challenge is to figure out who these individuals are so that you can subsequently contact them.

Proactive sourcing need not be exclusively tied to identifying prospective candidates through calling into organizations or using Internet resources. You can also source prospects via social networking – it's just a matter of asking people that you encounter to share whom they know that works at a particular organization or performs in a specific job function. I have attended many parties over the years, where in the course of casual conversations with people that I've never met previously, I have been able to obtain numerous worthwhile leads that were wholly relevant to job requisitions that I was seeking to fill. You simply need to take an interest in the people you meet, learn about what they do, and then remember to ask them who they know who might be relevant to projects on which you are working.

Securing candidates who are not actively working with other recruiters or broadcasting their resumes across the marketplace will greatly enhance the overall quality of your candidate network. This is not to suggest that you should or would want to altogether dismiss utilizing passive recruitment channels to aid you in filling openings. By incorporating some level of proactive sourcing into each business week, however, you will dramatically augment your candidate universe. Over time, if you remain disciplined about sourcing on a regular basis, you will become more responsive to your customers, bring greater value to your recruiting efforts, and face less competition in securing high quality candidate prospects.

Chapter 5: Compelling Voicemail Messages

As technological innovation has permeated the workplace, voicemail and auto-attendant based phone systems have become a simple reality of virtually every office environment. In most respects the days of walking into the office to find a small pile of "While You Were Out" message slips are gone. Voicemail allows anyone the ability to deliver a personalized greeting to external callers and to retrieve messages remotely, 24 hours a day. Furthermore, voicemail satisfies our seemingly insatiable desire to be in touch and accessible, a point underscored by the fact that most people have voicemail not just at the office, but also at home and on individual mobile phones. In fact, for most of us, it would be difficult to imagine life without the convenience of voicemail.

Voicemail has undeniably enhanced our ability to stay in touch and secure important messages. Like most technologies, however, voicemail has modified our behavior and how we interact with the world around us.

From the perspective of a recruiter making cold calls, voicemail is both a blessing and a curse. On the one hand, we can leave a detailed message for a prospective candidate saving us from having to repeatedly redial the person we are trying to contact. On the other hand, voicemail is utilized as a call screening tool, and we may find that we are "screened out" from getting a returned call if we are not creative in how we construct our messages.

Each of us can probably think of a time we got a message from someone, didn't recognize the caller's name or appreciate the intent of the message, and elected not to return the call. If the call was really important, we reasoned, the person would call us back.

Perhaps in listening to the caller's message, we sensed that it was a sales call.

For many people, voicemail has become a buffer between themselves and the world around them. We all probably know of an individual who, in fact, "hides" behind voicemail, opting to respond only to important messages rather than just picking up the phone when it rings.

Given the negative bias that most people have towards telemarketing, this should come as no great surprise. People don't like telemarketing calls for two reasons: 1) These calls consume time; and 2) Often times the person calling makes us feel pressured to make a commitment (purchase an item, agree to an appointment, etc.). As a result, we have collectively been conditioned to want to avoid these telemarketing approaches, not just at home, but also at work.

As recruiters, and ultimately as sales professionals, we have two basic options relative to leaving a voicemail message that will compel a prospective candidate to return our call. The first option is to leave a very detailed message that communicates the exact nature of the call. This type of voicemail message would sound something like this:

"Hi Tom, my name is John Smith, and I am a recruiter with XYZ Corporation. The reason that I am calling is because I am interested in speaking to you about career opportunities that presently exist with my firm. If you would call me back at 555-1212, I would appreciate having a chance to speak with you."

The problem with the direct approach is that in leaving a message such as the one above, you have elevated the prospect's voicemail box to the role of recruiter. This kind of approach is great, if you are highly confident that the prospect is indeed open to considering new opportunities. Regrettably, as I wrote previously, the people that you are most interested in recruiting often are not actively looking for a job or entertaining the possibility of making a job change.

In the example script above, the voicemail message offers detailed information as to the specific nature of the call, but is incapable of engaging the prospect in a discussion about their specific wants, needs, and career motivators. As a result the prospect is left to make a simple decision: Am I looking to make a job change or not? If they are not consciously looking to make a job change, the chances of a returned call are very low. In fact, a prospective candidate who listens to the script above is likely to think:

"Hmmm.....John Smith...recruiter...from XYZ Corporation....wants me to change jobs......I'm not interested......press the DELETE Key."

The thought process of a voicemail recipient, as reflected above, serves to highlight several other issues associated with the typical voicemail message that many recruiters elect to leave for prospective candidates. First, most voicemail messages tend to provide too much information about the exact nature and reason for our call and are too lengthy.

I have listened to a variety of voicemail messages left for prospective candidates by recruiters, and many of these messages are *even more descriptive* than the example provided earlier. Some of these messages delve into the detailed specifics of a role or various opportunities on which the recruiter is working, and go on for several minutes. These messages don't leave much to the imagination and are simply too long.

Furthermore, identifying yourself as a recruiter in the first ten seconds of a voicemail message initiates a subconscious thought process within a prospective candidate. This thought process is wholly oriented to deciding if they are open to hearing about new opportunities. If within this initial thought process they conclude that they are relatively happy in their current role, they may forego listening to the entire message, let alone return the call.

This reality ties into the second issue that many recruiters face in leaving voicemail messages. Most voicemail messages fail to be compelling. By 'compelling' I mean interesting. Your objective in leaving a voicemail message is to convey just enough information to spark a prospect's curiosity and have your call returned.

Remember, your number one objective is to have a meaningful conversation with a prospective candidate. Even if you conclude that the candidate is legitimately not interested in making a career change, you still want to have the opportunity to learn about this individual, their background, goals, and aspirations. If you can do this, you secure the ability to have follow-on discussions at a later date, perhaps with a more desirable result.

In leaving highly detailed voicemail messages, you not only risk *not* getting your call returned, but also risk the chance to engage an individual who may at some point in the future genuinely contemplate working with you to migrate into another role. Additionally, even if the prospect is not willing to entertain a job change, you still want the ability to network, as well as the ability to potentially obtain referrals.

Your ultimate goal in leaving any voicemail message is to provide enough information so that the prospect is compelled to return your call; nothing more, nothing less. If you are successful in getting returned calls you have a much greater degree of influence on whether or not the prospect determines that he or she is open to considering new opportunities.

How do you go about constructing and leaving a compelling voicemail message? Well, first of all you need to know exactly what you want to say and how you want to say it. You need to consider the content of your message as well as how you go about expressing the actual message itself.

To the extent that it is possible, you want to be cognizant of the speaking style of the message recipient. Some people have a rapid speaking style, while others have a much more deliberate or slower rate of speech. Some people come across as being highly extroverted and energetic, while others may seem rather soft-spoken.

Often, when you listen to someone's voicemail greeting, you can formulate various insights into their personality. For example, you may encounter an individual whose voicemail greeting sounds something like this:

FAST: *"This is Joe Smith, and I am unavailable to take your call. Please leave your name, number, purpose and time of call, and I will get back to you later."*

A very fast-paced message may indicate a Type-A personality, or reflect someone who is truly on the go. Alternatively, you may encounter a voicemail greeting that sounds more like this:

SLOW: *"Hello...you have reached Mary Jones, and presently I am either away from my desk or on another call. You call is very important to me, so at the tone please leave your name, number, and a detailed message and I will get back to you just as soon as possible. Thank you so much for calling and have a blessed day."*

A slower, deliberate voicemail greeting may suggest a more moderated personality type.

Studies have been performed on the effectiveness of adapting one's speaking style to that of the recipient of a communication. While the studies regarding the effectiveness of this approach are inconclusive, I have found that there is some merit to this technique. I am not suggesting that you rely entirely upon the speaking style of an individual's recorded voicemail greeting as an exclusive means of gauging that individual's personality. However, I do think an argument can be made for attempting to replicate a prospect's pace and style of speech as a means of presenting yourself in a manner that will resonate with the prospect.

If you call a prospective candidate, encounter a very soft-spoken greeting and elect to leave a gung-ho, hard charging, *"CALL ME BACK RIGHT AWAY"* type of message, you risk making the prospect feel uncomfortable and reduce the probability of getting your call returned. Likewise, if you call a prospective candidate, encounter a short, driven, staccato greeting, and opt to leave a slow, plodding message, the recipient is apt to conclude, *"I don't have time for this person."* The probability of your call being returned is greatly reduced.

In addition to modifying the pace and manner in which you deliver a voicemail message, you also need to be cognizant of the content of your message. Ideally, you want to provide some information, but again, only enough to make your message compelling. The information that you need to convey in order to optimize your chances of getting a returned call include: your name, a brief explanation regarding the purpose of your call, a specific timeframe when you can be reached, and finally a contact number where you can be reached.

The most important component of your message is your stated purpose for calling. The purpose of your call should relate in some manner to the individual you are trying to contact. If you secured the person's name via a referral, you can and should state this within your message. If you secured the person's name via research, you can say this as well. In addition, you can also say that you are working on a project or initiative that is the basis for your call. This does not mean, however, that you need to say that you are specifically interested in recruiting the prospect.

Additionally, you want to create a sense of urgency with respect to getting your message returned. From the standpoint of staying organized, it may make sense to suggest that the prospect return your call between specific timeframes during the day, when you are most likely to be available.

Also, you may want to provide the prospect with a cell phone number, as opposed to an office number that contains information regarding your company. This is a key point and should not be misinterpreted. There are instances where citing your company's name may be very productive and appropriate. As a rule, however, if you can eliminate potential objections in advance of your discussion, you should do so. If citing your company name has the potential to reduce the likelihood of getting a return call, then it's probably wise not to incorporate it into your message. Conversely, if using your company name could enhance the likelihood of getting a returned call, then you should certainly use it in your message.

So, when you put everything together, what does a compelling voicemail sound like? It should go something like this:

"Hi Tom, my name is John Smith, and we haven't talked previously. I am calling you today for a pretty specific reason. I am working on an initiative that might be of interest to you, and was hoping that I could speak with you for just a moment or two. If you could call me back at 867-5309 between 4:30 and 5:30 PM today, I would be very appreciative."

Or:

"Hi Sue, my name is Rita Jones, and we haven't spoken before.... I came across your name relative to a project that I am working on and was hoping that we might have an opportunity to speak briefly. If you could call me back at 867-5309, I would really appreciate it."

Or:

"Hi Sue, my name is Donna Evans. Sue we haven't talked before, but I am under the impression that you might be very relevant to a project that I am currently working on. My schedule is pretty hectic, but I should be available between 4:45 PM and 5:30 PM today, or tomorrow morning until 11 AM. If you could call me back at either

867-5309 or 555-1212, I would welcome the chance to speak with you. I promise not to steal more than a few minutes of your time."

Or:

Hi Andy, my name is Jeanne Young, and we haven't communicated before. In doing some research on a project, I came across your name and believe that you may be in a position to help point me in the right direction. If you could call me back at 867-5309, I'd appreciate the chance to map out the specifics of my project, and I pledge to keep our discussion brief.

Or:

"Hi Tom, my name is Jack Davis, and a mutual acquaintance, Tim Porter, suggested that I give you a call regarding a project that I am currently working on....I am going to be tied up for a good portion of the day, but I'm really hoping that we can connect for just a couple of minutes. If you can call me back at 867-5309, I should be available between 4:45 PM and 5:30 PM. If you are unavailable in this timeframe, please let me know a good time to reach you. I genuinely look forward to speaking with you."

The above messages are fairly concise and provide the prospect with a modest level of insight into the reason for the call. Effectively, the prospect knows only that you are working on a project or initiative that may relate to them in some manner. Each message underscores that you are not interested in consuming too much of the prospect's time. This point is further reinforced by your provision of a fairly tight timeframe when the prospect can reach you. In essence, you haven't given them a reason not to call you back and have hopefully provoked enough interest and curiosity to compel them to pick up the phone and dial your number.

Periodically, I am asked, *"Paul – aren't there times when people call you back and upon determining that you are a recruiter express disappointment that you didn't indicate this in the message?"*

In candor, this scenario has happened very rarely, and on the isolated occasion where it has occurred, my response has been, *"Mr. Prospect, with all the concerns about organizations monitoring their employees' voicemail and email, I chose to be deliberately vague for reasons of confidentiality."* On every occasion, the prospect's response has been, *"Oh, I hadn't thought about that. Thanks for your consideration."*

What if you leave a message but don't get a returned call? I know of one recruiter who told me about leaving a string of voicemail messages for a prospective candidate over a period of about two weeks. After getting no response, he determined that he would leave one more message that went something like this: *"Hi Tom, it's Matt calling again. I just checked my notes and this is the 11th voicemail message that I am leaving you. Just so you know, if I get to 14 messages, you will have helped me set a new personal record."* Remarkably, the prospect called back, laughing, and said, *"Okay, I got your message and you made me laugh – how can I help you?"* I don't advocate using voicemail to torture prospects, but I do give the recruiter who told me this story great praise, if only for his ingenuity and sense of humor in dealing with adversity.

In summary, voicemail is an obstacle with which all sales professionals must contend. Despite the fact that some people will never return your call, my experience has proven that the overall approach outlined within this chapter offers the greatest potential for getting returned calls from the majority of prospective candidates that you attempt to contact. I encourage you to formulate your own voicemail word tracks, consistent with your voice, personality and style. The overall format that I have presented works well and I encourage you to try it!

Chapter 6: Advanced Introductory (Cold) Calls

Once you have secured quality leads through networking and sourcing, the next step is initiating cold calls to prospective candidates. Admittedly, many recruiters don't like to make cold calls because the prospect of directly contacting someone they do not know or know very little about is intimidating.

Franklin D. Roosevelt is credited with having said, *"The only thing we have to fear is fear itself."* This quote is wholly applicable to the cold calls that recruiters should strive to make an integral component of each business day.

For many recruiters, cold calls are fundamentally uncomfortable for several major reasons including:

1) Fear of rejection. No one likes the prospect of being rejected. The mere term "rejection" invariably takes many of us back to a time in our adolescence when we were rebuffed by someone we had a crush on. In sales, (and, again, recruiting is a sales function) being rejected by a prospect is essentially the equivalent of being told to, "Go away." We can all recount an experience where we were the "Rejecter," who abruptly and unsympathetically terminated a call from a salesperson or telemarketer.

2) Fear of the "unknown." Closely related to a basic fear of rejection, the fear of the unknown typically results from a recruiter's anxiety about what will happen during a call to a prospect. Will the person be nice or rude? Will the person be qualified or unqualified? Will the gatekeeper screen the call or allow it to go through? The truth is you can never truly know what will happen when you initiate these calls; but recruiters who focus on what might or might not transpire during the call do so to their own detriment.

3) Fear of sounding unknowledgeable. In contrast to a highly trained professional performing in a particular job function, many recruiters are not necessarily subject matter experts within the domain for which they recruit. In other words, if a recruiter is charged with staffing information technology roles at his company, it is unlikely that he will possess previous hands-on experience designing, developing, and implementing software or database solutions. As a result, the recruiter may perceive that he has a credibility issue, because he is not a technical professional. Furthermore, it can be intimidating to communicate with talented professionals who can pose difficult questions that the recruiter simply isn't equipped to answer, especially if the search assignment is sketchy or lacking in detail.

4) Fear of intrusion or imposition. Some recruiters believe that initiating calls to prospective candidates at their place of work is a potential imposition. They don't want to feel as though they are intruding on a prospect's time. While I will address why you needn't fear Items 1, 2, and 3 above momentarily, I will speak to this last fear right now. As a recruiting professional, my job is to create meaningful introductions between talented individuals in the greater employment marketplace and specific hiring authorities within the organization for which I work. I am a sales professional. Rule number one in sales is this: <u>If you don't believe in the value of what you are selling, don't sell it</u>.

If I believe that my company is a quality organization and that I have something of substance to offer specific professionals in the marketplace, you better believe that I won't hesitate to pick up the phone and proactively reach out to these individuals whether I know them or not. Furthermore, if I believe in the overall excellence of my organization and the people who comprise it, I should be delighted to talk to others about the qualities, attributes and other distinguishing features that make my organization and its employment opportunities compelling. As I touched upon earlier, from where I stand a good recruiter must be something of a corporate evangelist, dedicated to spreading the word about great career opportunities to individuals who will indeed benefit by virtue of this knowledge. To me, in making proactive cold calls, the last thing in the world I am doing is intruding or imposing on someone's time. In fact, if anything, I am presenting them with what could well be a life-changing opportunity.

Cold calling success is expressly dependent upon how well these introductory calls are executed. By framing the call correctly, utilizing specific words, projecting yourself in a candidate-centric manner, and developing what I refer to as cold calling fluency, you should have every expectation that the outcome of most cold calls will be entirely positive.

Detractors may argue, *"Paul, I hear what you are saying, but at the end of the day cold calling is not effective."* To these individuals I must respectfully but completely disagree. Over my 20-year career in search, I have completed far too many assignments where the placed applicant emerged expressly and exclusively as a result of a timely and well-executed cold call. These individuals were passive candidates who, prior to my introductory call, hadn't given the remotest thought to identifying a new job opportunity. I came to them. I told them a compelling story about an organization and about a select opportunity. I imparted information that initially made them think and that ultimately made them act.

In the grand scheme of recruiting, nothing is more fulfilling than securing a high quality candidate as the result of a timely and engaging call. You start with nothing more than a name, a number, and perhaps a modest amount of information about an individual, and end up with something of tremendous significance – an A+ applicant.

Reeling in a high quality candidate is an adrenaline rush. Hearing a talented prospect say, *"Wow, I really hadn't contemplated the thought of making a move, but based on what you are telling me I absolutely am interested in talking further,"* is exceptionally gratifying. Proactive cold calls work.

The challenge for many recruiting professionals is that they have not learned how to conduct these calls in a manner that is effective, engaging, and oriented towards a long-term view. And this is the essence of what I will be addressing in this chapter.

To stay organized and effectively utilize your time, I highly recommend that you dedicate a block (or blocks) of time to conducting cold calls. If you can get into a rhythm of making these calls successively, you will greatly reduce the potential for call reluctance.

Additionally, if you need to make warm calls first as a means of ramping up to executing cold calls, don't hesitate to do so. Effective cold calls demand that you be focused. Effective cold calls require energy. Effective cold calls mandate active listening. If initially executing less demanding calls helps you to get into a flow or "rhythm" then that's fine.

What constitutes an effective candidate cold call? I am going to break down the cold call process and walk through the construction of a call script that will allow you to have a productive dialogue with virtually every individual you contact. The specific purpose or intent of these calls is twofold:

1. First, you want to engage prospects in a detailed career discussion that ultimately segues to understanding the candidate's willingness to entertain new career situations.

2. Second, and regardless as to whether or not a prospect is open to entertaining new situations, you want to cultivate high quality rapport. If a prospect is ultimately not open to considering new opportunities, you still want to learn about the individual's background and secure their permission to keep in touch over time.

Focused & Unfocused Candidate Cold Calls

There are two distinct types of candidate cold calls:

- Focused Cold Calls; and,
- Unfocused Cold Calls

A Focused Cold Call is one in which the recruiter is proactively calling a prospective candidate about a specific job order or requisition. And, as the name implies, an Unfocused Cold Call is one in which you are *not* directly recruiting on a specific job order or requisition.

Many recruiters prefer to make focused or position-specific cold calls, because they feel more comfortable being armed with a tangible job to discuss with a prospect. While there may be occasions when making a Focused Cold Call makes sense, I generally believe that this approach is flawed for two primary reasons.

The fundamental problem with position-specific cold calls is that this type of call is typically presented in a manner that assumes the prospective candidate is both <u>qualified</u> and <u>interested</u> in the opportunity at hand. A secondary issue is that the call is built around discussing one fairly specific role. As a result, the general thrust of the call is oriented to the "What Is," as opposed to the "What Could Be."

Let me explain further. Typically at the point when you are initiating calls to a prospective candidate, you have a nominal amount of information about the person. In fact, the knowledge you possess is likely to be oriented only to the work that the individual performs today. Let's say, for example, that I am recruiting for a mechanical engineer with prior experience in commercial product packaging, and through sourcing I find several likely prospective candidates. Prior to initiating a call, the most that I am likely to know about these individuals is that they perform in a job function that may be roughly similar to the role for which I am conducting a search.

What I cannot know until I speak with them is the overall degree to which each prospect's professional experience actually aligns with the role at hand. Additionally, until I engage each of the prospects in a discussion *about the manner in which they hope to see their career develop*, any presentation that I make about a particular job opening is effectively a crapshoot, because I have no idea of what they would regard to be important or enticing as relates to contemplating a new opportunity.

Again, Focused Cold Calls tend to emphasize selling a prospective candidate on an opportunity *prior* to formally qualifying the candidate or understanding whether he or she is sufficiently motivated to even entertain a career move.

This type of call might sound something like this:

Ring, Ring:

Candidate: *"Hello, this is Joe Candidate."*

Recruiter: *"Yes, hi Joe, my name is Sue Jones, and I'm a recruiter with ABC, Inc. I was calling you because right now I am working to identify a sharp Manager of Finance. We are a rapidly growing company that is looking for a real impact player who wants to assume a lot of responsibility. I don't know what your situation is currently, but I wanted to call to ask if you are open to new opportunities?"*

Candidate: *"Well, Sue, I appreciate your call, but right now I am really happy where I am. So no, I don't think I am your person."*

Recruiter: *"Well Joe, I understand that the timing may not be right for you, but I am really trying to dig on this role because it is a terrific opportunity. Do you know anyone else with your background who might be looking?"*

Candidate: *"Nope. I really would like to help you, Sue, but I can't think of anyone."*

<u>Recruiter</u>: *"Surely Joe, you must know someone that I can talk to…"*

<u>Candidate</u>: *"Sue, I'd like to help you, but I am not comfortable giving out names. Tell you what, give me your name and number again, and if I come across anyone who seems like a possibility, I'll pass your information along."*

<u>Recruiter</u>: (After hanging up the phone): *"Arrrrrrgh!!!!!"*

Sound familiar? The problem with the Focused Cold Call format is that this type of call puts "the cart before the horse." All too often, recruiters attempt to sell a particular job without understanding the wants, needs, and desires of their audience. If you don't take the time to understand a prospective candidate's situation, then you forego your chance to present your opportunity in a fashion that best aligns with the candidate's stated needs. You are effectively taking a stab in the dark that your opportunity may be of interest.

Some recruiters may argue, *"Well, Paul isn't it better to convey a specific opportunity at the onset of the discussion? After all, the worst thing that can happen is that the prospect can say that the role you have highlighted is not of interest, but even then the recruiter can still determine if there is some other type of opportunity that would be of interest."*

I do not deny that presenting a very specific opportunity to an individual via a Focused Cold Call could occasionally be highly appropriate – but these occasions are the exception. Based on years of experience trying different approaches, I simply don't believe that Focused Cold Calls allow a recruiter to communicate with a prospect from a position of strength.

Non-specific or Unfocused Cold Calls offer you the opportunity to emphasize learning about an individual's overall career status, experience and qualifications *before* raising a particular job opportunity. Furthermore, this call format allows you to fully understand and appreciate a potential candidate's career motivators in advance of promoting a particular job. Taking the time to understand a candidate's specific buying profile will dramatically improve your ability to present potential opportunities in a manner that optimally aligns with what a prospect has indicated is important or significant. In other words, using this approach allows you to present appropriate job opportunities in the manner that is most likely to resonate with a prospect.

I am by no means suggesting that in presenting an opportunity via the Unfocused Cold Calling approach that you should be manipulative or sugar-coat aspects of the roles upon which you are working. That is something I would never advocate.

What I am advocating is that by using the Unfocused Cold Call approach you are working from a position of strength. Simply stated, this call format is designed to help you engage all prospective candidates in a broad and upbeat career discussion. By taking an interest in a prospect's career and career objectives, you are better positioned to build a productive long-term relationship, regardless of whether the prospect is poised to explore near-term opportunities or not. Additionally, and perhaps just as importantly, the Unfocused Cold Call approach enables you to acquire important information that ultimately enables you to present your opportunities *with the candidate's stated needs in mind.*

In the Focused Cold Call script above, the primary intent of the call was to discuss a particular opportunity with a prospective candidate. Getting to know the candidate was a secondary issue. In contrast, the Unfocused Cold Call approach is first and foremost about the needs of a prospective candidate and secondly about job opportunities.

Before addressing the actual Unfocused Cold Call script, let's take a minute to understand the prospective candidate's environment and business mindset. Picture yourself performing the job of the individual you are going to contact.

Rarely is someone sitting at his/her desk, staring patiently at the phone and saying, *"Boy, it's 9:48 AM, I sure hope that a recruiter calls me."* While it would be nice for this to happen periodically, the simple truth is that most people are preoccupied with the daily demands of their job. The phone calls that they receive in a typical business day are fairly predictable. Depending on their function, they may get calls from colleagues, supervisors, clients, vendors, and family members. They may periodically receive a phone call from a recruiter, but it is not something that they are likely to anticipate.

Therefore, the tone and tenor of your voice and an attention-getting opening statement are very important to a successful call. Starting with an attention-getting opening statement will snap a candidate out of work mode and into a mode where they are fully concentrating on what you are saying.

Also, you want to make certain that your delivery is executed in a deliberate, confident, and metered fashion. I have listened to many recruiters rush through a sales presentation like this:

(Rapidly) *"Ah...Hi Tom, my name is Joe Smith, and I am a recruiter with ABC Recruiting firm. I am calling to ask you if you would like to hear about a really great job opportunity."*

It seems as if some recruiters believe that machine-gunning their way through a presentation will enhance the possibility of the prospective candidate saying, just as rapidly, *"Yes! I would love to work with you! When can we meet?"*

The truth is that when you talk rapidly, you sound anxious, which means that you don't sound confident. You risk having your message come across as a garbled and insecure sales pitch.

So, you need to draft and practice a professional sounding script that will help you have a meaningful dialogue with every prospective candidate that you contact. Before I go any further, let me speak to those of you who just read the last sentence and said, *"I*

HATE scripts! They make you sound canned. They diminish your ability to think on your feet."

To me, a script is nothing more than a tool. Most of the really talented recruiters I have known over the years take the time to map out or script key elements that they know they need to convey in a call. But a recruiter is not going to be effective if he or she drafts a cold call script and then proceeds to read it verbatim in a staccato manner.

Think of the exercise of building a script as being like taking a practice swing in golf, tennis, or baseball. The intent of the practice swing is to ensure that when you actually play the game, you hit the ball and hit it well.

In the sports I mentioned, you want to cultivate a replicable swing. In recruiting, you want to build out a quality script or bulleted selling messages that you flat out know "cold." Your objective is not to sound canned, but to deliver a compelling presentation in an entirely natural and completely fluid manner. This is something that comes with a great deal of practice.

Your cold call script will have three distinct phases:

- The Attention Phase
- The Objective Phase
- The Closing Phase

The Attention Phase

As I stated earlier, the individual you are contacting is likely consumed with work which means that you need to quickly capture his or her attention. When the prospective candidate answers the phone, you want to be very matter of fact and make an attention-getting introductory statement that sounds something like this:

"Good morning, John, my name is Rob Smith, and we haven't talked previously. I work in the software engineering market sector (or whatever niche you serve). Do you have a moment so that I can explain what prompted my call?"

This introductory statement will probably be enough to capture the prospective candidate's attention. At this point the candidate is wondering if they should be familiar with your name, as well as the exact nature of your call.

Alternatively, you might want to open your call by saying:

"Good morning, John, my name is Rob Smith, and we haven't talked previously. I deliberately wrote your name down this morning and was hoping that you might have a minute to speak."

This introductory statement is likely to have the prospect wondering, *"Hmmm. I wonder what prompted him to write my name down."* Or, in parallel to the voicemail messages presented in the last chapter, you might consider an opening along these lines:

"Good morning, John, my name is Rob Smith, and we haven't talked before. John, the reason I am calling is because I came across your name relative to a project that I am working on and was hoping that you might have just a moment to speak. Have I caught you at a good time?"

In the above introduction, additional intrigue is created by suggesting that the prospect *"may be relevant to a project"* on which you are working. Most prospects will find it difficult to not contemplate or be curious about what this might mean.

If the individual's name came from a referral who gave you permission to reference their name, you might want to open your call by saying:

"Good morning, John, my name is Rob Smith, and while we haven't talked previously, Sue Taylor suggested that I give you a call relative to a project that I am working on. Do you have a moment?"

If you got the individual's name via a confidential referral, you would logically alter your opening to say:

"Good morning, John, my name is Rob Smith. While we haven't talked previously, a mutual acquaintance suggested that you might be highly relevant to a project that I am working on. Do you have just a minute?"

If you utilize this last opening, be prepared for the prospect to ask you, *"Who would our mutual acquaintance be?"* Your response should be, *"John, I will be happy to address this, but first let me explain the purpose of my call."*

At the onset of some calls the candidate may say, *"Well, you have caught me at a bad time. I'm in a crunch to wrap up a project (go into a meeting, run out the door). What's this about?"*

In this case, you want to give *some* information, but *not* the entire purpose of your call. Remember, you want to have a quality conversation with this individual. I recommend that third party recruiters say something to the effect of:

"I am working on a project for a client and was hoping that I might be able to network with you. I know you are pressed for time right now, so rather than get into the specific details, I would prefer to find a time when you can speak without distractions. Can we set a time to speak later?"

If you are a corporate recruiter, you may wish to adjust your response to something like:

"I am working on an assignment in support of my firm's Accounting function (or whatever department or function is appropriate), and

was hoping that I might be able to network with you. I understand that this is not a good time to speak. Can we set a time to speak later? I pledge not to steal more than just a couple of minutes of your time."

More often than not, this explanation will suffice, and you can make an appointment to speak at a later time. Notice that at no point have you referenced your firm's name, and this omission is somewhat deliberate.

In my experience, the prospective candidate will not ask for the name of your firm at least 50 percent of the time. If they do ask, by all means give it to them. Remember, your objective is to present yourself in a manner that is distinctly different from the vast majority of recruiters in the marketplace.

Too many recruiters sabotage themselves by dumping too much information on the table at the beginning of the call. In the call script that I just outlined, the prospective candidate knows only that you have acquired their name and are interested in speaking.

In the Focused Cold Call example that I highlighted earlier, the recruiter's opening line told the candidate where she was calling from, the purpose of the call, and so on. This approach did not have an attention-grabbing opening, nor was the construct of the call particularly captivating.

A recruiter who leads with the name of their firm, particularly if they work for a third party recruiting organization whose name incorporates the words *"staffing, talent, search, recruiting or employment,"* or reveals at the onset of the call that they are a recruiter, runs the risk of having the candidate make a snap decision biased against the call. A prospective candidate who is relatively happy in his/her current role, upon hearing the word *'recruiter'* may automatically begin thinking, *"Okay, I'm happy in my job; how can I end this call?"*

The Objective Phase

After opening the call with your attention-getting statement, you want to proceed to the Objective Phase of the call. This component is oriented to telling the prospective candidate a bit about your role and the organization that you represent, as well as providing some insight as to the actual objective of your call.

For a third party recruiter, this part of the script might sound something like this:

"Joe, allow me to explain why I am calling. Again, my name is Rob Smith. I work on behalf of a distinct group of client firms that charter me to find highly talented professionals in the accounting marketplace" (or the market sector in which you work, such as IT, Healthcare, Legal, Construction, Medical Sales, and so on).

For a corporate recruiter, this segment of the call is where you would likely indicate the name of your organization. You can address this in the following manner:

"Joe, allow me to explain why I am calling. Again, my name is Rob Smith, and I work for XYZ Biotech. I am a corporate recruiter (corporate search specialist, etc.) chartered to identify highly talented professionals for critical roles within my organization."

As was illustrated in both examples above, recruiters should restate their name, simply because the prospect probably didn't catch it the first time. You also want to be sure to characterize your role and state that you are tasked with finding quality professionals for the market sector or organization you serve. You especially want to cite the fact that you are seeking high caliber individuals because this expression directly ties into your desire to leverage what I call a prospect's *"View of Self."* *"View of Self"* is effectively how an individual perceives his or her abilities and correlates with the prospect's ego or self-esteem. This self-perception will be addressed to a greater extent as you get into the second part of the Objective Phase.

The Objective Phase (Part II)

The second component of the Objective Phase is intended to highlight and reinforce a prospect's *"View of Self."* In this segment of the call, you want to communicate something along the lines of the following:

"Joe, in candor, I am looking to work with professionals who make a difference in the job they perform today, who possess ambition, and who want to get ahead. <u>I have reason to believe that your background may be aligned with opportunities on which I am currently working.</u>"

Or, if the individual is a referral:

"Joe, in candor, I am looking to work with professionals who make a difference in the job they perform today, who possess ambition, and who want to get ahead. <u>As a result of networking, my understanding is that you are a talented (Functional Role) and may be aligned with opportunities on which I am currently working.</u>"

The script above highlights features that are indeed important. You are absolutely looking to work with prospective candidates who *"make a difference in the job they perform today, who possess ambition, and who want to get ahead."* Anyone with a modest sense of self-worth is likely to reflect on these statements and conclude: *"That's me!"*

This reaction is reasonably predictable. In the training programs that I conduct, I often ask attendees to raise their hands if they regard themselves to be in the lowest 25 percent of performers at their company. No one ever raises his or her hand.

I then ask for individuals to raise their hands if they regard themselves to be in the bottom 50 percent of all performers at their company. Again, no one raises his or her hands.

Then, I will ask for people who perceive themselves to be in the upper 25 percent of all performers at their company to raise their hands. Without fail, virtually everyone raises his or her hand. And the reason that they do this is because each of us possesses a slightly biased perception of our own abilities, better known as an ego. So in effect, when you indicate that you are looking to work with highly capable performers, you are appealing to your prospect's ego.

The Closing Phase

We have addressed the Attention and Objective Phases of the Unfocused Cold Call script. Now we come to the Closing Phase, which goes something like this:

"Joe, the point of my call is twofold. First, I wanted to call to introduce myself and express that I am interested in learning more about your background. Second, I wanted to ask you a pretty straightforward question: If there were a really special situation in the market, one that could substantially advance your career, you would want to know about it, wouldn't you?"

You could also say:

"Joe, the point of my call is twofold. First, I wanted to call to introduce myself and express that I am interested in learning more about your background. Second, I wanted to ask you a pretty straightforward question: If there were a really special situation in the market, one that could substantially advance your career, is that something that you would be open to discussing?"

The difference between these closing questions is that the first example assumes that the answer will be yes. It is very difficult to say, *"No, I wouldn't want to know about something that could benefit me."*

The second script uses a close-ended question. The prospective candidate can more easily answer "Yes" or "No." Ultimately you need to own the script and put it into words that are comfortable for you. The actual close that you use (assumptive or close-ended) is up to you, and is largely dependent on your personal style. So, the script in its entirety will sound something like this:

Ring, ring:

Candidate: *"Hello, this is John Candidate."*

Recruiter: *"Good morning, John, my name is Rob Smith. We haven't talked previously, but I came across your name relative to a project that I'm working on and was hoping that you might have just a quick moment to speak. Have I caught you at a good time?"*

Candidate: "Ah, yes.....I have a minute."

Recruiter: *"Great, thanks Joe. Allow me to explain why I am calling. Again, my name is Rob Smith, and I work for XYZ Biotech. I am a corporate recruiter (corporate search specialist, etc.) chartered to identify highly talented professionals for critical roles within my organization."*

Candidate: "Okay....."

Recruiter: *"Joe, in candor, I am looking to work with professionals who make a difference in the job they perform today, who possess ambition, and who want to get ahead. I have reason to believe that your background may be aligned with opportunities on which I am currently working."*

Candidate: *"Uh huh..."*

<u>Recruiter</u>: *"Joe, the point of my call is twofold. First, I wanted to call to introduce myself and express that I am interested in learning more about your background. Second, I wanted to ask you a pretty straightforward question: If there were a really special situation in the market, one that could substantially advance your career, is that something that you would be open to discussing?"*

Now is a critical point in the call. You have gotten the prospective candidate's attention, laid out a fair amount of information about your call's purpose, and asked a pointed question. At this point you want to be absolutely certain to REMAIN SILENT. Silence is powerful.

All too often, recruiters ask a closing question, and rather than wait for the candidate to process the information and respond, the recruiter jumps in to augment or qualify the question that they have just put forth. As an old sales negotiation adage says, *"Whoever speaks first loses."* Now in reality, I am not implying that by speaking first and answering the question the prospective candidate has "lost" anything. But you have just put forth a potentially life changing question, and you need to allow sufficient time for the prospect to think about what he or she just heard and then respond. Talking further will only cloud the prospect's ability to contemplate your initial question.

If you ask the closing question and then interject a comment or qualifier prior to giving the candidate the chance to respond, you are subtly letting the candidate know that you are anxious. Would you have much respect for a salesperson whose approach seemed outwardly anxious or nervous, or who stammered or interjected an additional comment after asking you something important? Probably not, and that is why you should allow a prospective candidate a reasonable amount of time to process the content of what you have said before answering, even if it takes what may seem like an eternity (10 – 15 seconds) for them to respond.

"How Did You Get My Name?"

The likely responses that you will hear from candidates are not surprising: Yes, No, or Maybe. But before I get into the specific responses, let's handle the age old question of what to say when the prospective candidate asks, *"Where did you get my name?"*

Candidates ask this question for several reasons, the first of which is general curiosity. They have just gotten a call out of the blue, and naturally want to understand its origin. Again, in the call script above, you haven't provided a specific source for how you acquired the individual's name, so it's logical that the prospect is curious about the manner or method that you used to find him or her.

The second reason this question gets asked may be that they are actively looking, and they want to ascertain if your call is the result of a friendly referral, or if their job search has somehow leaked beyond a trusted circle of confidants.

Third, they may not be looking, but may be concerned that others in the organization could find out that they are getting calls from recruiters. As a general rule, I encourage you to be honest about how you acquired the prospective candidate's name. If you sourced it, you can simply say that you or your organization invests time and energy into ongoing market research, and that's how you got the person's name.

Over my career I have found prospective candidates via just about every means imaginable. Once, for example, I acquired a lead as a result of a woman calling into a morning radio program to participate in a contest. She cited her name and spoke briefly about her occupation. I called her later that day, explained that I had heard her on the radio and proceeded to set up an interview which took place a few days later.

On another occasion I decided to sell a used car myself, rather than trade it in. The individual who purchased it subsequently became a candidate who I placed a few months later.

I also remember executing a search that led me to an organization's Senior Vice President of Operations. When he asked me how I had gotten his name, assuming that he had been a high level referral, I felt as though I really disappointed him by responding, *"Actually, I got your name from a really helpful person at the switchboard."* He laughed and simply replied, *"Oh..."*

If the prospect's name was obtained from a confidential referral, explain that you got his/her name via a referral that resulted from active networking. Go on to state that while you can't reveal the name of your source for reasons of confidentiality, the person who provided the referral spoke highly about the prospect. You should also note that the person who provided the referral did not know whether or not the prospect was open to considering new opportunities, which you will find is typically the case. More often than not, prospective candidates will be very accepting of this feedback.

When They Say, "I'm Happy Right Now"

If the candidate immediately states that they are not interested in considering new opportunities, this is perfectly fine. You still want to attempt to establish rapport and learn something about their background for future use.

If they say, *"Actually, I am really happy right now and wouldn't want to consider other situations,"* you should acknowledge this and attempt to qualify their background with specific questions. This can be accomplished easily by saying something like:

"Wow, Joe, it really sounds like you must be in a special situation right now, and I can totally respect that. Do you mind me asking the specific role that you play today?"

Usually prospects will offer insight into the role that they presently perform and once you get them talking, it is fairly easy to ask any number of follow-on questions. The objective of engaging the prospect in this manner is to learn enough about this individual so that you can qualify the individual's overall experience (role, background, projects, etc.) and make some type of determination regarding the quality of the individual's experience as relates to current and anticipated openings.

Ultimately you will want to engage the prospect in a discussion about their future and the kinds of opportunities that they would theoretically be open to discussing. Additionally, you will want to establish some level of rapport as well as secure the right to contact the prospective candidate in the future.

I will address these elements in greater detail shortly, but first let me share a true story that validates the relative strength of the Unfocused Cold Call approach. I once worked on a search for a specialized mail order pharmacy organization that sought a senior IT executive. It was a very difficult assignment, because the client organization had formulated stringent criteria for what they perceived to be a mission critical role within the firm. After doing a fair amount of research, I contacted an individual who I suspected might be a dead fit for the role. Rather than leading with the fact that I was working on a position for which he might be qualified (Focused Cold Call approach), I deliberately opted to utilize an Unfocused Cold Call presentation.

The candidate was very polite, but firmly stated that he was very happy in his current position and wasn't open to considering new opportunities. I immediately put him at ease by explaining that this was fine, and as our discussion progressed, he shared a great deal of information both about himself and his role. He referenced that he had been in his current position for several years and was second in command of a 20 person IT shop. He felt challenged and respected, enjoyed the work he was doing, and was content in all respects.

As our conversation progressed, I transitioned the discussion to exploring the kind of role he might be open to entertaining in the future. I said, *"Dave, I totally respect that you are happy in your current role. From our discussion, I have to say that you are absolutely the kind of professional with whom I like to work. Even though I understand that you are not looking, if there were a perfect situation that you would want me to make you aware of at some point in the future, how might that opportunity look?"*

After thinking for a moment, Dave began to highlight the attributes that he thought would be important. He said, *"Well, Paul... it would need to be a role where I was running the entire IT organization. And, it would need to be an organization that was committed to using current tools and technologies. It would be important that I had an opportunity to roll out quality solutions. Also, I would want to be a part of the Senior Management Team. I have an MBA, and over time would want to contribute to the organization in a more significant manner - one that was greater than just the scope of IT responsibilities. Oh, and as long as we are talking about "ideal" situations, it would be nice if it were a little closer to home as I have a couple of young kids."*

As I took notes I was entirely cognizant of the fact that Dave's perceived ideal role was roughly the equivalent of the job requisition that had precipitated my call to him in the first place. As our discussion came to a close, I secured the right to contact him in the future by saying, *"Dave, I understand that you're happy in your current situation, but if I see an opportunity that aligns with the criteria you just referenced, I presume that it's okay to call you; is that correct?"*

He responded by saying that calling him in the future about opportunities was absolutely fine, but I could tell that he was primarily being polite – he really didn't expect to be hearing from me anytime soon. I could hardly wait until the following week to initiate another call to him.

I started the follow-up call by saying that while we had agreed that he wasn't really open to new situations, an opportunity had presented itself that so closely aligned with what he envisioned himself doing in a few years, that I had to call him to tell him about it. As I carefully mapped out the opportunity, I could sense that he was shocked to be hearing back from me.

Just days ago he had told me that he wasn't really open to new opportunities, after which he openly characterized what he perceived to be an ideal situation for the future. Now here I was calling to share an opportunity that in virtually all respects corresponded with what he indicated would be intriguing.

While acknowledging that he was more than a bit "taken aback" that I had contacted him again so soon, he was receptive to my call and to the opportunity I had just highlighted and agreed to meet with me.

Subsequent to our meeting, he agreed to interview with my client several days later. He called me after the interview, and I asked him, *"So, Dave, what did you think? Did I characterize the role accurately?"* Dave responded by saying, *"Yeah. You characterized it really well. I start in two weeks!"*

By utilizing the Unfocused Cold Calling approach, my call wasn't about a single opportunity, but rather was about him and what he wanted to do in the future. I am eminently confident that if I had initially led with the position or made a Focused Cold Call, I would not have realized the same outcome. I say this because psychologically, this individual was simply not in a place where he could genuinely entertain the prospect of making a move.

The notion of a new job just wasn't on the drawing board. I needed to get him thinking about what type of opportunity might serve as a legitimate catalyst for him to seriously entertain the concept of making a job change.

In other words, what I really did in my initial call was "grease the skids." By having him articulate the ideal types of scenarios that he would logically desire in the future, he effectively provided me with the information that I needed to ultimately present my original role in a manner that aligned with what he was seeking.

In my second call to him, I didn't embellish the opportunity at all. I merely presented it in a mode that highlighted the parallels between my client's role and what he had expressed as being the most important qualities and attributes of any hypothetical future job opportunity.

The above example highlights the fundamental power of Unfocused Cold Calls. This illustration is by no means an isolated event. Over the course of my career, I have used this calling approach to cultivate countless prospective candidates. Regardless of whether a prospect is interested in entertaining new opportunities or not, using the Unfocused Cold Call approach enables a recruiter to understand not only what type of role a prospect will be open to entertaining, but also how to optimally present the ideal opportunity.

Interpreting Cold Call Outcomes

As I previously characterized, when initiating Unfocused Cold Calls, you are likely to hear prospects respond to your closing question by indicating that they are either not interested in considering a job change, or that they are "actively" or potentially interested in entertaining new possibilities.

In Chapter Seven, Qualifying Candidates and Understanding Candidate Motivators, I address the specific steps you will want to take relative to qualifying and questioning any prospect, regardless of whether or not they are favorably disposed to considering new opportunities.

If a prospect indicates that he/she is not interested in considering other employment scenarios, the factors that have most likely influenced their reaction are:

A) They are content in their current role. It is entirely reasonable that an individual is indeed happy with the role that they play, the organization for which they work, and the composition of their team and management. If an individual is still feeling challenged by the role that they perform, the prospect of making a change has no inherent benefit in their eyes.

B) They just moved into their current role. Some prospects will indicate that they are not interested in considering new opportunities, because they have either recently made a job change or received an internal promotion. As such, the prospect of making another change is counter-intuitive.

C) The timing isn't right. Many individuals are not poised to consider new opportunities, because they are at a time in their lives when making a move is not practical. Family considerations such as pregnancy, child care, elder care, or potential relocation may make considering a change impossible. Commitments to a long-term project may also factor into the timing equation. I have had initial discussions with many highly qualified prospects who were both flattered to get my call and interested in hearing about opportunities, but making a move was not in the cards for them. These individuals were often deeply embedded into a project initiative that they believed would be irreparably damaged if they departed prematurely.

When a prospect concludes that he or she is simply not open to entertaining new opportunities, under no circumstances should you attempt to coax or pressure the prospect into reconsidering. Nor should you attempt to tell a prospect what *you* perceive to be in his or her best interests.

Believe me, they really mean it when they say, *"Gee, I appreciate your thinking of me, but I'm exceptionally happy in my current role."* At that juncture in time, they *are* happy in their current role. Take what the individual is saying at face value, at least at that moment.

The most frequently heard complaints from candidates about recruiters include: *"the recruiter was pushy," "the recruiter tried to pressure me," "the recruiter wouldn't take no for an answer."* At the onset of what you hope will become a long-term relationship, there just isn't any reason to act in a manner that undermines your ability to nurture a potentially very meaningful business association.

If a prospect indicates that the timing isn't right or that he or she is content in their current role, it is very important to acknowledge this respectfully. Doing so is the best means of steering the discussion to a mode where you can qualify the particulars of a given individual's background and experience. This approach is *extremely* important. It allows you the opportunity to highlight features of specific openings or opportunities that may be relevant to the individual's background, or just as importantly, to the backgrounds of potential referrals.

As I demonstrated earlier in characterizing the benefits of the Unfocused Cold Call approach, once you understand the specific composition of an individual's background and what they regard as being important to their future, you can subsequently contact them to discuss relevant opportunities. So, no matter how strongly you may feel about a particular opportunity or how much you may regard a specific position to be *'the next best thing to sliced bread,'* remember that what *you* think is of little consequence. If a prospect clearly indicates that they are very happy in their current role, take a long-term view and pursue the following steps:

1) Acknowledge that the prospect is happy in his/her current role;

2) Qualify the prospect's background – learn about their abilities and experience;

3) Define the future. Get them to map out what they perceive to be the ideal career opportunity or ideal next job move;

4) Build rapport. Find out something unique about the individual. Ask them about hobbies and other interests outside of work (learning these items can provide you with a touch-point in future discussions);

5) Secure the right to stay in touch/contact them in the future; and

6) Attempt to secure qualified referrals (See Chapter Eleven on Referral Acquisition).

If the candidate's response to your initial cold call closing question is, *"Yes, I would be interested (or potentially interested) in hearing about special opportunities,"* you will need to uncover the candidate's specific motivations for considering a career change. Qualifying candidates and ascertaining candidate motivators is carefully addressed in Chapter Seven, so I won't get into this issue here.

If you conclude through the course of an initial discussion that a prospective candidate's motivators seem solid and their experience relevant, you will want to set up a formal face-to-face meeting or a detailed phone interview. The benefits of a face-to-face meeting are many. By having the candidate actually come to your office, you obtain a measure of the candidate's commitment to the process. After all, they are now investing their time and energy to meet with you. Furthermore, it is much easier to establish meaningful rapport with a candidate in a face-to-face meeting than in a telephone discussion.

In preparation for this meeting, you should advise the candidate that he or she will need to do some preliminary homework. Specifically, you want the candidate to put some critical thought into their ideal role, key accomplishments associated with their current role, salary and/or benefits requirements, geographic concerns, etc. With respect to salary, you will need to have some appreciation for the candidate's requirements *prior to* bringing the individual in for a formal meeting. Chapter Ten will help you to address salary and compensation expectations at the onset of a relationship with any prospective candidate.

Additionally, you will want to advise the candidate that he or she will need to supply the names of several references capable of speaking intelligently about the candidate's work experience. You aren't interested in character references – only employment references. Ideally, you want references from supervisors, peers, and subordinates, if applicable. Chapter Eight will provide a great deal of insight on how you can leverage the Reference Check process.

In coordinating a face-to-face or detailed phone interview, you should advise the candidate to prepare to spend about one hour with you. The best times to set up these meetings are very early in the morning, over lunchtime, or at the close of the business day. Interviewing in these timeframes will help you to protect core calling hours for other activities.

Remember that sourcing and introductory/cold calls go hand in hand, but they ideally should NOT be combined into one phone call. The purpose of sourcing is to secure potential leads. The purpose of introductory or cold calls is to initiate contact with those leads to determine a prospective candidate's receptiveness to new career opportunities.

If you take the time to source on a regular basis, you will find yourself cultivating a stronger candidate pipeline. Adopting a structured cold call approach will enable you to initiate more meaningful conversations with prospective candidates. Furthermore, utilizing an Unfocused Cold Call approach will enable you to make the conversation entirely about a prospective candidate's career, not specifically about a particular position.

Remember, it does not matter if some of the prospects with whom you speak are psychologically unprepared to entertain making a job change. If executed well, you will find that your calls can actually serve as the catalyst for these individuals to meaningfully contemplate the idea of proactively exploring new career possibilities. Regardless of a prospect's ability to consider making a move, this introductory call approach will enable you to set yourself apart from other recruiter's who have weaker presentation styles or who rely upon position-specific, Focused Cold Calls.

The scripts that have been highlighted are merely examples of what you could say in conducting these calls. I highly recommend that you work on crafting your own scripts and selling messages so that they convey your voice and style. Practice makes perfect. Work on them until your delivery comes across as being both confident and fluid. You'll notice the difference, and most importantly, so will the candidate prospects that you contact.

Chapter: 7 – Qualifying Candidate Motivators & Utilizing the CAREER Questioning Approach

If you ask a room full of recruiters what they believe is the most important or critical facet of the recruiting lifecycle, I suspect that you would hear a host of different answers, including:

- The closing process;
- Offer presentations;
- Initial recruiting calls;
- The candidate interview process;
- Salary negotiation.

All of the above are undeniably important aspects of recruitment. But in my considered opinion, the most important and consequential component of the recruiting process is understanding a candidate's qualifications and appreciating their motivations for contemplating or actively entertaining a move.

Over the years, I have participated in the post-mortem analysis of various deals that imploded for one reason or another. Sadly, a number of them were my own! The goal of these exercises has been to understand what did or didn't happen that resulted in a deal going south. By conducting such exercises and by appreciating why a deal didn't come to fruition, I always hoped to learn something that could help me, or others, to avoid a similar negative outcome in future hiring transactions.

While conducting these reviews, I came to understand that occasionally some completely unforeseen event could prompt a candidate to terminate the search process altogether. For example, I recall working with one candidate who was fully prepared to make a move until a sudden and unexpected health issue with his child surfaced. The candidate concluded, rightfully, that given his child's health circumstances, making a job change was no longer in his family's best interests.

I can also recall a specific search where not one, but two extremely qualified candidates found out that they were pregnant almost immediately after I had presented their respective backgrounds to a hiring manager. In both instances, the candidates expressed that given their impending motherhood, it simply didn't make sense to pursue a career change.

Because I had presented their backgrounds sequentially, it became a bit comical calling up the hiring manager not once, but twice, to offer the same explanation regarding why these women were opting out of the interview process. This episode occurred in my 17th year as a recruiter, which supports my contention that although you may believe that you have seen "everything," chances are that you probably haven't.

More often than not, my post-mortem deal analyses typically revealed that the recruiter missed something critically important early on in the candidate qualification process; didn't assign enough significance to fully appreciating a candidate's stated goals or motivators; or failed to heed or outright ignored other indicators that should have served as a major red flag. Often, the recruiter in question was guilty of having heard what he or she _wanted_ to hear from the candidate, not necessarily what was being said. In other words, an awful lot of deals that end up imploding are destined to do so from the onset of the relationship between a candidate and a recruiter.

In order to make certain that all bases are covered and to reduce the potential for problems during the offer phase of the recruiting process, you want to engage every prospective candidate in a process of "Discovery." As defined in a legal context, discovery means to find out or learn something previously unknown or unrecognized.

While I am not recommending that you actually interrogate prospective candidates, per se, I am suggesting that you must have the ability to carefully, efficiently, and diligently qualify prospects at the onset of your relationship.

Implementing a replicable qualifying process that consistently poses thoughtful and insightful questions will provide you with two primary benefits. First, you will be better able to discern which prospects should actually be given the "candidate" designation. Separating prospects on the basis of how they respond to your qualifying questions helps to ensure that you are working with real candidates who have real motivations for considering change. Second, by concentrating on working with the right individuals, you will save yourself a considerable amount of time and potential heartache, especially during the back-end phases of the recruiting lifecycle.

After initiating contact with a prospective candidate and determining that a prospect is potentially interested in considering new opportunities, it is critically important that you pursue two distinct lines of qualifying questions. First, you must qualify that the prospect possesses the skills, abilities, and other attributes necessary to perform successfully in the role or roles for which you are recruiting. Second, after ascertaining that a prospect appears to be technically qualified, you must strive to understand the specific issues or factors that are compelling the prospect to entertain the possibility of making a career change.

To best appreciate a prospective candidate's background and motivations for considering a move, while also staying in a consultative selling mode, you can deploy a fairly straightforward yet structured communications approach. I advocate using what I call the CAREER Communications Approach, a qualifying and relationship building methodology that will allow you to consistently acquire essential information about every prospect with whom you speak while also engendering goodwill.

Before I get into the CAREER Approach, it is appropriate to share some general observations about candidate motivators. Individuals are compelled to seek new opportunities for a spectrum of different reasons. A partial list of motivators would include:

- A prospect's sense or belief that his/her career has stagnated;
- A prospect's perception that advancement is largely tied to the departure or promotion of a superior;
- Quality of life issues such as excessive work demands, a miserable commute, or extensive travel;
- Major life changes including the birth of a child, elder care, or family health issues;
- A prospect's perception that a clear growth path is not available or is wholly dependent upon a time-in-grade formula;
- A prospect's perception that existing corporate advancement structures and/or managerial factors are impediments to meaningful career growth;
- A prospect's concerns about corporate stability or viability;
- A prospect's concerns relative to peers or supervisors;
- A prospect's belief that he or she is under-compensated for work being performed.

Any of the above could be regarded as a very legitimate reason for an individual to consider new situations, and there are undoubtedly other reasons, as well. As a rule, however, you must determine the extent or degree to which prospective candidates have candidly addressed their particular motivators with their current employers. I can't reiterate this point enough, so I will say it again: **As a rule, you have to determine the extent or degree to which prospective candidates have addressed their particular motivators with their current employers.** The reason that you must make this determination is because you are attempting to secure a **validated motivator.**

A validated motivator exists only when a prospective candidate has <u>unsuccessfully</u> attempted to correct whatever he or she perceives to be deficient with a current role or employer. In other words, if a prospect tells me he wants to leave his current employer in order to substantially reduce his commute, I need to validate that he has explored commuting alternatives with his current employer to no avail. I need to know that the prospect has inquired about telecommuting or a modified work schedule, but has been told that this request can't be accommodated. I need to know that the current employer is either uninclined or incapable of offering the individual a remedy to whatever issue has been cited as the catalyst for contemplating a job change in the first place.

In many instances, prospects will acknowledge that they have unsuccessfully attempted to address their issues with superiors; if so, terrific. You theoretically have a validated motivator and can proceed forward knowing that a candidate has done his or her due diligence to resolve an issue with a current employer, but has not achieved a satisfactory outcome. If a prospect indicates that an issue has not been candidly addressed, strongly encourage them to do so. This discussion might sound like this:

Recruiter: *"Tom, I appreciate your sharing the reasons you are considering making a change. If I've heard you correctly, you have two primary motivators. First, you are looking to acquire some new responsibilities, as you have been performing in the same role for over three years now. Second, I gather that your commute has become very time consuming and that you are looking to reduce the amount of time you spend in traffic. Just out of curiosity, have you spoken with your Manager about these issues?"*

Candidate: *"Well, she knows that I want additional responsibilities, as we have talked about this several times over the recent past. She says she is working on it, but can't promise me anything. On the commuting issue, no, we haven't talked about this yet."*

Recruiter: *"Well, let's assume for a second that your boss was inclined to address these issues and figure out a solution – would that change your feelings about leaving?"*

Candidate: *"Hmmm. If she were able to address my issues in a timely manner, then yes, it could change how I feel. I'd really have to think about that."*

Recruiter: *"Tom, I am going to make a recommendation that I think you'll agree is in your best interests. I would suggest that you go back to your boss one additional time and reconfirm that nothing has changed with respect to getting the additional responsibilities you are seeking. Second, I would recommend that you also address the commuting issue very candidly to determine if there is any flexibility with respect to when you work. Making a career move is a big deal. I would love to work with you, but I need to know that you are moving forward with clarity. Does that make sense?"*

Candidate: *"Gee, I hadn't really thought to do that. For the most part, I have enjoyed being at my current company, but my boss gives me a lot of mixed signals, so I agree that it makes sense to do what you are suggesting – might as well find out where I stand."*

Some recruiters reading the above are apt to say, *"Paul, are you crazy? Why would you do that? Why would you send a perfectly good candidate prospect back to his manager to fix the problems that he has cited as his motivators for making a move?"* Again, the reason for sending a prospective candidate back to his or her manager is that you want to know that you are working with a candidate who has one or more *validated motivators*.

If a prospect indicates that an issue or multiple issues have not been candidly addressed, you need to encourage them to do so for several reasons. First, you want to mitigate the potential for a counter-offer. You don't want to get to the offer stage only to have the candidate tell you that they have decided to accept a counter-offer from their current employer because, *"they were able to address the very issues that were motivating me to consider new opportunities."*

Second, if an individual is unsuccessful in resolving a problem or deficiency with a current employer, any counter-offer that is subsequently put forth by the employer at the point of resignation is going to seem disingenuous. The candidate will be forced to reconcile why it took resigning to obtain a resolution to a problem that had earlier been characterized as being unfixable.

Third, sincerely recommending that an individual candidly communicate with their current employer about a career concern or issue keeps you in a consultative posture. You present yourself as being legitimately interested and concerned in helping the individual make informed decisions that best serve his or her career. In my opinion, a large part of being an effective recruiter is tied directly to fulfilling our ethical obligations to a candidate, and this translates to ensuring that they have considered the totality of their intent to make a move.

Actually, this philosophy benefits everyone – the candidate, the recruiter, and the employer. I believe that to be most effective in recruiting you have to follow the "Golden Rule" and treat people the way that you wish to be treated. You don't need to apply undue pressure or strong-arm tactics, regardless of the extent to which you believe a prospect would be better served by making an employment change.

Does this mean that you won't work to articulately convey the benefits of a particular opportunity? No. Does this mean that you won't work hard to put compelling information in front of a candidate so that he or she can make the most informed decision? No. But you also must accept that candidates will do what they perceive to be in their own best interests. This point further underscores why it is so critically important that you and the candidate both understand and work to eliminate any ambiguity around motivators. Failure to do so is an invitation for offer rejections, accepted counter-offers, and an awful lot of wasted time. (For a detailed analysis of counter-offers, see Chapter Eleven).

I remember getting a call from a talented woman who had been told to contact me regarding a team leader search that I was conducting. This prospect was technically sharp, articulate, poised – an A+ candidate in all respects. When we discussed her motivations for leaving her company, she indicated that the travel demands of her job had become significant, and that she had hit a point where she needed to get off the road. I asked her if she had discussed this with her management. She indicated that she had and was waiting to learn whether they would be able to accommodate her.

She candidly admitted that she really liked her company, her boss and peers, and the work she was performing. I suggested that she determine whether or not the travel issue could be resolved before we began to work together. Two weeks later, she informed me that her management had agreed to significantly reduce the amount of travel she was doing and had further agreed that she could work from home two to three days each week. Problem solved.

I was happy for her, and just as happy that I hadn't invested significant time in pushing her into hiring manager interviews that would not have progressed into anything meaningful. Sure, I would have loved to place her, but aside from the travel issue, she openly acknowledged that she liked her current employer and that's where her loyalties resided. In as much as I didn't place her, she remained very grateful for my honest advice and provided me with several excellent referrals.

On another occasion, I remember being referred to a top flight quality assurance and test manager for another search I was conducting. I contacted this gentleman, and he indicated that his primary motivation for wanting to entertain a move was tied to the fact that his firm was going to be acquired by a much bigger company. The uncertainty of how the acquisition would play out and how he would be impacted had prompted him to begin looking at other possibilities.

When I met with this individual, it was clear that he possessed superior skills, had a solid track record of growth, and was a respected manager. He was the kind of performer that any organization would want on its team. He stated that although he had heard good things about the acquiring firm, he was worried about where he would land in the new corporate entity. Senior management had told him that his status in the new organization would be determined over the near term. Given the overall strength of his background, I suggested that he wait to see what happened.

My rationale was that rather than having him engage in various interviews, he would be best served by finding out where he would end up and what that might mean to his career. Sure enough, he received a two grade promotion in the new organization. In his previous role he had been managing a team of about 20 people, but now he was charged with overseeing a group of 80.

As good a candidate as this individual would have been, I was grateful that I had not put forth a lot of time in working with him. It wasn't that I didn't like him, or that he wasn't marketable, but it was virtually inconceivable that I would have been able to show him a more compelling situation than the one that emerged within his own organization.

This story highlights another critically important point that warrants being mentioned. All recruiters must ensure that they are working "doable" deals, wherein prospective candidates are truly motivated and interested in making a move.

In the case of the quality assurance manager that I referenced above, he readily indicated that he *liked* his company. It wasn't so much a matter of him *wanting* to leave, but more an issue of the events impacting his company that prompted him to evaluate his options.

The merger of his firm with another company represented a massive unknown, one that would inevitably impact whether his candidacy would become viable. These factors naturally made the probability of getting a deal done precipitously lower, and the prospect of me wasting a lot of time significantly higher.

While there are no guarantees with respect to motivators, you ideally want to hear a prospect indicate that despite multiple attempts to address key job concerns with a current employer, no resolution has been achieved. To the extent possible, you want candidates to recognize and appreciate that larger systemic problems exist within their current employer as well as understand that these issues are unlikely to magically disappear.

Prospects whose driving motivation for entertaining a job change is largely oriented to "making more money" warrant careful consideration. Just about any entry-level business or economics class will tell you that an organization's payroll is its most controllable expense.

Increasingly, many firms are concluding that making a salary adjustment to secure the ongoing services of a valued employee is usually a better option than allowing the person to leave. If the candidate possesses specific skills or domain knowledge, the thought of losing this expertise is especially daunting and something many employers will go to great lengths to avoid. Recent studies suggest that the cost of employee turnover may run anywhere between 1.5 and 5.0 times a departing employee's salary depending on the role in which the individual performs.

You absolutely want to understand the resolve of any prospect whose primary motivator for making a move is directly tied to securing higher compensation. You must understand how they will react if their current employer matches or exceeds any offer extended by your organization (or client organization). If the prospect cannot definitively state that he or she would reject an overture to compel them to stay, you have a counter-offer scenario in the making. As a rule, regardless of the prospective candidate's stated motivator, you will want to ask yourself these important questions:

- Can this person's issues within their current environment be reasonably resolved?

- Has this individual proactively attempted to resolve the issues that have been cited?

- Do the prospective candidate's motivators make sense?

The CAREER Approach

The CAREER Approach to candidate discovery is comprised of six distinct phases that include:

- **C**andidate Phase
- **A**ttitude Phase
- **R**eality Phase
- **E**xploration Phase
- **E**ndorsement Phase
- **R**apport Phase

Candidate Phase

The first component of the CAREER Approach is the Candidate Phase. The Candidate Phase is principally oriented to understanding the technical and experiential attributes of a prospective candidate. In other words, this phase of the process is centered upon gathering basic information such as:

- Current job title;
- Tenure with current employer;
- Educational background;
- Specific skills or expertise;
- General overview of current project work; etc.

Because this book is written from a general recruiting perspective and is not oriented to a specific industry sector or functional discipline, I can't get into the specifics of how you should best go about qualifying the skills or basic technical qualifications of the particular individuals that you recruit. If you are a seasoned recruiting professional, however, I wholly expect that you know perfectly well how to qualify prospective candidates in your market sector or niche.

If you are new to recruiting, it is very important for you to immerse yourself in understanding what distinguishes a qualified candidate from an unqualified candidate in the industry or functional discipline you support. I would suggest that you attempt to aggressively acquire industry knowledge. This can be accomplished by reading trade publications, conducting informational interviews with domain experts, sitting in on candidate interviews with hiring authorities, and attending tradeshows/conferences.

In order to conserve time and energy and enjoy credibility in the eyes of potential prospects, it is essential that you rapidly cultivate some level of conversational fluency relative to the industry, function or discipline in which you are or will be recruiting. If you recruit for technical professionals, do you need to know how to program utilizing Java or C++? No, but you better understand what qualities distinguish or highlight true competence among the software professionals that you engage.

If you recruit for civil or structural engineers, do you need to understand the tensile strength of different concrete formulations? No, but again, you better understand what questions are significant with respect to qualifying and determining whether a prospect's background and experience is relevant to your opportunities.

You want to know as much as you can about the market sector in which you recruit. The more you understand about the industry in which you are recruiting, the more you will save valuable time in distinguishing qualified applicants from non-qualified applicants.

Remember, as is the case with just about every sales role, time is a recruiter's most precious commodity.

Secondly, the more you know, the more likely you are to be regarded as being credible. If a high quality candidate is contacted by three recruiters, whom do you think the candidate is going to be most interested in communicating with again?

- One who doesn't seem to understand the candidate's job at all?

- One who seems to possess a decent understanding of the candidate's job?

- Or one who really sounds like she knows what the candidate's job is all about?

Most candidates are very happy to talk about what they do, and are equally happy to explain nuances of the roles they perform, but this is often predicated upon the recruiter having at least a nominal appreciation for the domain in which a candidate works.

One of the most recurring criticisms of recruiters that I have heard from candidates is that, *"the recruiter didn't have a clue about what I do,"* or *"the recruiter was incapable of answering even the most basic questions about the job for which they were recruiting."* Candidates who make these types of statements often feel that they are wasting their time by communicating with a recruiter who doesn't understand their work domain.

Further, I think that many prospects subconsciously regard this as a respect issue. They may be inclined to think, *"If you respected me and the work that I perform, you would have taken the time to educate yourself so that we could meaningfully communicate."*

It has long been held that if you go out to dine at a Parisian restaurant and make the effort to speak the French language, you can usually anticipate better treatment than someone who simply presumes that the waiter will gladly communicate in English. Communicating with a prospective candidate is not dissimilar. By at least having some degree of conversational fluency about a given role or function, you convey to a prospect that you are at least trying to bring value to the relationship.

As your fluency improves, so does your credibility. During the 14 plus years that I recruited in the technology market sector, candidates often openly expressed that based on the content of our discussions they had assumed that I had prior software or hardware engineering experience. These remarks were attributable to the fact that: A) I did my homework to ensure that I possessed a reasonably detailed appreciation for the tools/technologies associated with the positions on which I was recruiting; B) I knew the right initial questions to ask; and, C) in listening to candidate responses to my questions, I knew the right follow-on questions to ask. Again, securing relevant domain knowledge is essential.

Once you have qualified a prospective candidate's actual skills and expertise, you will actively transition the discussion towards ascertaining the underlying factors that are compelling or motivating an individual to actively or passively contemplate making a job change. To accomplish this, you will progress to the Attitude, Reality, and Exploration Phases of the CAREER Approach. Each of these phases incorporates a variety of questions that are intended to engage the prospective candidate in a discussion about actual and near term career progression, likes and dislikes about current roles and employers, and the qualities or attributes that any new opportunity would need to offer in order to be viable.

Utilizing the next three components of the CAREER Approach (Attitude, Reality, and Exploration Phases) will help you answer these questions.

Attitude Phase

In the Attitude Phase, your objective is to engage the prospect in a dialogue about how *they feel* about their overall career progression relative to their current role and environment. You want to ascertain all relevant attitudes regarding the role they play today and what they envision or desire doing in the future.

The Attitude Phase provides you with insight into a prospective candidate's "View-of-Self" and will help you to better appreciate whether or not a given individual possesses the appropriate mindset to meaningfully consider the prospect of making a change. In addition to helping you to acquire an understanding for how the candidate feels his or her career is progressing, the Attitude Phase also helps you to assess an individual's ambition.

Ambition is an important candidate attribute. Given the choice, you absolutely want to work with individuals who are looking for upward mobility, increased visibility, and heightened levels of responsibility. Why? Well, for one reason, if a prospect lacks ambition or drive within the context of their career, chances are that they will not be particularly motivated to proactively entertain making a move. For some people, the idea of making a change may be as terrifying as it is exciting, and the status quo will become the path of least resistance.

Over the years, I have known various individuals who acknowledged that they were wholly satisfied with the role that they played in their current firm. They simply didn't aspire to greater levels of responsibility. These individuals were content and no longer interested in advancing their careers. Consequently, I could say little that would prompt them to seriously consider the possibility of making a change; they were entirely comfortable.

Let me be clear. It is perfectly fine with me if someone says that they are entirely happy or content in the role they play today. As a recruiter, I would rather know this sooner as opposed to later, so that

I can transition my relationship with an individual from that of a prospective candidate into a prospective source of referrals.

To engage a prospect in a dialogue regarding their career attitudes, you can pose any of the following questions:

- Are you happy with the way that your career is progressing?

- Do you feel you could be doing/accomplishing more?

- Do you feel that your career path is meeting your goals?

- What would you like to accomplish over the next three years or so?

These questions are very straightforward and are intended to initiate an honest dialogue. Interpreting prospect responses to these questions and asking the right follow-up questions can prove to be a bit more of a challenge.

For example, suppose you ask a prospect, *"Are you happy with the way that your career is progressing?"* They may respond by saying, *"I'm pretty happy,"* or *"I'm not happy."* Note that they haven't said, *"I am entirely and completely happy."* To make your questioning process more effective, you need to be ready to put forth follow-on questions that further qualify a prospect's responses. You can readily accomplish this by asking <u>What</u> and <u>Why</u> questions.

For example, suppose you ask: *"Are you happy with the manner in which your career is progressing?"* and a prospect replies, *"No, I feel I could be doing more."* You can ask a simple follow-on question such as: *"What do you mean when you say doing more?"* Alternatively, you could also ask, *"What would provide you with more fulfillment?"* Another follow-up question could be: *"Why do you feel you haven't gotten the additional responsibilities you are seeking?"*

As you progress through each of the phases of the Career Questioning Approach, remember that you don't simply want to accept superficial answers to your questions. You want to flush out all underlying motivators and fully appreciate what they mean. You want to probe as much as is necessary to fully understand a prospect's thought process, as well as what they regard to be important issues moving forward.

As demonstrated in the previous example, a great way to do this is by asking follow-on questions that ask the prospect to further qualify *what* they want or don't want and *why* these things are of consequence. In the example above, the prospect said, *"No, I feel I could be doing more."* Theoretically, you could choose to be satisfied with this response, and conclude: *"Candidate wants more responsibility... can't get this at current employer... motivator secured."*

While this might be true, you need to dig deeper to understand what this really means. Is the prospect frustrated because there is a lack of work to perform? Is the prospect in an environment that is highly bureaucratic where ability is secondary to the amount of time an individual spends at a certain position level? Has a promotion been delayed or has the individual been passed over for a promotion?

You cannot know the answers to these questions unless you dig deeper; but knowing the answers is of great significance and will influence your overall effectiveness in working with any individual. As I referenced earlier, you are essentially conducting 'discovery' which mandates that you be capable of asking thoughtful, probing questions that help you to accurately understand the prospect's mindset and thinking.

Reality Phase

As you discern a prospect's feelings about the possibility of making a change, you will migrate to the Reality Phase of the CAREER Questioning Approach. The Reality Phase is oriented to objectively understanding the realities of the prospective candidate's current role and acquiring insights into what characteristics would need to exist in any new situation in order for the prospect to seriously entertain a move.   In essence, you need to fully appreciate the prospect's current circumstances, as well as determine what they regard to be missing.   To do this, you can put forth the following questions:

- What are things you really like about your current role?

- If you could, what would you change about your current role?

- Are there barriers to success in your current environment?

Your overarching goal is to get a clear sense for whether a prospect perceives deficiencies in their current position or environment which would give them incentive to make a move. These questions help you to capture both positive and negative attributes of the prospect's current role and organization.

Exploration Phase

The Exploration Phase is intended to identify specific qualities and attributes that would be critical to any new role.   You may have acquired some understanding for this in the Reality Phase, but your objective now is to deliberately engage the prospect in a discussion about ideal job situations.   To accomplish this, you can ask the following questions:

- What do you feel are the real strengths in your background that you would like to leverage moving forward?

- What other qualities/attributes would be important in any new role?

- Describe your ideal scenario – what kind of opportunity would get you really excited?

You must secure clarity regarding the attributes and features that a prospect regards as being important to any new situation that they would entertain, which means that you may need to ask a host of additional questions in the Exploration Phase. Again, this is a great time to ask follow-on questions that further qualify *what* is significant to a prospect and *why* it is significant.

Suppose you ask a prospect, *"What other qualities/attributes would be important in any new role?"* and they respond by saying, *"I would really like to be in an environment where I have a mentor."* You can ask: *"What do you mean when you say mentor?"* or *"Why do you feel that having a mentor is important?"* or *"To what extent would having a mentor impact your future?"* Gathering this information will equip you to discuss appropriate opportunities with the prospect's stated needs and requirements in mind, while also letting you highlight job features that the prospect has suggested are of particular importance.

When you boil everything down, the Candidate Phase provides you with information about the prospect's background, experience and specific skills. The Attitude Phase gives you insight about how a prospect regards their current job and whether they possess sufficient ambition to consider moving into a new opportunity. The Reality Phase allows you to understand what a prospect likes and dislikes about their current job. The Exploration Phase enables you to appreciate key qualities and attributes that would be important in any future role.

Optimally, you will try to engage every prospect with whom you speak in these initial four phases of the CAREER Approach. A prospect who has an intriguing background, but is not ready to legitimately consider new situations, should still be walked through the Reality and Exploration questioning phases, if only to better understand what types of future opportunities might be compelling. The next two phases of the CAREER Approach are the Endorsement, and Rapport Phases

.

Endorsement Phase

In the Endorsement Phase you effectively want to "endorse" or compliment the prospect's background and how it correlates with current or pending requirements.

If you have determined that the individual's background aligns with opportunities on which you are working and that the individual has viable motivators, you will want to acknowledge this by stating something along the lines of:

Recruiter: *"Based on our discussion, Sue, I want to express that I am really impressed with your skills and experience – you have a terrific background. From our conversation, thus far, it would seem that if there were a really compelling situation that aligned well with your background and that addressed the reasons that are motivating your interest in making a change, that's something you would want to actively discuss, right?"*

Candidate: *"Oh, well thanks. I have enjoyed speaking with you, and yes, if there were an intriguing situation I would definitely want to consider it."*

Or you might say:

Recruiter: *"Steve, I have really appreciated the chance to talk with you today and have to acknowledge that you have an excellent skill set. Based on our conversation, I understand that right now you simply don't feel particularly challenged and don't see much opportunity for progression in your current setting, and that if there were a really compelling situation you would like to explore it, is that right?*

Candidate: *"Yes, I don't think I could have said it any better. I would absolutely be interested in exploring strong opportunities."*

The actual language you use to endorse a prospect's background and affirm that you correctly captured the major motivators is up to you. The key things are that you extend compliments honestly and appropriately and that you convey that you understand the prospect's motivations for considering a move.

When speaking with a prospect, and especially when restating motivators, don't be surprised if an individual complements you on being able to cohesively express what it is that is fundamentally prompting them to feel disengaged from their current employer. Motivators can be hard for some candidates to discuss fluidly, because they haven't necessarily been forced to think in a detailed manner about the factual aspects of why they want to leave.

Sometimes motivators may be conveyed in a disjointed and rambling fashion. Individuals know that on some basic level that they are unhappy or dissatisfied, but haven't necessarily had to process or articulate these sentiments in an orderly way. Of course, this is where you come in. Your goal is to help prospective candidates strip the emotion out of why they feel discontented and to help them communicate the factual basis of why they are determined to make a change.

Alternatively, if the prospect with whom you are speaking is not interested in exploring new situations, you can still offer an endorsement that is intended to build goodwill and help obtain the license to communicate with this individual in the future. To accomplish this, you can say:

Recruiter: *"Sue, I really appreciate the time that you have spent with me on the phone today. First of all, I want to express that I think you have a really outstanding background. You are absolutely the kind of individual and quality of professional that I am asked to identify. I understand that the timing is not right for you to contemplate making a change, but hope that you don't mind if I keep in touch periodically?"*

Candidate: *"Oh, I have enjoyed the discussion, as well. You're right....I'm really pretty happy right now, but yes, you are welcome to stay in touch with me."*

Recruiter: *"Sue, that's great. I'd like that, and let me also say that if I can ever be of assistance to you in any respect, please don't hesitate to call me. I am happy to help you if I can."*

Candidate: *"I really appreciate that and will keep your offer in mind."*

Rapport Phase

The final aspect of the CAREER Approach is the Rapport Phase. The Rapport Phase is intended to forge a human connection with every prospect. Regardless of whether or not you anticipate moving an individual into active candidate status, you want to learn something unique about every prospect that can serve as a touch point in future discussions.

At the beginning of the training programs that I conduct, I often ask the participants to briefly introduce themselves and to convey a personal passion outside of work. As you might expect, the responses are as intriguing as they are diverse.

One person will highlight that his passion outside of work is spending time with his kids; someone else will reference her love for travel; someone else will highlight an interest in particular sports; another person will profess a passion for supporting a particular charity, and so on. These expressed interests span the spectrum of possibilities, and are genuinely revealing. Each of these individuals discloses something that they regard to be of fundamental and personal importance.

Much later in the program, as we begin to discuss the need for recruiters to make a human connection with candidates, I will restate - person by person - what each program attendee referenced as his or her own personal passion earlier in the day. It usually doesn't matter if four people or 40 people are attending the program. With rare exception I have the ability to highlight each individual's stated passion outside of work.

I do this to underscore a point. If we want to work with people on what they inevitably must regard to be of critical personal importance (their career, for example), it behooves us to get to know something that is of consequence to them. Put another way: If we want someone to trust us, we need to be able to communicate in a manner that demonstrates that we are truly interested in them as a person, not just as a worker or employee.

At one training conference, after citing each individual's "passions," a program attendee approached me at the conclusion of the session. She said, "You must have completed one of those memory enhancement courses." I replied that I hadn't and remarked that anyone could do what I had just demonstrated – they simply needed to listen.

One of the most enjoyable aspects of recruiting is the people that we are afforded the opportunity to meet and engage. The people dynamic is what makes recruiting such a unique vocation, and understanding what makes people tick, what motivates them, and how they may fit into a new organization are all things that I find to be fundamentally intriguing.

In the Rapport Phase, you can ask very straightforward questions that will help you to learn something of consequence to the individuals with whom you speak. These questions might include:

- I know that a lot of your time is devoted to work, but just out of curiosity, what do you do for fun?

- I'm sure that work keeps you busy, but what are your interests or hobbies outside the office?

- From our conversation today, I realize that work is important to you, but what do you like doing when you're not working?

If my own experience is a reasonable indicator, most of the time you will find that individuals usually become a bit more animated as they reveal outside interests that are truly of importance to them. Some recruiters are bound to say: *"I'm not sure that I would be comfortable pursuing these types of questions.... They really don't have anything to do with an individual's ability to perform a job, and I wouldn't want to ask a person anything that could somehow later be construed to have been discriminatory."*

In the twenty years that I have been recruiting, I can't think of any occasion where I asked a person about their interests outside of work and discriminated against them based on the answers that they provided. Are they interested in gardening? Do they have a passion for speedboats or classic cars? Is there a profound love for the performing arts?

The benefit of asking rapport building questions is that answers often provide us with a touch point for subsequent discussions. What do you do if someone references a passion for their church or for a particular political cause? As long as you conduct yourself within the law and evaluate an individual on the merits of their ability to perform a job function, there is no issue.

At the risk of sounding like I am speaking from a soapbox, I will say that I think that we live in a world that is sometimes too preoccupied with being politically correct. I believe that if you exercise good judgment during the Rapport Phase, you have nothing to fear. From my vantage point getting to know someone as a person, learning something about them that will help establish trust, and discovering what someone regards to be a significant life interest are all incredibly worthwhile.

The amazing thing about asking rapport building questions is the extent to which there are common threads between us and the individuals with whom we are speaking. We are all human. It is only natural to want to understand and appreciate people in a way that allows us to more meaningfully engage them in the future.

In my training programs, I often tell a story about a fellow with whom I worked who had a love of radio controlled airplanes. I found this out simply by asking him what he did for fun. He ended up moving out of the area, but called me about three years later from Colorado when he was preparing to head back East.

He began the call by saying, *"Hi Paul – this is Dan Thomas – you probably don't remember me, but we spoke a few years ago."* My response was simply, *"Dan! Of course I remember you – have you been flying your planes much lately?"* Dan was absolutely blown away that I remembered him, and particularly because I immediately touched on something that was important to him.

I could cite countless stories of similar encounters and experiences. Effective human relations skills are critical to effective recruiting. Does this mean that you have to become "best buddies" with everyone you encounter? Of course it doesn't; but, to the extent that you are able to learn something about people who are in many respects entrusting you with their careers, you are well served to make the human connection.

As I stated at the onset of this chapter, it is tremendously important to understand candidate motivators and to discern all of the underlying reasons that a prospective candidate would consider making a job change. The consequences of not drilling down and getting a comprehensive appreciation for a prospect's motivations, wants, needs, and desires can be significant and result in a great deal of wasted time and energy.

I encourage you to exercise due diligence with every prospect you encounter. Ask probing questions; secure underlying motivators; qualify what prospects mean when they provide a superficial response to a specific question; and utilize the CAREER Approach. Just as importantly, make the human connection. If you work diligently in this critical facet of the recruiting process, you will unquestionably realize better quality candidate relationships and experience far fewer surprises on the back end of the process.

Chapter 8: Reaping Reference Check Rewards

Conducting high quality candidate or applicant reference checks is unquestionably a critical element in the recruitment lifecycle, and reference checks should be a key component of any recruiter's daily or weekly plan. Increasingly, however, many organizations have elected to outsource the reference check process to third party vendors. This trend is attributable to a common perception held by many firms that reference checks are a low priority administrative task to be performed only at the point where a candidate is poised to receive an employment offer. Other organizations have come to regard references as being totally inconsequential – after all, no intelligent candidate is going to offer anything other than good references, right?

In the training programs that I conduct, the reference check process is prioritized for the simple reason that reference checks, if conducted properly, yield numerous peripheral benefits to every recruiter. Well-executed reference checks enable you to:

- Have "warm" calls with a spectrum of individuals that may uncover other prospective candidates or sales leads;

- Earn respect from active candidates, prospective candidates, and customers;

- Verify that your candidates are who they say they are; and

- Acquire information that enhances your appreciation for a candidate's abilities and the market sectors in which they work.

This chapter examines all aspects of the reference check process and discusses best practices for conducting a comprehensive reference check call. But let's start with the fundamental reason behind making this essential call. Reference checks are conducted to verify that a candidate's written and oral statements about his or her background are true.

A February 2006 "Pittsburgh Post Gazette" article, by Patricia Sabatini, suggests that some experts believe "up to 50 percent of resumes contain false information." While it is impossible to know the exact extent to which prospective candidates embellish their resumes, there are many recent examples of highly public misrepresentations that have destroyed careers.

A U.S. Olympic Committee Chairman resigned after it came to light that she had listed a Ph.D. that she hadn't earned; a Washington, D.C. Fire Chief resigned because he claimed a college degree that was never awarded; a newly appointed Notre Dame football coach was forced to resign within days of being hired because of material misrepresentations on his resume; and the CEO of Radio Shack was forced to resign for claiming two degrees that were allegedly never awarded.

Thankfully, my own experiences indicate that most job candidates tend to be fairly truthful about their work experience and academic backgrounds. Nonetheless, we need to verify that what they have represented about themselves and their abilities is consistent with reality.

When should you conduct reference checks in the recruiting process? Ideally, complete reference checks should be conducted *prior to* presenting a candidate to a hiring authority. Too often recruiters pursue reference checks after a candidate has been presented to a hiring authority for consideration or at the point where a formal employment offer is about to be tendered – contingent upon favorable references.

Conducting reference checks only after presenting a candidate to a hiring manager unnecessarily puts your credibility at risk if a problem or issue is subsequently uncovered. If you do identify a problem through reference checks or through any other form of background investigation (credit checks, criminal background checks, degree verifications), you are ethically obligated to divulge any inconsistencies to your client. The following true story highlights this point.

Several years ago, I worked with a candidate who had a unique aeronautical systems engineering background. After several interviews with the candidate, the hiring manager indicated that he intended to make an offer. He thanked me for transmitting completed reference checks and requested that I also verify the candidate's college degree.

The hiring manager knew that performing degree verification was outside the parameters of my firm's recruiting services agreement, but explained that a degree was mandatory for this particular opening, as the project was with a Department of Defense client. Having already completed several reference checks, all very favorable, I was happy to take care of the degree verification process.

My candidate had listed two bachelor's degrees: one in aeronautical engineering and the other in computer science. My client requested that I have the candidate submit transcripts for either of the degrees that had been noted on the resume.

I called the candidate, and he was very pleased that an offer was imminent. I explained that all we needed to do was submit transcripts verifying one of his four-year degrees. I quickly sensed that something was wrong when the candidate stated that his college transcripts were *"somewhere in his basement,"* and that it *"might take a few days"* for him to find them.

Up to this point, the candidate had not only expressed that he was completely sold on the company, but had additionally been pushing hard to get an offer, indicating that he was ready to accept the job and go to work immediately following his two-week notice period. Now he was saying that it *"might take a few days"* to find his transcripts. I knew that something just wasn't right.

I had previously obtained his permission to complete references and/or a background check, so I decided to call the registrar's office at each of the two colleges he had attended. I immediately learned that the candidate didn't possess either of the degrees that he had alleged, and that his collegiate experience was limited to a few classes at both schools.

Having had my worst fears confirmed, I contacted the candidate to respectfully advise him of what I had learned. He insisted that there must have been some type of gross mistake, and that he would resolve the misunderstanding immediately, after which he would be back in touch with me.

I politely hung up the phone with him and immediately dialed my client's number. I explained what I had learned and recommended that the discussions with my candidate be terminated. I went on to apologize and express my genuine disbelief about the events that had just unfolded. I found it very hard to believe that my candidate felt the need to perpetuate a fabrication even after being confronted with the fact that I had learned the truth about his actual college experience.

My client indicated that he appreciated my call and my honesty and indicated that he did not hold me or my firm at fault. Needless to say, years later I am still waiting for this particular candidate to call me back with proof that he had earned his degrees.

The good news in all of this was that *I had* completed the reference checks well prior to performing the degree verification. The candidate's references were good. Although the deal unraveled in the 11th hour, I was able to preserve some measure of credibility, because I had completed reasonable due diligence on the candidate well in advance of presenting his background to my client. The manager knew that I had attempted to validate the candidate's work experience, and that it was ultimately beyond my control that the candidate had elected to lie about his academic background.

So, from where I stand, the number one reason to conduct reference checks is to maintain professionalism and to establish your credibility as a recruiter who makes the effort to confirm that your candidates are who they say they are. Of equal significance is the fact that reference checks are effectively a final evaluation of your candidate. Aside from validating that a candidate is representing his or her background accurately, you are afforded the opportunity to assess the quality or depth of a candidate's experience. It is much more desirable to have a reference reveal that your candidate is not necessarily as good as he or she might have first appeared than to risk submitting an unqualified individual to interview with a busy hiring manager.

References provide you with a wealth of information that may actually help you "sell" the candidate. Reference data can strengthen your presentation of a candidate to a customer and can be equally effective in overcoming potential hiring authority objections about some aspect of a candidate's background.

Sometimes candidates will downplay or disregard their personal achievements that may reveal important skills or qualities that they possess. By talking with references, you'll be surprised to find hidden abilities or accomplishments that never surfaced during the detailed candidate interview. By gaining these insights, you are better able to sell the "complete" candidate.

As a case in point, several years ago, a high technology client charged me with identifying a key Software Development Manager. The firm's Chief Technical Officer outlined a number of critical success factors for this role and was fairly explicit in stating that the appropriate candidate would have to come from another commercial telecommunications product company. In executing the assignment, I came across one individual who embodied virtually everything that my client sought, with one critical exception: he lacked high volume commercial grade telecommunications product experience. Instead, he had experience working on lower volume telecommunications solutions for secure government applications.

Knowing that the missing product experience would be an issue in my client's eyes, I set about conducting detailed reference checks. Every reference I checked was adamant that the candidate in question was one of the very best software engineering managers with whom they had ever worked, characterizing him as "meticulous," "smart," and "results oriented." I became convinced that this individual could successfully perform in my client's position, and that the quality of his work and overall ability would more than overcome a lack of specific experience in developing high volume commercial telecommunications software. I submitted the resume along with the reference data that I had collected and then initiated a call to the CTO.

After speaking for a few moments about what I had learned and why I was compelled to submit this individual for consideration, my client didn't hesitate to push back by saying, *"Paul, I hear what you are saying, but this candidate doesn't have the commercial telecom experience I need, so I am going to pass on interviewing him."* Undeterred, I said, *"With all due respect, I know that this is a critical hire for your firm. Based on my interview with this individual and the uniform quality of his references, I'd be doing you a disservice if I didn't ask you to reconsider. I believe that this candidate can more than overcome your concerns.... In fact, I believe so strongly in this individual's ability that if you agree to meet with him and determine that he lacks what you are seeking, I will buy you lunch at the restaurant of your choosing – pick anyplace you like."*

The CTO reluctantly agreed to meet with my candidate a few days later, after which he called me. *"How did the meeting go?"* I asked. After a short pause the CTO responded by saying, *"Well, I guess I am the one who owes you a lunch."* They hired the candidate a week later, and he quickly became a star within the organization.

Just as some items of consequence may not arise in your initial interview with a candidate, these items may not come up during hiring manager interviews either. But sometimes they do. Over the years, in debriefing hiring managers following a candidate interview, I have discovered things about candidates that I simply didn't know. These items were not necessarily negative in nature; in fact often they were positive items that simply hadn't emerged during the interview process.

As demonstrated in the above story about the software development manager, conducting reference checks in advance positions you to bolster or support key elements of a candidate's background that may be important in the eyes of a hiring manager, or to counter potential objections that a hiring authority may have relative to an aspect of a candidate's experience.

To help further illustrate this point, I'll share an instance where reference data proved to be pivotal in helping a colleague close a deal. Scott (the recruiter) had recently interviewed a talented candidate for a pharmaceutical sales manager position. The candidate seemed to have all the tools necessary to do the job, and she possessed a terrific personality.

Scott fully believed that the candidate would make an ideal employee for the hiring manager he was supporting and embarked on conducting reference checks. Because one of the key traits that the hiring manager sought for this role was competitiveness, he made sure to inquire about it within each of his discussions with the candidate's references.

On the very first reference call, he asked her former manager to characterize the candidate's overall competitiveness. The manager laughed and responded, *"Well, I'm sure she's told you that she medaled in the Olympics."* *"No, she didn't,"* Scott exclaimed. *"What else has she not told me?"*

He ended the call having discovered several additional positive traits that the candidate possessed. When he asked the candidate why she had never told him about her Olympic medal, she replied, *"I guess I didn't think it would be relevant."*

It *was* relevant, and it allowed Scott to emphasize key attributes of significance to the hiring manager during the candidate presentation. The moment the manager asked him if she was competitive, he smiled and quickly convinced the hiring manager that she was likely one of the most competitive people in the world.

The manager brought her in for an immediate interview and ultimately made her an offer on the spot. Clearly, the reference process played a pivotal role in the hiring manager's confidence in the candidate, as well as in Scott's ability to speak about the candidate with conviction.

On another occasion, a hiring manager had asked me to identify a key product support specialist with very strong network technology skills. I contacted an individual who seemed very appropriate for this opportunity. Upon formally interviewing this person, however, I learned that he had quit his current job three weeks earlier. When I asked him what had prompted his departure from his last employer, he said, *"Well, I knew that I wanted to go in a different direction with my career, and I saw leaving as an opportunity to pursue a new job search while also taking an extended break with my family."*

I really liked and respected this fellow, and he seemed remarkably genuine in explaining his decision to leave his job without having another one in hand. I explained that I was going to need to check his references, and he cheerfully smiled and said, *"No problem, I have absolutely nothing to hide."*

The hiring manager from my client firm was exceptionally scrutinizing, and I knew that the circumstances regarding the candidate's departure from his last firm would have to be fully explored and validated. The candidate provided me with five references.

The references of greatest interest were two supervisors from his most recent employer. In initiating these reference check calls, I quickly determined that indeed, my candidate had been a highly respected and valued employee.

After several minutes of discussion, I inquired about the circumstances regarding this individual's recent departure. The Vice President of the organization responded by saying, *"Tom hit a point where we were no longer in a position to challenge him technically and he decided that it was a good time to make a move. I am never going to stand in the way of people trying to advance their career, but I did try to convince him that he should continue working for us until he landed something new. He felt that this was a good time to do a job search and take a break with his family. I told him that leaving might create concerns among prospective employers, but he insisted that everything would work out."* The VP acknowledged that he would rehire Tom without hesitation and truly regretted that his environment couldn't offer Tom additional growth opportunities.

Well, everything did work out. I presented Tom's resume to the hiring manager, along with three detailed reference check summaries. The hiring manager called me directly and said, *"As soon as I saw Tom's resume I noticed that he had just left his most recent position, which prompted a "red flag" – until I read his references. I definitely would like to have him in to interview."*

The interview took place a few days later, at which point I received another call from the hiring manager. *"I just wanted to let you know that I made Tom an offer at the end of our meeting, and he starts in three weeks,"* he stated. *"He wanted to complete his extended break with his wife and kids, and I have no problem with that."*

References As Leads

References can also help you to cultivate warm candidate leads. The fact that you are conducting reference checks in the first place affords you the opportunity to separate yourself from competitors, many of whom are not engaged in this facet of the recruiting process. If you are thorough and professional when conducting your reference checks, you have an opportunity to gain real credibility not only in the eyes of the candidates whose references you are checking, but also in the eyes of the references themselves.

A reference check call has great potential to transition into a recruiting call for two reasons. First, you are initiating a call that provides you and the reference contact with a common basis point, namely the candidate about whom you are calling. By default, this means that you are initiating a warm call.

Second, you hope to gain credibility and cultivate rapport over the course of your general discussion with a reference by asking high quality questions regarding the candidate's background and abilities. Again, being thorough and asking insightful questions goes a long way towards conveying a positive image of your abilities and professionalism as a recruiter.

Regardless of your industry niche, it is highly probable that the candidates with whom you work are going to cite similarly skilled individuals as references. Accountants will cite other accountants; software engineers will cite other software engineers; nurses will cite other nurses, and so on.

There simply is no easier way to introduce yourself in a non-threatening manner to a potential candidate prospect than through a warm ten minute phone call regarding a colleague. In addition to validating a candidate's background and experience while talking with a candidate's references, you peripherally hope to identify other highly qualified professionals that can be recruited either now or in the future. This approach is especially effective if a recruiter specializes in a highly focused niche market sector.

References are the fastest way possible to build a network of quality prospective candidates. I have found it best to conduct at least three reference checks per candidate, but I typically ask a candidate for five or six references. One reason I ask for five or six references is to reduce the number of call backs that I must make. I know that at least one of the references that a candidate has provided will either be out of the office, in a meeting, or otherwise inaccessible.

Obtaining five names enables me also to expand my potential network of contacts. It's fine if a candidate isn't in a position to provide five or six references, but as the saying goes, *"If you don't ask, you don't get."*

Of additional importance is asking for the right mix of references. Some recruiters and organizations only request supervisory references, but I believe that references should also be acquired for immediate colleagues and senior peers (someone who performs in a similar function as your candidate, only they've been doing it longer or have a greater range of responsibilities).

The supervisor reference check, of course, introduces you to someone who should be able to validate various aspects of a candidate's experience and performance. If you are a third party recruiter, conducting a reference check with a supervisor also gives you the opportunity to speak with a potential hiring manager.

The immediate colleague reference can introduce you to another potential candidate with skills that are likely very similar to your current candidate. The senior peer reference potentially introduces you to an even more experienced version of your candidate. The other benefit derived from speaking with a senior peer is that they may be able to offer greater insight into the specific abilities and work habits of your candidate, because many individuals are inclined to initially seek assistance from a senior peer rather than a manager when working through project issues or problems at work.

Securing references from candidates can be accomplished in a number of ways, including formal employment applications, candidate data sheets, or reference disclosure forms. I prefer using a detailed reference disclosure form such as the one that appears in Figure 8.0 on page 153. This form is designed to capture a great deal of information about individuals cited as references, and it includes a background check disclaimer at the bottom of the form (the need for which I will discuss later in this chapter).

How can you leverage reference checks from a candidate acquisition standpoint? For the purposes of illustration, let's suppose that you specialize in recruiting electrical engineers. If you interview five candidates per week and perform three reference checks on each one (consisting of one supervisor, one immediate colleague, and one senior peer) by the end of the week, you will have ten potential engineering candidates in addition to five engineering managers who could also be prospective candidates (or potential clients). Each new candidate has the ability to provide three or more references. If you can turn every new reference into a candidate that provides an additional three references, at the end of just one month those initial five candidates could theoretically enable you to speak with 155 new engineers and 75 engineering managers.

From the standpoint of practicality, it's highly unlikely that you would be able to convert every single reference into a candidate or that you would want to work with every single reference that you contact, but there is no denying that from a candidate acquisition standpoint, the reference process has limitless possibilities. Even if your conversion rate is only 20 percent, you will still end up securing 31 new engineering candidates and 15 new engineering manager candidates – immediately.

Figure 8.0

Candidate Reference Disclosure

Candidate Name: _____ Email: _____

Candidate Address: _____ State: _____ Zip: _____

Work Phone: _____ Home Phone: _____

1. Reference Name: _____ Title: _____ Relationship: _____
   Employer: _____ Email: _____ Years Known: _____
   Address: _____ State: _____ Zip: _____
   Work Number: _____ Ext: ____ Home Number: _____ Mobile Number: _____

2. Reference Name: _____ Title: _____ Relationship: _____
   Employer: _____ Email: _____ Years Known: _____
   Address: _____ State: _____ Zip: _____
   Work Number: _____ Ext: ____ Home Number: _____ Mobile Number: _____

3. Reference Name: _____ Title: _____ Relationship: _____
   Employer: _____ Email: _____ Years Known: _____
   Address: _____ State: _____ Zip: _____
   Work Number: _____ Ext: ____ Home Number: _____ Mobile Number: _____

4. Reference Name: _____ Title: _____ Relationship: _____
   Employer: _____ Email: _____ Years Known: _____
   Address: _____ State: _____ Zip: _____
   Work Number: _____ Ext: ____ Home Number: _____ Mobile Number: _____

5. Reference Name: _____ Title: _____ Relationship: _____
   Employer: _____ Email: _____ Years Known: _____
   Address: _____ State: _____ Zip: _____
   Work Number: _____ Ext: ____ Home Number: _____ Mobile Number: _____

I formally provide my consent to (Organization Name) to contact the references I have provided above for the purposes of gathering information about me relative to my pursuit of new employment opportunities. This contact may include investigation of information concerning my previous employment and any pertinent information regarding my personal and professional conduct. I release all parties from any liability for any damage that may result from furnishing same to you. I understand that false or misleading information given in my application, resume or interview(s) may result in dismissal or refusal of employment. I also understand that I have the right to request a full and accurate disclosure of the nature and scope of this investigation.

Signed: _____ Date: _____

If you were able to sustain this conversion rate over time, you could potentially cease cold-call recruiting forever and recruit strictly off of references, and that's why it makes eminent sense to try to conduct reference check calls on a daily basis.

How many reference checks you conduct each day will be determined by the overall flow of new candidates into your recruitment pipeline. Generally, I strongly advise that a recruiter attempt to complete somewhere between three and seven reference checks daily, or between 15 and 35 each week. These numbers will vary depending on your job duties. Someone who only works on the candidate side of the process (doesn't work extensively with hiring authorities) may be able to handle a higher volume of reference checks than someone engaged in all facets of the recruitment lifecycle (candidate and hiring manager interface).

Again, if at all possible, it is preferable to perform reference checks *before* presenting a candidate to a client. Aside from the credibility and professionalism reasons cited previously, failure to check references before the offer stage can be extremely costly. A regrettable experience that I endured several years ago may help to illustrate the importance of timely reference checks.

In executing a General Manager search for a long-standing client, I identified a senior executive from a Fortune 500 company who seemed to possess all of the necessary characteristics and experience for my client's opportunity. In addition to having a lengthy initial discussion with this individual I also conducted a subsequent and more detailed interview, which was very positive. Everything seemed positive, including the candidate's willingness to relocate back to the East Coast.

I advised the candidate that I needed to complete reference checks prior to introducing his background to my client. He indicated that providing references from his current employer would be very difficult, given that he was a member of the firm's executive team, but offered to give me references from former employers instead. He sent me the names of two preliminary references in a timely manner.

The first reference I contacted provided an outstanding commentary on the abilities of my candidate. This individual had been a subordinate of my candidate, but was now at the Senior VP level. He made no bones about the fact that he regarded his former boss to be a true mentor. Upon completing the reference check, I thought to myself, *"Wow, this guy is really good."*

I attempted to call the second reference and left a detailed voicemail message requesting a return call. About this time, the candidate called me to say that he was heading to the East Coast on business. I openly advised my client that I had not yet finished my due diligence on this particular candidate, but on the basis of my initial reference check and the relative quality of the candidate's experience, they agreed to push forward with an initial meeting. This enabled them to take advantage of the candidate's availability, as well as to conduct his interview in context with other candidate interviews.

After setting up the interview, I advised my candidate that I hadn't been able to reach his second reference and requested additional references. He indicated that he would get me a couple of additional people with whom I could speak, but then asked if doing reference checks at this juncture wasn't premature. I didn't think much of his question and simply indicated completing reference checks at the onset of the process was not uncommon, particularly for a position at this level.

The initial interview date arrived and, per plan, I went and met the candidate for lunch. Because he was based on the West Coast this was our first face-to-face meeting, after which I walked away thinking, *"This guy is really impressive."* He was cordial, articulate, and responsive. He even brought up the fact that he still owed me additional references and remarked, *"I haven't forgotten about them and am simply waiting for a couple of individuals to get back to me."*

His initial interview went extremely well. The client really liked this candidate a great deal and asked that I coordinate a second round of discussions. In doing so, I reiterated to my client that I was still working on obtaining additional references.

I decided to try calling the reference that had been provided to me originally one final time. This time I got through.

I told the reference who I was and why I was calling. He abruptly said, *"You've caught me at a really bad time, and I simply can't talk right now."* I don't know if it was something in his voice or the style of his delivery that caught me off guard, but I responded, *"Gee, I'm sorry, and I understand that you can't speak right now. Is it possible to set a time to speak with you later?"* After a long pause, I added, *"Or is this just not something you are comfortable doing?"*

A moment later the reference responded by saying, *"No, I am fine with speaking to you. How about calling me at 2:30 PM today?"*

I called back at the appointed time, and after a moment of small talk the reference said, *"Paul, I have thought about this, and I really don't feel comfortable functioning as a reference. Don't get me wrong, he's a great guy, but it has been so long since we worked together that I just don't feel comfortable functioning as a reference."*

As I hung up the phone my radar was in overdrive. This outcome was not good at all. I called my candidate and said that I had talked to the other reference that he had originally provided, but that this individual expressed that he could not perform in this capacity. Without missing a beat, my candidate replied, *"Well, he must still be unhappy with me that I didn't get his firm on my company's approved vendor list."* He elaborated on what had transpired, and I found myself surprised with how fluid and genuine his explanation seemed.

I asked for additional references including someone from his current company, and he said that he would provide them. His second round interview with my client was just two days away. He reiterated that he needed to be extremely careful about providing a reference within his current firm, as no one had a clue that he was looking at new situations.

In my heart of hearts, I sensed something was wrong, but I couldn't put my finger on anything specific. This candidate had been responsive throughout our relationship, had done everything he had pledged to do, and had gone out of his way to coordinate his initial interview with my client to parallel with his business travel. Even his response to one of his references opting out had been so smooth and rational that I found him to be very believable. But still, something was bothering me.

The second interview went well, and the client called to indicate that pending the completion of additional references, they were ready to make an offer. I conveyed this news to the candidate who cheerfully promised me that references would be forthcoming the next day.

The next day came, but there was no call or email with the additional references. I tried my candidate's cell phone – our standard means of communicating – and listened as it rang repeatedly before going into voicemail. This individual almost always answered his cell phone. On the rare occasion that I was forced to leave a voicemail, the transfer was immediate without any ringing.

I decided that I would call him at his office which was something that I hadn't needed to do over the course of our relationship. His office number had never been reflected on his resume or in any of our email correspondence, but I managed to track down a direct dial number for him at his company via the Internet.

I dialed the number, and a female voice answered and correctly identified the business unit that my candidate oversaw. I asked for my candidate by name and she responded, *"He is no longer employed here."* BOOM! In the two seconds that it took for her to utter those words, everything came together. He had lied about being employed. Something had happened that resulted in his departure, and he was hiding it. I thanked the woman who answered the phone and hung-up in disbelief.

Then I immediately picked the phone back up and called the main number for the company's headquarters. After requesting and being transferred to payroll, I completed a quick employment verification check by asking for my candidate's dates of employment. I learned that this individual's last day of employment had occurred several months earlier and well before my relationship with him commenced. Now everything made sense. My candidate was holding out on providing references, presumably because he had been terminated from his Senior VP role at his most recent employer.

I now had the unfortunate responsibility of calling my client firm and advising them of the circumstances. They were in complete and total disbelief that an individual would perpetuate a lie of this magnitude. The candidate's frequent references to business meetings and other activities that were taking place at his alleged "current" employer were a complete sham. Performing employment verification was outside the parameters of a typical search engagement with this client, so my client didn't specifically blame me for what had transpired; but they were understandably unhappy, and I couldn't blame them one bit.

Fortunately, I had introduced another very strong candidate that my client elected to hire. While the final outcome reinforces my belief that things inevitably happen for a reason, the façade put up by my original candidate created a massive waste of time and could have significantly damaged my relationship with a long-term client.

There's actually more to this story, including my follow-up discussions with the candidate, but rather than detail the remainder of this tragedy here, if you are interested in reading the gory details go to the following website address:

http://artofrecruiting.com/referencestory.htm

My reason for sharing this story is twofold. While I had secured one very positive reference, I should have been more diligent in securing others prior to presenting the candidate to my client. And I should have assigned greater significance to the individual who opted out of performing as a reference. While everything worked out in the end, I could have avoided a great deal of aggravation for both myself and my client had I more diligently pursued reference checking from the onset of the process.

You should secure references for every individual that you are going to interview, and you should absolutely execute reference checks on any candidate that you intend to have interview with hiring authorities. Remember, you conduct references not only to verify a prospective candidate's qualifications (versus your first impressions), but also to acquire additional prospective candidate leads.

Unless you are recruiting new college graduates, you should only be interested in acquiring professional references as opposed to character references (former teachers or professors, members of the clergy, family relations, etc.). You need to advise your candidates that you are interested only in talking with individuals who have the ability to speak about the candidate's actual experience in a relevant work setting.

Legal Considerations Associated with Reference Checks

A number of legal considerations are associated with conducting reference checks. Many individuals involved in the recruiting process are unaware of the fact that, from a legal perspective, reference checks are actually a form of background investigation covered by the Fair Credit Reporting Act of 1970.

The law states that recruiters who engage in reference checking are participating in the compilation of an investigative consumer report. Specifically, the Act states: "The term 'investigative consumer report' means a consumer report or portion thereof in which information on a consumer's character, general reputation, personal characteristics, or mode of living is obtained through personal interviews with neighbors, friends, or associates of the consumer reported on or with others with whom he is acquainted or who may have knowledge concerning any such items of information. However, such information shall not include specific factual information on a consumer's credit record obtained directly from a creditor of the consumer or from a consumer reporting agency when such information was obtained directly from a creditor of the consumer or from the consumer."

The Act goes on to state: "The term 'employment purposes' when used in connection with a consumer report means a report used for the purpose of evaluating a consumer for employment, promotion, reassignment or retention as an employee."

Furthermore, the Act stipulates that, "a reference can be any written, oral, or other communication of any information by the agency bearing on a candidate's credit worthiness, credit standing, credit capacity, character, general reputation, personal characteristics, or mode of living which is used in whole or in part to establish eligibility for employment purposes."

The Fair Credit Reporting Act of 1970 mandates that recruiters disclose to candidates that reference checks will be performed and that the candidate is allowed to request "a complete and accurate" disclosure of the "nature and scope" of the investigation that was performed. The disclosure notification to the candidate must be made in writing.

Earlier, in reviewing the Reference Disclosure Form (Figure 8.0), I noted that a reference disclosure notification had been placed at the bottom of the form. This section is where the candidate acknowledges that he/she understands that references will be checked. In typical government fashion, the law stipulates that the disclosure must be made in writing and within at least three days *after the date* on which a reference check was completed.

Again, this notification process is easily completed if you are interviewing candidates face-to-face and are having them fill out applications. As is reflected on the Reference Disclosure Form cited earlier, you can simply include a statement on the application outlining the candidate's rights and have the candidate read it and endorse it on the spot. If you do not have the luxury of meeting your candidates face-to-face, then you should develop a form letter or email template that outlines the candidate's rights and send it to each candidate prior to conducting reference checks. The statement should read as follows:

"You have the right to request a complete and accurate disclosure of the nature and scope of the investigation conducted by us." Note that the candidate does <u>NOT</u> have to give written permission to check references.

Certain information cannot be conveyed to third parties. "If the salary of the candidate on whom you are conducting a reference check will not exceed $20,000, then the following *may not* be disclosed: Bankruptcy actions more than 10 years before the reference check and none of the following if they occurred more than seven years before the date of the reference check: Suits, Judgments, Paid Tax Liens, Accounts placed for collection, Arrest/indictment/and conviction records."

Any candidate has the right to dispute the accuracy of the results of a reference or background check. In this event, the recruiter must reinvestigate the information in dispute within a reasonable time period.

The actual notification and disclaimer language that you incorporate into your own reference disclosure form or employment application can be as simple as:

I formally provide my consent to (Organization Name) to contact the references I have provided above for the purposes of gathering information about me relative to my pursuit of new employment opportunities. This contact may include investigation of information concerning my previous employment and any pertinent information regarding my personal and professional conduct. I release all parties from any liability for any damage that may result from providing this information. I understand that false or misleading information given in my application, resume or interview(s) may result in dismissal or refusal of employment. I also understand that in accordance with the Fair Credit Reporting Act of 1970, I have the right to request a full and accurate disclosure of the nature and scope of this investigation.

Now you may be wondering, *"What happens if I fail to comply with the Act?"* If taken to court by a candidate, you could be held liable for an amount equal to the sum of actual damages sustained as a result, plus punitive damages, plus attorney's fees. While this is a low probability scenario, it's also a risk not worth taking in the ever more litigious society in which we live.

The benefit of complying with these legal obligations is twofold. First, little effort is required to be in compliance. Second, you can distinguish yourself and your organization by complying with the Act.

In my experience, candidates are not accustomed to receiving any indication or notice stating that they have the right to request a full disclosure of reference checks performed in context with their job search. Candidates don't typically know that references are governed by the Fair Credit Reporting Act of 1970. Some candidates will point blank tell you, *"I have never seen reference disclosure language like this."*

Incidentally, it's worth mentioning that in all the years that I have been recruiting and conducting reference checks, I have only had two candidates out of thousands actually request to know what their references stated about them. If the candidate does request the disclosure of the investigation, the rules are simple: You must disclose *what* was said, but you do not have to disclose *who* said it. This allows you to preserve the confidentiality of the individual who provided the information. Furthermore, you may need to paraphrase information that was shared or speak in generalities in order to keep the identity of specific references confidential.

Conducting The Reference Check

What questions should you ask in conducting a reference check? The reference check call can be broken into three different phases: The Opening, Questioning, and Closing Phases. In initiating a reference check call, I suggest that you open the call along these lines:

"Bill, this is John Smith with XYZ Company. We haven't talked previously, but I specialize in working with software design professionals and was interested in speaking with you for a few moments because you have been listed as a professional reference for Lisa Patterson.

Lisa and I have been speaking recently about select employment opportunities, and I was interested in talking with you about her experience. I was hoping that in speaking with you I might gain some additional insights into her background. Have I caught you at a point where you have just a few minutes?"

It's very important to initiate the call in this manner. Many recruiters state that they're conducting a reference check and move immediately into questioning mode. Explaining who you are, and the market sector within which you recruit, will hopefully provide incentive for the individual with whom you are speaking to spend time with you after the actual reference check is complete.

Most of the time, the reference has no idea if you're from a recruiting firm, a reference checking firm, or an employer. Ideally, you want to plant a seed in the reference's mind, one that implies that you possess relevant marketplace expertise and that there may be reason to speak beyond this particular call.

Additionally, whether the reference is a peer or manager, the fact that you're conducting a detailed reference check establishes credibility. A thoughtful, well-executed reference check suggests that you and your organization are discriminating and conduct business in a manner synonymous with quality. How you conduct the reference check and the nature of the questions you pose will have a great deal to do with how the reference regards you.

Now you want to move into the questioning phase. The types of questions that you ask will say a lot about how much emphasis you place on references, as well as your professionalism. Below are some questions that I've found work best. An example of the Reference Check Form that I use is displayed on pages 165 – 166 in Figure 8.1 and Figure 8.2. This Form, along with the Reference Disclosure Form (Figure 8.0), can be found on ART's Forms Disk Product, available at (www.artofrecruiting.com). The questions are as follows:

1) *Characterize the length and nature of your professional relationship with the candidate?*
You want to verify that this is a professional relationship, and not the candidate's friend, relative or social connection. Clearly the information you gather from a professional reference will be much more meaningful. Also, you want to know how long the reference had exposure to the candidate, and in what capacity. You will want to pay close attention if the reference's exposure to the candidate is of a relatively brief duration, or the reference and the candidate have not worked together for a number of years.

2) *What was the candidate's job title?*
You not only need to verify the title, but also want to learn how that particular title fits within the organization's structure. Titles are meaningless without a point of reference, as they vary widely from company to company.

Reference Check Form

Completed By: _____

Candidate Name: _____   Date: _____

Reference Name/Title/Employer: _____

Reference Phone Number: _____

1. Characterize the length and nature of your relationship with Candidate?

2. What is (was) his or her title and specific responsibilities?

3. Is there an adjective that you think accurately describes the Candidate?

4. Characterize the Candidate's professionalism (Demeanor, Ethics, Conduct)?

5. How you would characterize the Candidate's written & verbal communication skills?

6. Did the Candidate get along well with peers and management? Were there ever any issues?

7. Can you think of a time when he/she was integral to the success of a particular project?

8. Has he/she ever had to sell ideas to peers or management? What was the outcome?

9. Has he/she ever been in a supervisory role? If so, characterize overall effectiveness?

Figure 8.1

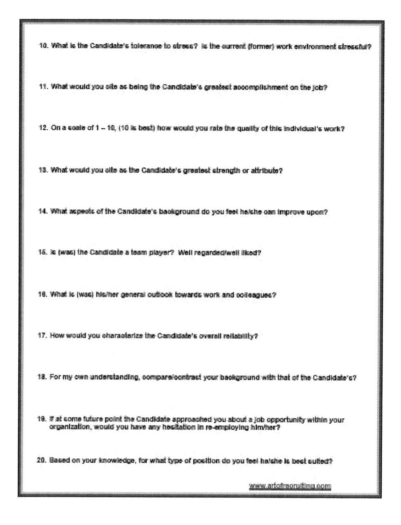

10. What is the Candidate's tolerance to stress? Is the current (former) work environment stressful?

11. What would you cite as being the Candidate's greatest accomplishment on the job?

12. On a scale of 1 – 10, (10 is best) how would you rate the quality of this individual's work?

13. What would you cite as the Candidate's greatest strength or attribute?

14. What aspects of the Candidate's background do you feel he/she can improve upon?

15. Is (was) the Candidate a team player? Well regarded/well liked?

16. What is (was) his/her general outlook towards work and colleagues?

17. How would you characterize the Candidate's overall reliability?

18. For my own understanding, compare/contrast your background with that of the Candidate's?

19. If at some future point the Candidate approached you about a job opportunity within your organization, would you have any hesitation in re-employing him/her?

20. Based on your knowledge, for what type of position do you feel he/she is best suited?

www.xxxxxxxxxx.com

Figure 8.2

3)   *Characterize the candidate's primary job duties and responsibilities?*
You want to know what the candidate's job actually entailed. This answer should give you a fair amount of insight that may help you sell the candidate's background to prospective employers.

4)   *Is there an adjective that you would use in characterizing the candidate?*
This is a great question because it underscores what the reference really thinks about your candidate. Furthermore, if the reference answers that the adjective that best describes your candidate is "tenacious," you are poised to respond by saying, *"Wow, what makes you say that?"*

5)   *How would you characterize the candidate's image, interpersonal skills and presentation ability?*
For recruiters who do not have the luxury of meeting candidates face-to-face, it's better to find out now if any issues exist in this regard, rather than having a hiring authority tell you something negative following an interview. Pay particular attention for roles that require a lot of outside interface, such as sales. If your candidate doesn't project a professional image, you need to know this now.

6)   *How would you characterize the candidate's oral and written communication skills?*
It's all well and good that the candidate can speak with you, but how do they communicate with others on a daily basis at work? Again, you're looking for both the good (to help sell the candidate) and the bad (to possibly rule someone out).

7)   *Did the candidate get along well with peers and management? Were there ever any issues?*
This question will help you to understand how a candidate tends to fit into work environments and will also help you to discern if the individual is a team player or is potentially divisive.

8)   *Has the candidate ever had to sell ideas to peers or supervisors? What was the outcome?*
If this candidate is an exceptional leader or innovator, you want to know so that you can convey this information to the hiring authority.

9)   *Has the candidate directed the activities of others? If so, how many direct reports did he/she have?*
This question helps you to verify the level and scope of a candidate's overall responsibilities.

10)   *On a scale of 1 – 10, with 10 being the best, how would you rate the quality of the candidate's work and overall performance?*
This question gives you a baseline numeric rating for your candidate. If a reference says, *"I would say that overall, Lisa is an 8 out of a 10,"* you can follow-up by asking, *"What would propel Lisa to a rating of 10?"*

11)   *Characterize the candidate's professionalism (Demeanor, Ethics, and Attitude)?*
You want to know that your candidate takes work seriously and is regarded as being highly professional. If the potential exists that the candidate has questionable ethics or doesn't project a positive professional attitude, you need to know this now.

12)   *What aspects of the candidate's background do you feel he or she should strive to improve?*
Just as there are no perfect people in this world, there's no such thing as a perfect employee. You need to know your candidate's weaknesses to ensure that there isn't a significant shortcoming that would impair overall performance. You need to identify any major issues that would inhibit the candidate's ability to perform in the role for which he or she is being considered.

13) *In your view, what was the candidate's greatest accomplishment on the job?*
This question is intended to help you understand what makes your candidate special and will help you to most effectively present your candidate to a hiring authority.

14) *How would you characterize the candidate's overall reliability?*
You need to know if your candidate is regarded for getting work done in a timely and consistent manner.

15) *What is the candidate's ability to tolerate stress? Is the current/former work environment stressful?*
Some people thrive in fast-paced environments, and others do not. It is important to qualify the extent to which your candidate can tolerate stress.

16) *Would you have any hesitation in re-employing the candidate?*
This is a pretty straightforward question, but one that must be asked. If the reference hedges in answering the question, you may need to investigate a bit further.

17) *Based on your knowledge of the candidate, for what type of position do you feel he/she is best suited?*
You want to hear the reference's perspective on whether or not your candidate would be a good fit for the position for which you're currently recruiting. You may want to specifically outline the role for which the candidate may be considered and ask, *"Based on the role that I just highlighted, and based on your knowledge of Lisa, do you have any reservations about how she might perform?"*

The questions highlighted above may be more numerous or more in-depth than what you are accustomed to asking when conducting reference checks. These questions are designed to help acquire broad insight about a particular candidate. The information you acquire can be utilized to make a compelling presentation to a hiring manager.

Also, don't be surprised if you begin to receive comments from candidate references indicating that they have not previously participated in such a thorough reference check. Remember, a secondary reason for conducting a detailed reference check is to generate a favorable impression from the individual you have contacted to provide a candidate reference. You want to be regarded as an extremely thorough and professional recruiter who is truly dedicated to finding the best match for the candidates and hiring authorities with whom you work.

And now you have arrived at the close of the reference check call. You started out by introducing yourself and highlighting the market sector(s) in which you specialize. You then migrated into questioning mode. Now, it's imperative to bring the conversation back around to the individual reference with whom you are speaking. You will set this up by asking the reference the following:

"Thanks for your time Bill. Your responses to my questions have really helped me obtain a better understanding of Lisa's experience. I do have an additional question that I hope you don't mind answering. Just for my own understanding would you mind telling me a bit more about your specific experience, and how your background is similar or different from Lisa's?"

Over the course of answering the questions posed previously, you may have already received some measure of insight regarding the role that the reference plays. The intent of this final question is to gather more information about perceived similarities or differences between the backgrounds of your candidate and the reference.

At this juncture, the reference will likely respond by saying that he or she specializes in ABC aspect of software development and has been working on a similar project to Lisa in the XYZ Department, etc. Take careful notes, because you have effectively asked the person providing the reference to qualify his or her background. The references response will help you to determine whether or not you want to potentially pursue this individual as a prospective candidate.

After the individual has provided additional information on his or her background, you can quickly ascertain whether or not this is someone that you should get to know better. If so, you can say:

"Bill, I appreciate the overview you provided on your background. I have to say that your experience sounds really impressive, which raises a question. If at some point in the future there were a unique situation that might significantly advance your career, would you be open to talking about it?"

As I referenced earlier in the chapter on Advanced Introductory Calls, Bill can respond in one of three different ways: Yes, No, or Maybe. If he says, *"No, I'm really happy where I am right now, and things are going well,"* you can respond by saying, *"I totally understand and I think that's great. Nonetheless, I have really enjoyed our conversation and would like to keep in touch with you in the future, if that's okay?"*

Most likely, Bill will say it's perfectly okay to stay in touch. At this point you want to close by thanking him for taking the time to speak with you about Lisa and reiterating that you look forward to seeing her candidacy move forward.

If Bill indicates that he would be open to speaking with you about potential opportunities, you need to exercise great care to separate any further discussion about Bill's background from the original premise of your call which was to conduct a reference check. The best way to handle this is to say: *"Bill, I would welcome the chance to speak with you, but the intent of my call today was primarily to discuss Lisa's background and experience. I would feel more comfortable if we selected an alternate time to speak further.... I'm sure you understand."* Most candidates will say that they fully understand and respect the premise of the call and agree to set up an alternate time to speak further.

A great deal of subtlety is at work here. On the one hand, you really do want to complete a comprehensive reference check on your candidate. On the other hand, you don't want to miss an opportunity to engage what could be another highly qualified candidate. From an ethical perspective, however, it is entirely <u>inappropriate</u> to consider putting a current candidate into competition with an individual that was provided as a reference.

If a candidate calls to say that they understand you may be speaking with one of their references about new career opportunities, you should acknowledge this without hesitation. But you should also make it clear that under no circumstances are you going to place the candidate into a competitive situation with a reference who is also interested in speaking with you. And you should absolutely honor this commitment.

In summary, the reference check process allows you to consistently qualify the skills and abilities of candidates with whom you are actively working. References also enable you to establish a host of other contacts within your market niche in a credible and professional manner. Additionally, increased reference check calls can help you to dramatically optimize your pipeline of prospective candidates.

I hope that this chapter has given you greater insight into the many benefits associated with the candidate reference check process. By ensuring that reference checks are a component of each business week, you will validate candidate skills, improve the quality of candidate presentations to hiring authorities, build greater credibility in your market sector, and increase warm call volume, all of which are ingredients for achieving heightened levels of recruiting success.

Chapter 9: Referral Acquisition Techniques

Referrals are the life-blood of recruiting. Whether you are conducting cold calls, indirect sourcing calls, networking calls or candidate interviews, the ability to consistently and successfully solicit the names of other potentially qualified referral prospects is an essential aspect of successful recruiting. Many individuals engaged in recruiting, however, either don't consistently employ a strategy to obtain referrals or utilize inefficient techniques.

Throughout this book, I have addressed the significance of implementing a consultative approach and working to forge some measure of rapport with everyone you contact in the course of your recruiting activities. The most fundamental reason for doing this, of course, is to construct the foundation of a relationship that can be cultivated and leveraged over time. By taking a legitimate interest in the people you engage, you will not only build rapport, but will also engender some measure of trust. Establishing meaningful rapport and building trust are the keys to obtaining referrals.

In contrast, for recruiting professionals who employ a purely transactional selling style and who make constructing long-term relationships with candidate prospects a secondary priority, referral acquisition will be an ongoing and frustrating challenge. The intent of this chapter is to address the candidate mind-set relative to recruiter referral approaches and to present effective referral acquisition methods that will help you further broaden your ability to identify prospective candidates.

Referral Acquisition From Prospects Not Interested in Making a Job Change

When speaking to prospects who indicate that they are not interested in considering new employment opportunities, many recruiters are apt to pursue referrals by putting forth questions like this:

1. *"Is there anyone else you know who's looking?"*

2. *"Can you refer me to anyone else who might be looking?"*

3. *"Do you know anyone else with XYZ skill set who's looking?"*

4. *"Who do you know who might be interested in hearing about ABC opportunity?"*

The basic problem with the first three referral acquisition questions listed above is that they are close-ended. Close-ended questions allow the respondent to offer a simple "Yes" or "No" answer. And, more often than not, the answer to these questions will be, "No."

Further, all four questions above are qualified by the phrases, "who's looking," or "who might be interested." Life would be great if recruiters could consistently be pointed to others "who might be looking" or "who might be interested" in the opportunities they represented. But do you really care whether someone is "looking" or not? In the interest of always wanting to further broaden your network of contacts, your ultimate concern should be oriented to caring only about whether someone has the requisite skills, qualities and other attributes that are relevant to the position(s) on which you are working.

If you ask qualified or close-ended questions when seeking referrals, you are essentially allowing the individual from whom you are requesting a referral to function as a filter. Many individuals will opt for the safety of offering no information rather than run the risk of providing information to someone (a recruiter) who, for all intents and purposes, represents a complete unknown.

The simple truth is that many people are fundamentally uncomfortable with providing the names of friends and colleagues because on some basic level they either don't trust the individual asking for referrals, or because they don't want to impose on others, or both. As a result, most individuals will respond to a close-ended or qualified question by saying, *"Gee, I'd like to help you, but I don't know anyone who's looking"* or *"Hmmm, there really isn't anyone I'm aware of who's looking right now."* In fairness, some professionals honestly don't know of anyone who is looking or "who might be open to hearing about an opportunity."

Individuals will sometimes respond by saying, *"You know, there are a couple of people who come to mind, but I would feel more comfortable giving them your name, and if they are interested they can call you."* While courteous, more often than not, this sort of response is a dodge, as the individual from whom you are seeking referrals is highly unlikely to pass your name along. They aren't comfortable giving you a name because they don't know you, and it is unlikely that they will pass along your name because they really don't want to get involved as an intermediary between a colleague and a recruiter – and why should they?

All of us have gotten a call in the past from someone offering a service or product that simply wasn't of interest to us at that moment in time, whereupon the caller requested referrals. Consider how you felt in that moment. How did you ultimately handle the referral request?

Maybe you provided the salesperson with a lead. If you did, it was probably because you liked the caller's presentation style and on some level trusted the individual. I suspect, however, that many of us can think of an occasion where we were reluctant to give referrals, because we either felt uncomfortable with the timing of the request or the person making the request.

Gauge Your Audience – Know When To Ask

The first rule of referral acquisition is: Know when to ask and when to hold off on asking. If you make a recruiting call to a passive candidate who acknowledges that he is not looking, but who embodies the qualities and experience you are seeking, you must determine whether or not you have built sufficient rapport within your introductory discussion to meaningfully ask for a referral.

If the prospect doesn't open up significantly or seems guarded in the course of your initial conversation, you may be better off not asking for a referral in that particular call. You might be better served by calling the individual back in a few days or in a couple of weeks. Or if the individual is someone who has the capacity to point you to a number of different leads, you may want to allow the relationship to incubate over an even longer period of time.

How to grow the relationship is ultimately up to you. Throughout my career, countless individuals who weren't open to making a job change subsequently became true business friends instead. If someone is good at what they do, I try to find a reason to stay in touch. Sometimes the reason is simply tied to the fact that the individual has unique domain knowledge or experience. My follow-up calls are oriented to getting their perspectives or insights about industry trends. These follow-up calls are completely non-threatening and allow me to nurture the relationship.

On other occasions, I will use something that I have learned about an individual's interests as an on-going touch point to affirm my interest in them as a person. Regardless, over time I become more than just *"the recruiter who, upon determining that I wasn't interested, pressed me for the names of peers."* Over time, I become a known quantity that can be trusted. Over time, I have the ability to call these contacts and cut right to the point: *"Joe, I am working on a new assignment – who should I be talking with who has XYZ experience?"*

There are no perfect or bullet-proof approaches that will consistently yield referrals from every passive candidate prospect. Your best option is always to take the time to project your expertise, explain the market you serve, characterize the opportunity that you are working on, and describe the kind of person you are looking to identify. Then, you want to explain to the individual with whom you are speaking that he or she might be in a position to help you. This question can be framed in innumerable ways, but I believe that asking someone for a networking contact, as opposed to directly requesting a referral, constitutes a less threatening approach. Specifically, at the conclusion of your call you can say:

"Tom, I have really enjoyed the chance to learn about your background and understand that the timing is not right for you to consider new opportunities. I look forward to keeping in touch, and please know that if your circumstances ever change or if I can ever be any help to you, I'm happy to do so. In complete candor, your background aligns closely with the kinds of roles that I am working on, and I am hoping that you can help point me in the right direction. As someone with a number of professional contacts, who else would you recommend I consider reaching out to, if only for the purposes of networking? Obviously anyone that we discuss will be handled with the utmost confidentiality."

Referral Acquisition from Active Candidates

Because you can quickly build rapport-oriented relationships with active candidates who work in your industry or market sector, these individuals are often invaluable sources for other high quality prospects. Referral acquisition from active candidates can be accomplished using either a Direct or Indirect Approach. Whereas the Indirect Approach is geared towards creating an expectation that you will obtain referrals at some point in the future, the Direct Approach is a real-time referral solicitation.

Earlier, I referenced that a big component of referral acquisition was tied to knowing when to ask. There will be circumstances when it may make more sense to use one approach versus the other based on the candidate with whom you are working. Regardless of the approach you select, it's best to express your interest in obtaining referrals from active candidates towards the closing portion of either an initial face-to-face meeting or a detailed phone interview.

The Direct Approach

As your initial meeting or detailed phone interview with an active candidate draws to a close, it is both logical and appropriate that you formulate a plan to stay in touch or establish a time for a follow-up discussion or status update. At this juncture, you should review the contents of your meeting and attempt to affirm the candidates comfort level with what has transpired. Then you can segue into actually asking for referrals. This conversation might flow as follows:

Recruiter: *"Sue, I have really appreciated the chance to spend time with you today and look forward to working with you. In an effort to make sure that we are on the same page, I want to verify a few items. First, are you comfortable with the content of our discussion today?"*

Candidate: *"Yes, I have enjoyed the opportunity to meet with you (or talk with you on the phone)."*

Recruiter: *"Great, and are you comfortable with how the process will flow moving forward?"*

Candidate: *"Yes, it seems just fine."*

Recruiter: *"Terrific. And, finally, are you comfortable with me personally?"*

Candidate: *"Oh, absolutely. I have really appreciated the time you have spent with me and the depth of our discussion."*

Recruiter: *"Sue, I really appreciate that. I want you to know that I am excited to be working with you, and to the extent that I can help you, I am very happy to do so. I would also like to ask you a favor. As you might imagine, I am working on an array of positions right now, and I am hoping that you can help me build my network. Because business networking is such an integral part of what I do, I am always interested in talking with talented professionals such as yourself, regardless of whether they are open to considering new opportunities or not. As someone with a host of professional and industry contacts, who else would you suggest I consider networking with? Obviously, anyone that we discuss will be handled with the utmost confidentiality."*

In reading the script outlined above, you undoubtedly recognized several set-up statements. You must verify that an active candidate *is* comfortable with the content of the overall discussion that has taken place, and the manner in which the process will move forward, as well as the fact that they are comfortable with you personally. If the candidate has any concerns, this is the point to get them on the table. You are asking the candidate for feedback and need to know that they are satisfied with everything that has occurred up to this point.

Furthermore, if the candidate affirms that she is comfortable with the content of the discussion, the action plan that has been formulated, and with you personally, it becomes exponentially more difficult to object to providing referrals. Even if the candidate's gut feeling towards offering referrals is negative, it is far more difficult for him or her to act upon this sentiment having just offered you an endorsement seconds earlier.

The Indirect Approach

The Indirect Approach is less about asking for specific referrals, and more about setting the stage to acquire referrals at a subsequent point in time. In the Indirect Approach, you want to convey the idea that at some juncture you may reach out to an active candidate for assistance relative to other positions you may be working on. Specifically, you can say:

"Terry, I have really appreciated the chance to talk with you today and look forward to working with you. Because so much of what I do entails networking with quality people like you, I want to ask a favor. As you might expect, I am working on a variety of different positions. Is it okay to contact you from time to time for the purposes of networking about professionals you may know who could be relevant to other assignments I may be working on?"

Or you can say:

"Terry, as you might expect, networking is a huge component of my job. While I have no intent of asking you for referrals today, I want you to know that if you think of other quality individuals who I might benefit by speaking with, or who might benefit by speaking with me, that I absolutely welcome referrals. Additionally, I want to make sure that it's okay to contact you for the purposes of networking, if I encounter a role where I think you might be able to help me."

In both of the scripts above, you are basically doing nothing more than establishing a mutual understanding that you intend to solicit referrals in the near or distant future. In essence, you are setting the stage to acquire relevant leads at some point down the road. The other benefit to using an Indirect Approach is that it allows you to make referral acquisition a secondary priority, or an assumed outcome of your business relationship with the candidate. The Indirect Approach employs a fair amount of subtlety, but be assured that it works just as well and, in many instances, better than the Direct Approach.

Potential Objections To Providing Referrals

You will encounter occasional objections from active candidates who are reluctant to provide referrals regardless of the actual solicitation format you employ. The most common objections include:

- *"I really don't feel comfortable giving out names yet."*

- *"I would prefer to call them first and give them your name."*

- *"I would prefer to see what you can do on my behalf before giving out names."*

As I suggested earlier, if a candidate is not comfortable providing you with names, there really isn't much to be gained by applying pressure. Instead, it would be better to simply say, *"Jane, no problem. I hope over the course of our relationship, we will get to a point where you are comfortable helping me build my network of contacts."* Pressing too hard or making an active candidate uncomfortable is entirely counter-productive and will diminish your ability to construct rapport.

If the candidate prefers to provide your name to others, you can say, *"If you are more comfortable passing my name along, that's fine. To ensure that the call gets routed by my receptionist, however, do you mind providing me with your colleague's name? I won't initiate contact without your permission."*

If the active candidate offers a colleague's name, you should act in good faith and wait for the referral to contact you. If you are not contacted within a reasonable timeframe, simply call the active candidate to obtain their permission to call the referral directly. You can simply say, *"Sue, when we met last week, you were kind enough to mention Tom Jackson's name and suggested that you would pass my name along to him. I know that people get busy, and I hadn't heard from Tom yet – do you mind if I reach out to him directly?"*

At this point, don't be surprised if you hear, *"Oh, gee – I meant to speak with Tom, but haven't had a chance. Go ahead and contact him, but I would appreciate it if you don't mention my name."*

A candidate who states that he prefers to see what you can do on his behalf before providing the names of referrals, is most likely saying that he doesn't want to create direct competition for any role that he himself is interested in pursuing. If you encounter this concern, plainly indicate that you will not place any referral into a competitive situation with the active candidate and honor your commitment.

If the background and experience of a referral and the active candidate are approximately the same, you must allow the active candidate to progress through the interview process to some definitive conclusion (an offer acceptance or a determination that the active candidate's background is not a fit). Only then can you ethically reach out to the referral that has been provided by the active candidate. Ideally, you may be working on several very similar opportunities that further protect the active candidate from any possibility of competing with a referral.

Another approach is to ask an active candidate for a referral whose experience or role is not immediately similar to his or her background. This approach mitigates the potential for active candidates to feel that citing a referral may introduce competition to their own candidacy for a particular role.

For instance, if you are working with a candidate whose background is oriented to marketing, you might say: *"Tom, obviously your background and experience are focused on product marketing. I am also working on a senior level sales role. Some of the key attributes associated with this role include (cite attributes). As someone who's had a lot of exposure to sales professionals, who would you recommend I consider contacting about this opportunity, if only for the purposes of networking?"*

In Chapter One, I highlighted the fact that internal employee referrals are often the most effective way for employers to acquire talent. In my travels, however, I am consistently surprised that many organizations lack a communications plan that specifically engages current or new employees to regularly recommend former colleagues or new business contacts for existing openings.

I recall speaking with a corporate recruiter who was struggling to identify prospective candidates for a Product Manager role. I inquired whether her firm participated in any industry tradeshows. *"Yes, actually we participate in several large shows each year,"* she responded. In discussing this further I asked her if she had ever tasked the executives who attend these trade shows to capture the names and contact information of individuals they encountered from competitive organizations. *"I hadn't really thought to do that,"* she replied.

This response is not unique. Just about every company has employees that have the capacity to contribute to the referral acquisition process. These individuals simply should be reminded that they need to adopt a recruiting mentality while attending conferences, tradeshows or other functions that facilitate networking. I don't mean that these individuals must directly engage in recruiting individuals that they may meet, but that they can help support their company's mission by simply passing along the names of other professionals they encounter and regard positively.

Additionally, recruiters should focus on soliciting referral leads from new hires, perhaps especially when they first join the organization. Again, the mode of securing referrals from a new hire should not be oriented to, *"Who else do you know who might be looking or who might be interested?"* Instead, the better question to ask is: *"Who at your last firm impressed you?"* Or *"Who at your last firm performed in XYZ job function, and what did you think of him/her?"*

Regardless of whether you obtain referrals from individuals who are not poised to entertain a job change, individuals who are active candidates, or people that you have hired or placed, it is important to gather as much information as possible about the person being referred. Let's say that you solicit a referral for a senior marketing position on which you are working and are given the name of John Smith. While it's nice to know the name of someone with whom you may want to speak, understanding the particulars of John Smith's experience and accomplishments will not only help you to better qualify his background and relevance to your opening, but will also help you to execute a much more effective introductory call. When you reach out to communicate with John Smith, it will be extremely clear that you have done your homework, which will enable you to obtain credibility and build rapport more rapidly.

When you call a referral prospect, you will inevitably be asked, *"How did you get my name?"* As I recommended in Chapter Five, Advanced Introductory Calls, you want to answer these inquiries as truthfully as possible. Some people who provide referrals will indicate that it's absolutely fine to cite their name when you initiate contact with their referral. Others, uncertain as to whether or not the person they have referred will be receptive to a recruiter's call will prefer to remain anonymous. Obviously, you must honor all requests for confidentiality.

If you contact a referral prospect and are asked, "How did you get my name," you can respond in several ways. If the referring party is an active candidate, simply say, *"In truth, your name came up in a discussion with another individual with whom I am currently working. Because they are actively involved in a job search, I am not at liberty to divulge this individual's name, but I can say that this person holds you in high regard, which is what prompted my call."*

If the referring party wishes to remain anonymous and is not an active candidate, you can say, *"I do a lot of networking and your name was referenced in confidence. As is often the case, the person who cited you as a contact had no idea as to your current status and only suggested that you were very capable and might be relevant to a project I am working on. Does that make sense?"* Usually, at this point, the referral prospect will say, *"Oh, okay – that's fine,"* and you can then transition the discussion back to one oriented to learning more about the prospect's background and experience.

I began this chapter by referencing the sales axiom that, "Referrals are the life-blood of recruiting." Throughout my career, I have been the beneficiary of countless referral leads that have tangibly and favorably impacted the outcome of many recruiting engagements. I've always gone out of my way to express tremendous appreciation to those individuals who have provided me referrals. In as much as I have been the grateful recipient of qualified candidate leads, I have been just as grateful that the people providing referrals have extended me something of much greater consequence: their trust.

If you are not actively pursuing referral acquisitions or have attempted to do so without great success, I highly recommend that you consider utilizing some of the approaches that have been highlighted in this chapter. Again, you are unlikely to identify referral acquisition approaches that will work 100 percent of the time. But if you project yourself and the assignments on which you are engaged in a professional manner, treat referral acquisition as a basic "networking" activity, and thoughtfully solicit the assistance of others, you will significantly enhance your ability to access passive candidate prospects and optimize your overall recruiting effectiveness.

Chapter 10: Salaries, Offers & Closing The Deal

In the hierarchy of painful experiences that a recruiter must endure, having an offer turned down is perhaps second only to having a prospective candidate accept a counter-offer from his or her current employer. In both instances a great deal of time and energy is expended on courting a particular prospect; and in both instances, when all is said and done, the recruiter and employer have nothing to show for their efforts.

In many organizations, particularly those that actively use performance metrics, a great deal of attention is paid to recruitment closing ratios. Closing ratios essentially reflect the overall efficiency in the relationship between extended offers and accepted offers. In a perfect world, a recruiter would like to see a 1:1 ratio where every offer extended is ultimately accepted. But, alas, we don't live in a perfect world. Inevitably, candidates (in their own mind) will always have very plausible reasons for rejecting employment offers. At times these reasons will seem exceptionally logical; at other times they will appear to be incredibly irrational. Sometimes, however, the offer negotiation process is flawed from the onset, dramatically reducing the likelihood of a recruiter obtaining an accepted offer from a candidate. This chapter outlines specific approaches that a recruiter can pursue to optimize key facets of the offer negotiation, extension and closing processes.

Many professionals who play a role in the talent acquisition process (Hiring Authorities, Human Resources Representatives, and even some Recruiters) believe that in-depth discussions regarding a candidate's compensation or the negotiation of critical components of a potential offer should begin in the later stages of the recruitment lifecycle. Let me be clear – these individuals *do see* value in acquiring *basic* knowledge of a candidate's current compensation at the front-end of the recruiting process. Often, however, they perceive that detailed aspects of a prospect's desired compensation should only be explored and addressed after a candidate has successfully navigated through one or more interview cycles, favorable references have been secured, and background checks have been completed.

In reality, the offer negotiation process should begin during your initial discussion with a prospective candidate. Some individuals may say, *"Now wait just a cotton pickin' minute. Why would you attempt to negotiate an offer with a prospect when you don't even know if they will make it through the interview process? Isn't this potentially a tremendous waste of time?"*

To be clear, I am ***not*** suggesting that a recruiter attempt to talk with a candidate about the finer points of a hypothetical offer in an initial or introductory discussion. I ***am*** suggesting that the recruiter who thoroughly explores and validates basic candidate compensation expectations at the onset of the recruitment lifecycle is: A) more likely to fully understand what kind of offer will be required to land a desirable candidate, and B) more likely to make an informed judgment about whether or not the candidate's compensation expectations are achievable. The recruiter who does his or her due diligence relative to understanding a candidate's current and desired compensation at the front-end of the recruiting process is far less likely to encounter last minute surprises culminating in an offer being rejected.

Securing Clarity Regarding Current Compensation

For most people, compensation is regarded as personal or confidential information, which explains why most of us don't walk around discussing what we earn with others on a day-to-day basis. For some engaged in the recruiting process, having a detailed discussion with a prospective candidate about current or future compensation can feel awkward. Even within the context of a job search, many candidates are naturally guarded about discussing "money." On many levels, this sense of discomfort makes sense. For example, suppose a total stranger walked up to you on the street and asked, *"Pardon me, what's your annual income?"* You would likely look at this individual as though he had three heads. Because you don't know this person, you are unlikely to trust him. You have no compelling reason to share this information.

We can all probably think of a time when providing income information made us feel vulnerable even though there was an entirely logical reason for providing it. I remember an occasion many years ago when I was looking to buy a home. I had been in recruiting for less than a year, and my wife and I would regularly hit the road on weekends to look at homes. It seemed that every agent with whom we spoke was principally interested in determining if we were qualified buyers.

As we were only in our mid-20's, I can look back and appreciate why they wanted to know our annual salaries; but at the same time I found this chronic questioning about our income to be really intrusive. After all, I reasoned, why on earth would we be investing time searching for a home if we couldn't afford to buy one?

One Saturday, we found a great new neighborhood that we really liked. Upon expressing preliminary interest at the on-site real estate office, we encountered yet another agent who carefully looked us over and asked, *"So.... what is your annual income?"*

Irritated, my response was, *"We are well qualified to purchase this home, if that's what you're asking. But just out of curiosity, what's your income?"* I was tired of hearing this question and decided to turn it around on my inquisitor. The realtor smiled and immediately responded, *"Well, last year I guess I made about $365K."* I laughed and responded, *"That's pretty damn impressive."* We bought the house and made a friend in the process.

From a purely economic perspective, compensation is an expression of the value that an organization assigns to an employee for the work that he or she performs. From an emotional perspective, the level at which an individual is compensated can and does tie into their sense of self-worth and/or ego. This fact is perhaps especially true if an individual feels under-compensated. As you might expect, in all my years in recruiting, I have yet to encounter anyone who felt that they were over-compensated.

Despite the potential for awkwardness with some candidates, recruiters obviously have a legitimate reason for inquiring about a prospective candidate's compensation level. This information is critical to understanding whether an individual will fit within the organization's defined compensation structure. Compensation will always be a key criterion in the candidate selection process.

The recruiter/candidate relationship is usually predicated on at least some nominal level of trust. Candidates recognize that they will be asked about compensation at some point in the process. So it's reasonable to expect to be given some baseline information when you ask a candidate about their current compensation structure.

I highly recommend that you candidly inquire about the prospect's current compensation level at an appropriate juncture during your initial discussion -- after you have determined that a candidate is seemingly qualified for the opportunity on which you are recruiting, and after you have had a chance to build at least a bit of rapport. You can simply ask, *"With respect to compensation, where are you presently?"* or *"What is your current salary?"* Or you can frame the question a little bit differently by asking, *"What is your current compensation, and what are you looking for moving forward?"*

I have found that it is best not to dance around the *"what are you making"* issue, but to simply ask the question candidly and directly. Many candidates are likely to briefly pause before answering this question, as they invariably recognize that the conversation is now going to become a great deal more personal.

Most candidates will give a fairly straightforward answer to your question. Some candidates will provide a very crisp and timely response, while others may feel a little uncomfortable and hedge slightly while they formulate their answer.

Others will try to be a bit more evasive and vaguely characterize their compensation, saying something along the lines of, *"Well, right now I am in the upper 5-figures;"* or *"My overall package puts me in the upper $70's."* If you get one of these more ambiguous responses, it will be important to drill down further to fully qualify what the candidate means by *"upper 5-figures"* or what comprises the *"package in the upper $70's."*

Sometimes the candidate's answer will not merely consist of base compensation, but will also contain information about bonus compensation or select benefits that they receive from their current employer and regard to be noteworthy. As recruiters, the more information that a candidate shares with us, the better positioned we will be to determine what may or may not be attainable.

Occasionally, you may encounter a candidate who very deliberately does not want to share current compensation data. While any number of reasons could account for this, the most common one is a candidate's perception that he or she is underpaid. If a candidate feels underpaid, it is unlikely that he or she will want future compensation to be in any way based on current compensation. Sometimes a candidate who is reluctant to share detailed compensation information will say, *"Rather than focus on where my salary is today, I would prefer that we talk about what this role can pay."*

Some recruiters and hiring managers may take this type of response as an affront and feel that the candidate is hiding something or is essentially saying, *"I don't trust you."* And the truth is that they probably *haven't* hit a comfort level where they regard the recruiter or hiring authority to be entirely trustworthy.

Honestly, if a candidate doesn't want to divulge current compensation at the onset of the relationship, I really don't care. What I do care about is taking the time to understand the level at which a person needs to be compensated and whether or not this level is achievable based on the individual's experience and the position at hand. After I have forged a level of trust with the individual, I can always revisit the issue of what they are currently being paid.

A shrewd candidate who doesn't want to disclose current salary may respond to a compensation inquiry by saying, *"I am not comfortable sharing my current salary at this point, but I would be curious to know what the range is for the position you are seeking to fill?"* Out of a desire to be helpful and keep the conversation flowing, some recruiters will immediately answer, *"Sure – the role is currently set to pay in the $65K - $85K range."* In my opinion, this is a huge mistake. If you cite the upper end of the compensation range for a particular role, you better believe that most candidates' salary expectations will gravitate to the higher end of the range. Because it is critical to manage expectations, you never want to unnecessarily divulge information regarding the high-end of a compensation range.

The better thing for a recruiter to say is, *"Well, the compensation structure is fairly broad and is based on an individual's background and experience. With that in mind, and without forcing you to commit to anything, why don't you tell me what you are seeking? Then I can tell you whether or not I think we are in the same ballpark."*

This question alters the flow of the discussion and forces the prospective candidate to address the compensation question. You want the prospect to tell you what they want or need first, and then you will be able to provide the best possible response, without creating a specific compensation expectation.

For example, if you know that a position will pay $75K - $90K, and the candidate says that she is seeking $84K, you can simply say, *"Great, I think we are pretty much in the right ballpark* (depending on their experience, how interviews progress, etc.)." On the other hand, if the candidate says, *"I guess that I really want to be at a base of $95K,"* you can respond, *"Hmmm. We may have a problem. I'm pretty confident that this role actually tops out below what you're looking to be paid."*

At this point, the prospect will likely ask, *"Well, what can the position pay?"* You can then respond, *"Again, the compensation structure for this role is tied to a number of factors, but generally speaking it will likely pay in the XYZ range."* In this example, XYZ might be *"the mid to upper $80's."* Notice that the 75K - $90K range is deliberately NOT indicated. That's because, although the high end of the range is $90K, in your heart you may realize that the likelihood of actually getting to that level is slim to nil. This reality is particularly true if the role is within an organization that attempts to formulate offers that are at or below a salary grade mid-point. The candidate's response will be either, *"Well, for the right situation I might consider that"* or, *"Boy, I am sorry to hear that. There's just no way that I could consider that salary level."*

If the prospect says, *"I would consider that range,"* you are positioned to at least move the discussion to the next phase. If the prospect says, *"That's really below my expectations,"* you can either allow them to opt out of consideration or further qualify the candidate's expectations, while also offering realistic counsel. Your objective should be to:

- Learn how the person has formulated specific perceptions about what they are worth; and

- Provide factual input, if appropriate, about factors that play into how compensation is formulated and governed within your organization (or client organization).

Working the CAP – The Compensation Analysis Process

Before you can meaningfully address future salary expectations, it is very important to understand a prospect's current compensation realities. The best way to understand a candidate's compensation status is to implement a standardized Compensation Analysis Process (CAP).

When to perform Compensation Analysis is ultimately up to you and will likely be dependent upon how a candidate responds to initial inquiries regarding current compensation. After gathering basic compensation information and determining that a candidate is roughly within or near the given salary range, some recruiters may elect to conduct a more detailed compensation analysis during a face-to-face or detailed telephone interview. Alternatively, you can choose to hand the prospect a Candidate Compensation Worksheet at the onset of an on-site interview. I will discuss the Candidate Compensation Worksheet momentarily.

How far should you dig into a prospect's anticipated compensation in an initial phone discussion? It's really a judgment call. However, a recruiter certainly needs to know enough about a prospect's current and anticipated compensation to determine whether or not the person fits within the salary parameters of a particular opening.

If the individual is priced considerably higher than what has been budgeted for a specific position, then it may not make sense to continue the interview process unless mitigating circumstances would motivate the prospect to adjust his or her salary expectations. For example, if a candidate wants to reduce the amount of time she spends on business travel, she may well be open to modifying her salary expectations to achieve this goal. Likewise, a candidate who expresses that he is unable to acquire new skills in his current position may be willing to adjust his salary requirements if a new role will provide the opportunity for meaningful professional growth.

However, if a prospect acknowledges that he or she expects to be making more money than a role can accommodate, you should candidly explain that you have a concern regarding the prospect's anticipated compensation. You might say something like this:

Recruiter: *"Tom, I really appreciate that you have provided me with some insight on how you are presently compensated. Based on what you have shared, I have a concern. The position for which I am recruiting tops out in the upper $80's range, which is below where you are right now. This is a great opportunity that I would love to discuss with you further, but I want to make sure that I'm not wasting your time. Please understand that I just want to be as candid as possible."*

Sometimes a candidate will state that they are open to talking further as long as the compensation level for a new role is relatively comparable to their present situation. At other times, the candidate may concur with the recruiter's assessment that it doesn't make sense to talk further, because they are not prepared to work at a reduced compensation level.

For prospects who indicate a willingness to take a salary hit for the right opportunity, you must exercise due diligence in fully understanding the individual's motivators. As I highlighted earlier, sometimes candidates do have compelling reasons for taking a new position at a reduced compensation level.

For example, I recently worked with a senior executive who expressly stated in our opening discussion that compensation was not a driving issue. Because he had made enough money throughout his career, his primary motivator was to affiliate with an organization where he could be involved in interesting work and make an impact. He was wholly genuine in expressing this sentiment throughout the recruitment lifecycle.

On another occasion, I was contacted by an individual who no longer wanted to live in the San Francisco Bay Area. He had a young family and was tired of worrying about earthquakes. He and his wife had determined that they wanted to move to Virginia where they had family. As a result, he was willing to be very flexible on the salary issue and ultimately accepted a position for less than he had been making in the Bay Area.

Again, assessing the validity of a candidate's intent regarding desired salary is a judgment call. As I said earlier, people generally don't perceive themselves as being overpaid and generally don't want to see their compensation reduced. A candidate's statement that he or she is willing to accept lower compensation is something that needs to be considered carefully. The last thing any employer wants is an employee who ultimately becomes resentful about not being paid the perceived market rate for work being performed.

I have found that the best way to fully appreciate a candidate's current and desired compensation is to utilize a standardized Compensation Analysis Process (CAP). Figure 10.0 and Figure 10.1 on pages 196 – 197, reflect a sample CAP worksheet. The subject matter areas addressed include:

- Gross Annual Compensation (Current Year/Last Year)
- Base Salary (Current Year/Last Year)
- Bonus (Anticipated for Current Year/Actual for Last Year)
- Bonus Criteria
- When Bonus is paid

The information gathered in sections one through three of the CAP worksheet is intended to provide a recruiter with a reasonable understanding of a candidate's present compensation scenario. The next portion of the worksheet seeks to discover if a candidate has a pending review and if so, what the anticipated increase might be. This information is important. Many candidates with a pending salary review are logically going to factor any anticipated raise into their desired salary figure.

Figure 10.0

Candidate Compensation Worksheet 1

Candidate Compensation Worksheet

Candidate Name: .... Associate: ....

Date: ....

1. ***Cash Compensation***

   Gross Cash Compensation (this year) ....

   Gross Cash Compensation (last year) ....

2. ***This Year's Base Salary*** ....

   Last Year's Base Salary ....

3. ***This Year's Bonus*** (Projected) ....

   Last Year's Bonus ....

   What is bonus based on? ....

   When is bonus paid? ....

   Total Projected Annual Compensation ....

4. ***Reviews***

   When is your next review? ....

   # of Review Cycles? Annually or Biannually? ....

   Anticipated Annual Salary % Increase? ....

5. ***Stock Options***

   Do you have stock options presently? ....

   If so, how many? ....

   What is the value? ....

   What is the Vesting Schedule? ....

www.artofrecruiting.com

Figure 10.1

Candidate Compensation Worksheet   2

6. **_Tuition Reimbursement_**
   How much is provided annually?

   Do you actively participate in the program?

   Do you have to pay it back when you leave?

7. **_Other Benefits Information_**
   Do you have a 401K?

   Does your company match?

   What is the matching schedule?

   What is the vesting schedule?

   Do you have a Pension?

   Any Healthcare Premiums that you pay?

   Amount of Vacation You Receive?

   # of Paid Holidays You Receive?

   Any Other Noteworthy Benefits?

8. **_Future Considerations_**
   What are your salary expectations for a new position?

   What is that number based on?

   Lowest Acceptable Offer?

   Any outstanding debts to current employer?

9. **_Counter-Offer Considerations_**
   Have you ever received a counter-offer?

   Would you consider a counter-offer? (Why?)

www.artofrecruiting.com

Over the years, I have worked with a host of candidates who failed to mention an upcoming salary review until I brought up the issue. These individuals were not trying to be evasive in most instances. They simply didn't think to mention it. By getting a pending review out in the open, these candidates were able to comprehensively address future salary considerations. It is far better to get this information out on the table at the beginning than to have to deal with it when an offer is extended. The last thing that you want to hear upon extending an employment offer to a candidate is, *"Oh....I forgot to tell you that I have a review coming up next month."* Remember, nothing is worse than having surprises crop up on the back-end of a deal, especially those that impact salary expectations.

The CAP worksheet also addresses benefit differentials that may impact a candidate's desired or anticipated compensation. Most candidates will want to offset any perceived loss in benefits by increasing their future base compensation.

Consider Jane Candidate's situation, for example. Her present employer provides a non-contributory 401K plan (the company contributes an amount equal to ten percent of Jane's salary regardless of what Jane contributes). Jane's prospective employer only offers a 401K contribution match of up to five percent, with the match component entirely dependent upon Jane's contributions to the plan. In Jane's eyes, accepting a position with the prospective employer will result in the perceived loss of a benefit equivalent to ten percent of her current salary. Understandably, Jane is going to want this loss to be addressed equitably.

This example underscores the need to thoroughly evaluate and understand all the elements of a candidate's current and anticipated salary, including benefits. Careful consideration of these elements allows for a true apples-to-apples comparison between a candidate's current compensation and any offer that may emerge from the interview process. Understanding what a candidate makes in totality will enhance your ability to effectively formulate a competitive offer.

The ultimate goal of the Compensation Analysis Process is to mutually forge an understanding of exactly what the candidate presently makes as well as what the candidate will accept in a future compensation scenario. After navigating through the worksheet and identifying the specifics of a candidate's present situation, you will want to engage the prospect in a more detailed discussion about desired compensation. This discussion might flow in the following manner:

Recruiter: *"Sue, we have talked about the work that you are currently doing and the types of future opportunities that you would find most appealing. We have also discussed your current compensation structure. In terms of future compensation, what are you looking for, moving forward?"*

Candidate: *"Well, as you know, right now I am at a base of $90K, plus bonus. With respect to new jobs, I expect to see an increase in base salary that puts me at or above $100K."*

Securing baseline information on a candidate's current compensation is imperative; but recruiters often fail to really dig to understand the variables associated with compensation or factors that may influence desired compensation. In the sample dialogue above, we learned that the prospect is at $90K and is looking for an increase to at least $100K. What we haven't determined are the specifics of bonus compensation or what additional factors are motivating the prospect to seek a $10K plus base pay increase. Let's follow the dialogue a bit further:

Recruiter: *"Sue, that's very helpful. You reference that you get a bonus. What does that amount to and what is the bonus based upon?"*

Candidate: *"My bonus is up to ten percent of my base and is determined by a combination of factors that include company performance and individual goals."*

Recruiter: *"And with respect to the bonus, what percentage have you actually received?"*

Candidate: *"Last year I got eight percent, and this year I received seven percent, mostly because the company failed to meet revenue goals. All of my personal objectives were achieved."*

Recruiter: *"Okay, that's fine. So, just to be clear, is your expectation for future base compensation oriented to the $100K number, or are you expecting additional money from some sort of a bonus?"*

Candidate: *"Well, right now my total compensation is really about $96K including bonus. I would like to be at or above a base of $100K, but would also expect either a bonus scenario, or in lieu of a bonus structure, I would want my current bonus factored into formulating my base."*

Recruiter: *"So does that mean that you are really seeking a total compensation structure that puts you somewhere beyond $105K?"*

Candidate: *"Yes, I guess now that I think about it, that's realistically where I see myself and what I would be expecting."*

The recruiter in the above discussion has determined the candidate's actual compensation, as well as her anticipated or desired compensation. During this discussion, the recruiter must assess whether or not the candidate's expectations align with what the organization can or cannot accommodate. The recruiter needs to also address all of the other contingencies that might impact a candidate's salary expectations. I touched upon some of these items briefly (pending reviews or bonuses, specific benefits of note). Other discussion items are reflected on the CAP worksheet and include outstanding debts to the current employer (tuition reimbursement, moving expenses, etc.). It is absolutely imperative to cover all bases relative to current compensation and benefits NOW, and not later.

Another effective negotiation exercise is to talk with candidates about Lowest Acceptable Offer Scenarios (LAOS). Every candidate should be walked through LAOS (not the country, but the process). It is essential to understand at what compensation level a candidate says, *"That's lower than what I would be willing to entertain."* LAOS discussions can sound something like this:

Recruiter: *"Steve, I know in your current role you are making a base of $136K and have a bonus potential of up to 15 percent. You have also indicated that for new opportunities you are ideally seeking to be at a base of $150K, plus bonus; is that right?"*

Steve: *"Yes, I would say that's pretty much where I am and what I am seeking."*

Recruiter: *"Okay, just for the purposes of discussion, what if the opportunity can only pay up to $145K, plus bonus. How would you feel about that?"*

Steve: *"Well, it's less than I really want, but I wouldn't rule it out."*

Recruiter: *"Fine. Again, just so that I fully understand your thought process, what if the opportunity were at a compensation structure of $142K, plus bonus?"*

Steve: *"Honestly, I would have to really think about $142K, but I definitely wouldn't entertain anything lower than this."*

Recruiter: *"I totally understand. Obviously there are a lot of considerations that factor into an offer. Again, my reason for asking is out of a desire to know what compensation levels you would consider and wouldn't consider. Based on what you have indicated, $150K or higher is optimal, and anything less than $142K is not something that you are open to considering. If something were between $142K and $150K, you would at least be open to entertaining it, is that right?"*

<u>Steve</u>: *"Well, I would prefer to be on the higher end, but yes, depending on the situation, I wouldn't rule out an offer in that range."*

Again, the ultimate goal of addressing compensation in a detailed manner at the front end of the recruitment process is to appropriately manage a prospective candidate's expectations, while also eliminating the possibility of last minute surprises. And remember that while you are assessing whether or not a candidate aligns with an opportunity from a skills and compensation perspective, most candidates are making the same assessments about the organization with whom they are interviewing. A notable distinction, however, is that it is typically considered poor form for a candidate to make detailed inquiries about compensation, especially at the front end of the interview cycle. So it is incumbent upon the recruiter to take the lead in facilitating this discussion in an open, honest, and factual manner.

Figure 10.2, on page 203, reflects the logical flow of engaging a prospective candidate in a discussion about compensation. If a candidate's compensation expectations are too high for a given role, it is best for you to determine this as quickly and efficiently as possible and to politely and candidly explain this to the prospect. An organization will engender no goodwill by having a candidate participate in a lengthy interview process only to discover that he or she is priced well beyond what the organization can pay.

In these situations, candidates are correct to ask, *"Why couldn't this have been determined earlier, before I invested hours in an interview process?"* Even worse situations occur when an employer determines that a prospect is beyond what they can pay, but proceeds to put forth a "low-ball" offer anyway without regard for any resulting fallout.

Figure 10.2

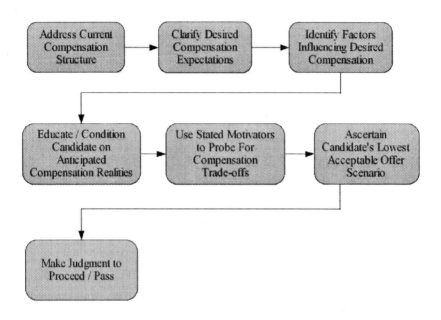

If a candidate's salary expectations are seemingly unrealistic, it is absolutely appropriate for you to attempt to understand whether external factors are influencing an individual's compensation expectations. Recruiters and employers must understand that most job candidates are in a disadvantageous position when it comes to figuring out what they should ask for when a company questions them about desired salary. Job seekers lack access to what I regard as factually grounded qualitative data that says: If you perform in role (*a*), possess experience (*b*), and live in geographic area (*c*), you should be making (*x*) income. As a result, candidates are often left to consider the input of:

Career Guides and Salary Surveys
Relatives & Spouses
Another Employment Offer
Peers & Colleagues

If you are a careful reader, you have noticed that by combining the first letters of these external data sources, the acronym CRAP emerges. While I am honestly not suggesting that these external data sources are entirely worthless, I do believe that often times they only serve to further cloud an already emotionally charged issue.

I appreciate and respect that every candidate should strive to make an informed compensation decision. Some candidates, however, assign too much significance to input from outside sources that are simply incapable of considering the many variables that impact compensation levels.

Career Guides & Salary Surveys

Numerous candidate-oriented career guides, articles, and websites address the salary negotiation process. The perspectives and approaches presented by these sources are as different and unique as the authors themselves. Undoubtedly, many of these guides have merit. But I have also seen salary negotiation tips for candidates that recommend approaches with which I simply do not agree.

I recently read a candidate salary negotiation article advocating that a candidate should resist giving any indication of what he or she is seeking until it becomes eminently clear that an offer is forthcoming. I have read other material that suggests that candidates should "aim high" when discussing desired salary, as expectations can always be modified later.

I fully respect and appreciate that salary negotiation is indeed a "negotiation," and that some give and take is likely to occur. But the process of an employer and employee moving forward together is in many respects not dissimilar to marriage. It is a relationship that should be grounded in trust and candor, not in manipulation.

My best advice for a candidate or an employer is to speak honestly, truthfully, and respectfully regarding their respective compensation needs and concerns. While difficult, it is helpful if both parties can strip the emotion out of the process and focus on the logical rationale behind their motivations and desires relative to compensation. An old saying about negotiating states: *"If all parties in the negotiation feel a little bit uncomfortable with the final solution, they're probably in the right place."*

I have a number of concerns with salary surveys. For example, at what point does a salary survey capture a data sample that is statistically significant? What is the margin of error associated with the ranges that are cited for a particular position? How do these surveys account for the spectrum of different titles that companies use to characterize what a particular role pays within different industry sectors? Salary surveys may offer some insights about how a particular role might be compensated by some organizations, but I don't regard them as the voice of authority on salary by any means. There are simply too many factors and variables in play.

I recall speaking, years ago, with a recruiter who worked at a firm that produced periodic salary surveys as a means of securing new candidate leads. Individuals who requested the survey would have to provide their own contact information and other basic background information. The survey wasn't based on hard factual data that had been organized and tabulated, but was the result of several individuals sitting down and providing "gut-feel" ranges for an array of different position titles in a particular geographic region; obviously, the approach was not particularly scientific.

Relatives & Spouses

Relatives and spouses, however well intentioned, often haven't got a clue about the realities or dynamics associated with a salary that might be offered to a loved one. As admirable as it is that a relative or spouse wants to see their family member well-compensated, their opinions and input are typically emotionally based and rarely grounded in logic.

I distinctly remember an occasion where a colleague of mine was working with a talented woman for whom an offer was imminent. In the eleventh hour, the candidate's husband, a stockbroker, called in to say that *he* would now be negotiating on his wife's behalf. He had little interest in hearing the recruiter's views about what the market would or wouldn't accommodate relative to salary. It took just two days of him playing "hardball" with the prospective employer before they said, *"Forget it."*

Another Employment Offer

A candidate who cites having another employment offer at a particular salary level may indeed have a valid indicator of market worth. Then again, validity in this instance depends on the qualities and attributes of the organization that tendered the offer and whether or not the candidate really perceives the offering firm as being a viable employer.

For example, I once worked with an individual who said, *"I'm currently at $100K, but just got an offer from another firm at $125K. I feel that this is indicative of my market value."* This remark prompted me to ask several questions, the first of which was, *"Do you see yourself wanting to move forward with the firm that has put forth the offer?"* After a short pause the individual responded, *"Well, it's an okay firm, but it's in another city and I would have to move."*

"Do you want to move?" I asked. *"Well...not really,"* he responded. *"Do you think that this offer was possibly motivated by the firm's desire to induce you to seriously consider making the move?"* I countered. *"Yes, I think that's possible,"* he replied. And on went the discussion, at the end of which he had modified his requirements significantly. This particular candidate was really attempting to leverage an offer that he was very unlikely to accept.

Peers & Colleagues

Recruiters face yet another challenge from candidates whose unrealistic salary expectations have been influenced by peers and associates. I have had numerous compensation discussions with candidates who have effectively said, *"Well, a friend of mine just went to XYZ Company, and he says that he got a 30% increase in pay. So, I figure that if he can get that, I probably should expect that as well."*

I remember once replying to an individual who made this sort of comment, *"Well, you may want to seriously consider going to work with your friend!"* Joking aside, I explained that the compensation evidence I had seen from working with others with similar backgrounds and experience levels suggested that he was fairly compensated already. While he could anticipate a reasonable increase in making a move, it wouldn't be in the neighborhood of what his colleague had quoted. His response was, *"Okay, what salary level should I be looking to achieve?"*

You can deploy several strategies that will help a prospective candidate who has unrealistic salary expectations to obtain a more grounded view regarding compensation. Early on in my recruiting career, I was frequently frustrated with candidates who expressed what I perceived to be entirely unrealistic compensation expectations. What frustrated me most was that I didn't really have an effective way to help these individuals view salary and compensation in an unemotional and logical manner.

After a great deal of thought, I began to contemplate the factual basis of compensation. In doing so, I came to conclude that there are "five realities" or factors that have significant bearing on salary including:

1. An individual's academic background;
2. An individual's years of relevant experience;
3. An individual's specific area of expertise;

4. An employer's internal salary structure; and
5. An employer's perception of what the overall marketplace would pay for a specific skill set.

I discovered that sharing these "five realities" with candidates who had inflated salary expectations was a very effective way to force them to think about compensation in a more holistic manner. Doing so helped candidates consider more than just the emotional aspects of what they perceived to be equitable.

In communicating with candidates who are clearly "aiming high" with respect to their desired or anticipated salary, I recommend that you carefully listen to what they have to say. Then you should honestly express your concern that they might be pricing themselves out of consideration. You should also attempt to determine how they have arrived at their target compensation number in a manner that doesn't come across as being condescending or patronizing. This conversation might progress along the following lines:

Recruiter: *"Terry, I understand from our discussion that you are presently making $85K, but feel that you really should be making $110K, which is a 30 percent increase over where you are presently. For my own understanding, do you mind explaining how you arrived at this number?"*

Candidate: *"Well, I have talked to a couple of colleagues, and I have also been doing research on the internet. Oh, and my wife has talked to a couple of people she knows, and that's how I sort of determined that $110K was a good target."*

Recruiter: *"Terry, I really appreciate where you are coming from. In a perfect world, I would love nothing more than to see you realize your goal of making $110K annually, but I would be doing you a disservice if I didn't share the "five realities" of compensation. You have to realize that in formulating any offer, an employer must consider: an individual's academic background; an individual's years of relevant experience; an individual's specific area of* *expertise; the employer's internal salary structure; and the employer's perception of what the overall marketplace will pay for your specific skill set. Does that make sense?"*

<u>Candidate</u>: *"Well....yeah, I guess I hadn't really thought about those factors. What do you think is a more appropriate number for me to be considering?"*

Over the years, I have had countless discussions with candidates that flowed very much along the lines of the illustration above. Additionally, it pays to be able to discuss the concepts of salary equity and salary compression.

The American Heritage Dictionary defines equity as: "The state, quality, or ideal of being just, impartial and fair." Many employers invest considerable resources in formulating a compensation structure that pays employees equitably and considers an array of factors (role, responsibility, tenure, etc.). It would be unfair for an organization to bring a new hire on board at a salary level that was exceptionally higher than other employees performing the same work. Significant internal issues could arise when tenured employees discover the compensation disparity – and believe me, they will find out!

Salary compression occurs when an organization pays nominally different salaries to similarly skilled employees without regard to their years of experience, length of affiliation with the organization, or educational background. Salary compression issues can often create salary equity concerns. For example, let's say that Tom is an Engineer with a M.S. degree, who has worked at ABC, Inc. for seven years and makes $90K. ABC, Inc. then hires Roger at $88K for an opening in the Engineering Department. Roger is also an Engineer, but he doesn't have an advanced degree and possesses only four years of total experience. Assuming that both individuals are performing in a similar job function, Tom isn't likely to be too thrilled that someone with lighter credentials and less overall experience is being compensated at almost the same level.

From a recruiter's vantage point, it is very productive to be in a position where you can explain to candidates the various factors that play into how employers consider the issue of compensation. Providing candidates who have unrealistic salary expectations with factual perspective is a true opportunity for you to conduct yourself in a consultative manner and to hopefully lay the groundwork for what will be a win/win situation.

Make The First Offer The Best Offer

Because compensation is such an emotionally charged issue, I learned long ago that it is in neither party's best interest to engage in a long and protracted salary negotiation process. Prolonged negotiations suck the life out of whatever goodwill has been established between a company and a prospective employee over the course of the interview process. A drawn out negotiation process may prompt a prospective employee to feel that the employer is cheap, and the prospective employer may begin to feel that the candidate is using "nickel & dime" tactics. No one ends up feeling great about the process or the other side's motivations.

We witness this scenario with ongoing regularity in professional sports. Team A refuses to offer Player B the type of contract that Player B feels he is due. Player B complains to the media that Team A is 'disrespecting' his past accomplishments. Team A begins to leak concerns in the press about Player B's attitude, and on and on it goes. Sometimes the issues are resolved and everyone makes up – more often, bitter feelings develop, and the two sides must part ways.

I have always believed that an employer should attempt to make the first offer the best offer. It is important to highlight that when I say "best offer," I mean a thoughtful, well-intentioned offer that legitimately considers the candidate's current total compensation and future compensation objectives, as well as the impact the individual will be making. I have seen companies "low-ball" an applicant just to see if the individual would accept a lower salary.

Regardless of any company's inherent need to control costs and be profitable, this sort of approach is terribly short-sighted and will never create candidate goodwill.

Smart employers strive to make offers that are fair and equitable. As I expressed previously, any worthwhile employment relationship should be grounded in trust. If one side feels that they have been taken advantage of, any hope of long-term loyalty is greatly diminished. Employers that utilize "low-ball" tactics fail to realize that they risk making a highly negative impression upon a candidate. From a candidate's perspective, organizations that extend "low-ball" offers will be judged as "cheap" and guilty of wasting the candidate's time. The company will have done nothing to engender goodwill, and the candidate will actively strive to reinforce his or her negative impressions to peers, colleagues, and associates at every opportunity.

Again, if compensation appears to be an issue, it's always best to create an appropriate expectation regarding this at the onset of the relationship. This way, if the candidate elects to proceed with the interview process, he or she does so knowing that the organization may be incapable of producing an offer that fully aligns with the candidate's objectives.

The Recruitment Progression Chart reflected in Figure 10.3 depicts the emotional state of prospective candidates as they progress through an interview cycle. Not surprisingly, many candidates find the process of interviewing with a potential employer to be stressful. Preparing for interviews and taking time off from work may only add to a candidate's anxiety level.

Over the course of an interview cycle, the intensity of the process tends to peak at the point where an offer is tendered and the candidate must make a decision to accept or decline. Needless to say, this decision-making juncture is emotionally charged.

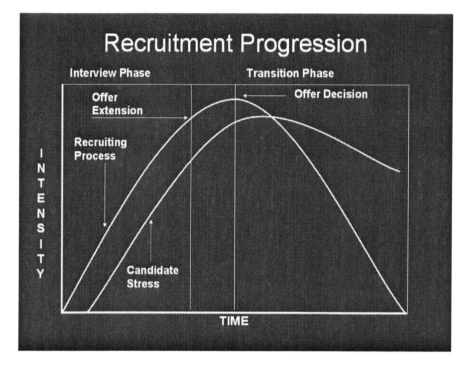

Figure 10.3

Both the employer and the prospective employee have formulated many expectations of each other over the course of the interview process. A key consideration is whether or not their compensation expectations are aligned. If not, it is unlikely that an employment offer will be accepted. This reality further underscores the importance of addressing compensation at the front end of the process, when there is less stress, less anxiety, and less emotion.

Extending the Offer

As a fundamental rule, I recommend that employers and recruiters *not* extend written employment offers unless: A) the offer elements have been "trial closed," and B) there is a very high likelihood that the offer will be accepted. I continue to be amazed by the number of organizations that employ a formulaic offer process, where consideration of the individual candidate's stated needs and requirements are largely secondary to the organization's offer generation process. In these situations, after the candidate interviews and the organization elects to proceed to the offer stage, a static formula is used to produce the offer based on an array of considerations (academic background, years of experience, position grade, etc.). Input the information about the candidate, press the button, generate the offer, and transmit the offer package. Efficient? Yes. Tailored to the needs of the candidate? Not necessarily. Personal touch? None at all.

In executing a trial close, you need to verify that the candidate is fully prepared to accept the job provided that the anticipated offer elements align with stated expectations, as determined through the Compensation Analysis Process. Only after the offer has been verbally closed should it be placed in writing and only as a formality following a candidate's verbal acceptance. This strategy offers numerous advantages.

First, walking through the key offer components verbally allows you to get immediate feedback on the candidate's actual interest in moving forward with the organization and, thus, the probability of closing the deal. This is the point to get any issues or concerns with the offer on the table.

Second, by verbalizing the offer components, you give the candidate a chance to think about what has been presented, ask questions, and inquire about potential modifications. In my experience, once an offer has been put in writing, it is as though the offer elements have been codified and cannot be changed.

Think about it; human nature is to look for closure. In the eyes of many hiring managers or HR executives, when an offer is placed in writing, it is "done." No one wants to revisit something that they regarded as being completed or finalized. You will never hear a hiring authority or HR executive say, *"Gee, I can't wait to go back and modify Sally Smith's offer letter."* In fact, if anything, the person responsible for affecting the offer changes is likely to be perturbed at having to go back to deal with this again. It is far better to float the prospective offer verbally, get feedback, address any questions or concerns, make modifications if necessary, gain approval/acceptance from the candidate, and then (**and only then**) place the offer in writing.

Third, you gain some degree of leverage by discussing offer elements at a high level without committing them to paper. I have witnessed many employers produce and transmit written offer letters and then provide candidates up to two weeks to make a decision. To me, this is not only counter-intuitive, it's counter-productive.

An analogy: Let's say that after dating a wonderful woman named Joni, I concluded that I would like to ask her to marry me. While presenting her with an engagement ring should I say, *"Joni, I love you and I think we would be great together. Here's an engagement ring. Take a couple of weeks and let me know if you would like to get married?"*

NO! If I am going to ask someone to marry me, I want to know how they feel right away! Not in two weeks. If there are issues, I want to know about them now. Likewise, in presenting an offer you want to capitalize on the momentum and presumed goodwill that has existed throughout the interview process and get some kind of definitive feedback now.

Communicating offer elements to a candidate should be done in a very straightforward and upbeat manner. You can say something like this:

Recruiter: *"Sue, I want you to know that all of your interviews have gone very well and everyone believes you would be a tremendous addition to the team. There is definitely an interest in pushing the process forward. As I previously explained, at XYZ Corporation our process is a little different than some other organizations. I'd like to walk you through what I believe will be the key components of a potential offer to ensure that they align with your expectations. Based on our prior discussions regarding your goals and objectives relative to compensation, I really think that what I am about to share with you will be very appealing. So are you ready to take some notes?"*

Candidate: *"Wow, I'm excited to hear this news. Yes, I have a pen and paper ready."*

Recruiter: *"Terrific. Because we have previously talked through the benefits package, I am not going to spend much time on that, but know that if you have any questions or concerns about benefits, I am happy to address them. With respect to compensation, and in line with what we previously agreed would be a realistic salary for this role, my expectation is that a formal offer is likely to fall between $73K and $76K. Additionally, this role is bonus eligible, so you could expect a bonus, based on performance, that would likely fall between seven and twelve percent.*

Furthermore, you would be eligible for a pro-rated review in six months. Historically, people in your position category have been seeing increases between five and eight percent. This again is based on individual and company performance, so there are no absolute guarantees on increases. As you know, vacation starts at three weeks per year, and all insurance premiums are covered (etc., etc., etc.) So, how does that sound to you?"

Candidate: *"Well, it sounds really great overall. I'm excited. Is it possible to get this in writing?"*

Recruiter: *"Sue, that's a great question. Basically, what I wanted to do today was map out what a likely offer is going to look like so that you can reflect on it, and I can address any questions or concerns you may have. Based on what I have characterized, if you are ready to proceed forward and accept this position with my firm (or my client), it will be no trouble to get you a written offer immediately. I'm sure you can appreciate that unless you are ready to move forward, it doesn't make sense to ask the hiring manager and HR Department to invest time in pulling together the written offer package."*

Candidate: *"I hadn't thought about that. So, yes, that makes sense to me. All in all, I think that the offer that you have verbalized sounds great, but I would like to sleep on it, if that's okay? Can I give you a call tomorrow?"*

Recruiter: *"Absolutely. Take the time you need to reflect on what has been put forth. The key thing is that you make a decision that feels right. XYZ Company thinks you would be a phenomenal addition to the team, but we don't want you to feel any pressure. That's why I wanted to provide you with the likely offer components so that you could think about it, and make the best decision for you, your family, and your career. One other thing would be helpful; so that I can keep Tom, the hiring manager, posted, can you share your overall "gut" feeling about moving forward?"*

Candidate: *"Well, I really appreciate this approach, and you can tell Tom that my 'gut' feeling is extremely positive. I look forward to talking tomorrow morning."*

Recruiter: *"Sue, I appreciate your candor, and I am excited for you, and again, XYZ is excited at the prospect of having you on the team. Let me know if you have any questions. Otherwise, I look forward to speaking with you tomorrow."*

Most of the time, any issues of consequence or specific concerns about a proposed offer will emerge within this discussion. You may receive candid, factually-based objections that will require careful consideration. But if you have done your due diligence in ascertaining the candidate's salary expectations, no significant surprises should occur. If you sense any hesitation on the part of the candidate, you should candidly inquire if the candidate has any reservations or concerns. You may need to do a bit of detective work to bring these issues forward for discussion to determine if they can be overcome.

Making the Important Inconsequential (and Vice Versa)

In addressing specific concerns regarding a theoretical offer, another concept to consider is that of *making the important inconsequential, and conversely, making the inconsequential important.* For example, if I am discussing compensation with a candidate who really wants a base salary of $80K, but my company can only offer a base of $78K, the candidate may conclude that a $2K shortfall is a lot of money and therefore is important. But $2K amortized over time looks a lot less significant.

That $2K nets out to $500.00 per quarter or roughly $167.00 per month. But over 365 days, $2K is less than $5.50 per day – about the cost of a good cup of coffee and a blueberry muffin each morning. If we factor in taxes, the perceived disparity between desired and actual compensation drops even further. For most people $2K in gross compensation really translates to something between $1250.00 and $1550.00 after taxes (assuming a federal tax rate of 22 percent to 27 percent).

In offering the above explanation to a candidate you may find that he or she acknowledges what you are saying, but expresses that the delta between what they want and what they are being asked to consider is too great. Just as frequently, however, you will find candidates expressing that they are not going to let a salary gap of $5.50 a day stand in the way of moving forward with an opportunity that they want.

Alternatively, you may encounter situations where the seemingly inconsequential becomes very important. I recall working with a candidate who was mildly disappointed that his salary offer was roughly $3,000.00 less than what he had hoped to receive. The offer was in the range of what he had earlier deemed to be acceptable, but he acknowledged that he had hoped to be paid at the higher end of his range. This individual was a new father who spent about two hours each day commuting. The employer that he was considering was approximately ten minutes from his home.

I admitted that I, too, had hoped that the base salary might be just a bit higher. Then I quickly transitioned the discussion to address the savings he would realize by having a dramatically shorter commute. I had calculated that he was spending almost 530 hours in his car getting to and from work. In his new role, the commute would drop to about 87 hours annually, gaining him over *eighteen* 24-hour days to do with as he wished – like spend time with his new son. Furthermore, the fuel savings and reduced wear and tear on his vehicle were also worth thousands of dollars. Needless to say, when we wrapped up our discussion he was correctly under the impression that he hadn't left anything on the table, but had walked away well ahead.

I hadn't manipulated the conversation at all. I merely helped him look upon his circumstances and the offer elements from a slightly different vantage point.

Again, the process of verbally presenting probable offer components provides you with an opportunity to trial close the likely offer scenario, obtain immediate feedback, and determine specific concerns. This approach allows you to place any subsequent written offer into its final form only when you know it will be accepted.

At the end of the example call presented earlier, the recruiter executed a soft trial close by asking the candidate to share her "gut" feeling. This is a very low pressure approach, enhanced by the recruiter's emphasis on the importance of the candidate making the decision that is right for her. Some recruiters might take the trial close a step further by asking for permission to accept on the candidate's behalf, provided that the candidate's stated salary expectations are met. This approach is perfectly fine, as well, provided that you enjoy excellent rapport with the candidate.

In situations where you know that a candidate has multiple offers, you should utilize the exact same approach of trial closing offer components before providing a written offer. Sometimes organizations and recruiters feel like they must jump through hoops to present a written offer to a prospect who has multiple offers.

I would submit that most candidates will ultimately do what they perceive to be in their best interests. The key issue associated with a candidate who holds multiple offers from other organizations is whether or not they fundamentally want *your opportunity* over the others that are in hand. What is the best way to find out what a prospect is thinking? Ask them.

Recruiter: *"Tom, I understand that you have a couple of other outstanding offers, which in many respects speaks to the degree to which you are perceived to be a true performer. As you know, my company (or client) holds you in extremely high regard. We think you would be a great addition to the organization and could have a stellar future here, but what's really important is what you think. How do we stack up against the other organizations you are considering? I ask this principally because I want to make sure that we have answered any outstanding questions or concerns that you have, as well as to better understand where we stand in terms of your overall interest. Can you share what you are thinking?"*

Tom: *"I really appreciate your candor. You are correct. I do have a couple of other offers pending right now. However, I am very interested in your organization. The role I would be playing, the people, the luxurious office setting have all been very impressive."*

Recruiter: *"Understand that I am not trying to pin you down, but in comparison to the other opportunities you are evaluating, where does my firm stand?"*

Tom: *"I would have to say that right now your firm is my number one choice."*

Recruiter: *"Tom, that's great, because from my side all of the feedback that I have been receiving about you has been uniformly positive. Let's discuss next steps."*

If the candidate says, *"Gee, there are a number of things about your firm that I like, but I'm trying to weigh everything,"* you must immediately go back into investigation mode. It is critical to find out what specific qualities or attributes relative to the other organizations are of greatest significance to the candidate.

In addition to verbally trial closing the offer, you must pursue a "down stream" discussion with your candidate before placing it in writing. The objective of this conversation is to ensure that the candidate has fully considered what must transpire in conjunction with the acceptance of an employment offer. Specifically, you must confirm that:

1. The candidate has selected a start date;
2. The candidate is poised to resign;
3. The candidate has already or is prepared to "shut down" any and all discussions with other potential employers; and
4. The candidate has reaffirmed that he or she will not entertain a counter-offer from a current employer.

If the candidate responds to each of the above items in the affirmative, a written offer should be extended in a timely manner. To effectively address the above issues, you can say, *"Sue, I'm really excited that you are prepared to move forward with the offer that we have discussed. As a means of insuring that we have covered all bases, I wanted to make sure that you had given some considered thought to the following items:"*

1) *"Have you selected a start-date?"* You may have to help the candidate pin down the best date based on the desired notice period, internal project schedules, etcetera.

2) *"Are you prepared for the resignation process, and do you need any help in formulating a thoughtful resignation letter?"* Again, you must be willing to bring a value-add and help the candidate craft a cohesive resignation letter, if necessary.

3) *"Have you terminated discussions with other organizations that you have been considering?"* This question is critical. To avoid any last minute surprises, the candidate should express no hesitation in shutting down discussions with other firms. If you haven't previously asked who else the candidate has been speaking with, do it now for future reference.

4) *"Are you prepared for the possibility of a counter-offer; and more importantly, are you prepared to politely refuse such an offer?"* Chapter Eleven is dedicated to addressing Counter-Offers. The question posed here is to simply reaffirm that the candidate is on-board with leaving their current employer.

You may want to consider some additional strategies relative to written offer presentations. These strategies are especially helpful in closing those deals that superficially seem "closed," but that still retain an uncertain or unsettled feeling.

One approach worth considering is to have the Hiring Authority personally extend the written offer. If you feel that the Hiring Manager can help close the deal, don't hesitate to engage him or her in the process. Over the years, there have been numerous instances when utilizing this approach has yielded tremendous dividends.

On some occasions, I have set up meetings (over breakfast or lunch or at the close of the workday) between a Hiring Authority and an individual candidate expressly for the purpose of having the Hiring Authority directly present a written offer to a candidate. In addition to projecting a highly personal touch, the Hiring Authority is best poised to reiterate the construct of the position for which the candidate is being considered and can also reinforce the positive aspects of moving forward.

Given that the Hiring Authority will be the candidate's direct supervisor, he or she is also in a position to help the candidate realize the most seamless transition and is, in many respects, the very best mechanism to offset the potential for an accepted counter-offer. In the eyes of many candidates, a potential Hiring Manager is synonymous with the new employer and can be instrumental in helping a candidate to realign his or her allegiance. Any well-timed communication from the Hiring Manager to the candidate immediately prior to or during the offer extension phase of the process can dramatically enhance the odds of closing the deal.

Another approach is to have the candidate stop by your office to pick up the offer letter (provided that the individual is in the same geographic area). Again, this approach provides a personal touch, and the act of coming to your office further reflects a degree of commitment on the candidate's part. While not guaranteed, it is far less likely that a candidate is going to invest the time to personally pick-up a written offer unless he or she is committed to moving forward.

The Transition Period

Once the offer has been extended and accepted and the candidate has tendered her/his resignation, your job is not done. I have seen recruiters make terrible mistakes during the transition period. The biggest mistake that a recruiter can make during this timeframe is to not proactively remain in touch with a candidate who has accepted a new position.

For some candidates, the transition period is the time when second guessing occurs, and this is absolutely the time when many candidates need a friend and welcome hearing a reassuring voice. This is also the point at which many candidates will confront "the fear of the unknown." Fear of the unknown is a powerful force and prompts some candidates to question their own decision-making ability. After all, they are casting away the status quo to embark on a new situation that while theoretically defined will remain somewhat fluid until they have acclimated to their new environment. As irrational as it may seem, I have witnessed fear of the unknown prompt candidates to renege on an accepted offer at the last minute.

While staying in touch is important during the transition, you need to do more than simply call to say "hello." It is extremely important to be as blunt and candid as possible at this juncture. In fact, you need to pointedly ask the candidate: *"How are you feeling about everything? Are you feeling nervous?"* If the candidate is having any doubts or second thoughts, you need to know as soon as possible. Some candidates simply need to be reassured that everything is going to work out fine.

Again, if geography permits, another thing that a wise recruiter can do to help effect a positive transition is to get the candidate to stop by to complete pre-employment paperwork, participate in a meeting, pick up project literature, or attend a corporate social event.

Any activity that puts the candidate into his or her new setting and allows for interaction with peers or managers is worth pursuing. This interaction will help the candidate further align their loyalty to their new employer. For example, I have had clients request that a candidate drop by to pick-up product documentation to facilitate a faster ramp-up on a particular project effort. In these instances, the employer came across as being interested in the new hire's near term success. When the candidate came by to visit, various individuals within the organization were able to reiterate how pleased they were to have the individual joining the team. Taking a personal interest in the candidate and making the candidate feel as though they "belong" are simple things that can make a huge difference.

This chapter has covered a great deal of ground and has hopefully given you some valuable insights on how to meaningfully optimize the salary negotiation, offer presentation, and closing processes. The key is to appreciate that compensation is an emotionally charged issue for candidates. By implementing a thoughtful and structured approach to addressing compensation and by discussing compensation in an open, pragmatic, and non-judgmental manner, you will be better positioned to help candidates formulate salary expectations that are grounded less in emotion and more in the realities of the marketplace. Furthermore, by trial closing offer elements before extending a formal written offer, you can pre-empt a variety of issues and ultimately save yourself a considerable amount of time and energy. Finally, by maintaining contact following offer extension and acceptance, you can help ensure that each and every candidate actually begins work on their designated start date.

Chapter 11: Counter-Attacking Counter-Offers

Accepted counter-offers are among the most demoralizing, stressful, and indeed painful events that a recruiter can face. Think about it. For recruiters, the counter-offer experience is the emotional equivalent of arriving at the summit of an imposing mountain, only to lose your footing and subsequently plummet 10,000 feet into an abyss.

If you ask seasoned recruiters to describe their least favorite recruiting experience, dealing with a counter-offer is usually at the top of the list and with good reason. You have invested valuable time and energy into a complex search process. Resources have been allocated to identifying, qualifying, and meeting a capable candidate and presenting him or her to a motivated hiring authority. The interviews have gone well. The hiring manager wants to hire the candidate and asks for your counsel in presenting an acceptable offer.

You soon find yourself excitedly presenting an offer to the candidate. You have rehearsed what you're going to say carefully. Because you have done your homework, you know that the proposed offer falls into the candidate's acceptable salary range. You also know that all of the candidate's concerns and potential objections have been effectively addressed. By all rights this deal should be a "slam dunk."

You present the offer, and the candidate is euphoric and announces his intention to accept the job. You prepare the candidate to resign and mention that the candidate may face a counter-offer, but you work to reinforce all of the motivators that have led the candidate to consider leaving in the first place. Everything is going according to plan.

The candidate agrees to call you immediately following the resignation to let you know what happens, but is confident that everything will be fine. The candidate even remarks that the likelihood of a counter-offer is very low, given what has transpired when other people have resigned.

The candidate tells you that he will check in with you in the early afternoon to tell you how it went. The afternoon arrives and you patiently await the candidate's call. As the afternoon progresses, you become anxious.

Something is wrong; you just feel it. You think of a million possibilities as to why you haven't heard from the candidate. You pick up the phone and dial the candidate's number. After several rings, your candidate answers. You try to sound upbeat and say, *"Hey, it's me, your old recruiter pal. I hadn't heard from you and thought I should give you a call. How did the resignation go?"*

After a long pause the candidate responds, *"Yeah, I'm sorry, I should have called you. I know that I said that the counter-offer wouldn't be an issue, but they have really been making me think about some things that I hadn't considered."* As the stark reality of the situation hits you, you recall the words of Jim Lovell, the Commander of the ill-fated Apollo 13 flight: *"Okay Houston, we've had a problem here."*

Does the scenario sound familiar? I honestly hope that it doesn't sound too familiar, because counter-offers are truly debilitating. Within my first three months of recruiting, I experienced a counter-offer scenario that I couldn't have anticipated, and it left an indelible impression.

I was working with a senior engineering professional, and being new to the business had carefully followed a checklist to make certain that I didn't miss anything relative to this individual's candidacy and resignation process.

I had worked hard to establish and build a solid relationship. I had presented him with a great opportunity at a very successful firm, and after a series of successful interviews, he very happily accepted a quality job offer. I had discussed the possibility of a counter-offer, and he assured me that he had made up his mind and was moving forward with the new opportunity.

Over a celebratory lunch at a restaurant just one day after my candidate's resignation meeting with his employer, I reiterated this line of discussion. When I asked him at lunch how his resignation had gone, he remarked, *"Well, it went about as you would expect, they were disappointed – asked if there was anything that they could do to change my mind – that sort of thing, but I told them that my decision was firm."*

I was happy that my candidate seemed so matter of fact and concluded that I had nothing to worry about. Having only recruited for a short time, this was the biggest deal I had ever closed. I told my candidate that I would check in with him in a few days to see how he was doing.

I called him again at the end of the first week of his notice period with his soon-to-be former employer. He reiterated that everything was fine; in fact, he said that everyone was leaving him alone and not pressuring him at all about staying. I was very happy to hear this and went home feeling great.

I didn't bother calling him again until the end of the second week of his notice period. I left a message at his home wishing him well on his first day of employment at his new company. I had no trouble assuming that this deal was done. Surely, I thought to myself, if there were even a hint of a problem, I would have heard something by now.

The following Monday morning is a day in my recruiting career that I will never forget. My phone rang at around 8:15 AM. It was the hiring manager from my client company. My first thought was that he initiated the call as a simple courtesy to let me know that my candidate had arrived for his first day of work without issue.

What I heard next stunned me. The hiring manager advised me that the candidate had called and told him that he would not be joining the company and had elected to stay with his current firm. The hiring manager was extremely upset, and while not directly blaming me for this sudden turn in events, he clearly wanted to vent his disappointment.

Understandably, I was completely taken aback. I wondered what on earth could have happened. I called the candidate. When he answered and realized who was on the phone, his voice took on a very apologetic quality. *"I'm sorry,"* he said, *"But I really didn't know how to tell you."* All I could say to him was, *"What happened?"* This is when I learned that companies can be deviously clever in putting forth counter-offers.

I discovered that my candidate's employer had a specific methodology for pursuing counter-offers with individuals that they wanted to retain. It was a rather simple, but brilliant approach. When my candidate resigned, he received a very typical response: *"Boy, we are very disappointed to be losing you. Is there anything we can do to keep you?"*

Then for the next seven days of the candidate's notice period, nothing more was said. No direct efforts were made to talk my candidate into staying. The net effect of this "business as usual" approach was that my candidate felt that he no longer needed to keep up his guard with respect to a potential counter-offer; clearly one would not be forthcoming.

On the Wednesday of the second week of the notice period, something significant happened. My candidate was called into his Project Vice President's office for an impromptu meeting. Upon arriving, he realized that in addition to the Project Vice President, who was his direct boss, a Director, and a Group Vice President were also in attendance.

My candidate initially assumed that the purpose of the meeting was to finish transitioning project responsibilities prior to his departure. But my candidate was soon to learn that an entirely different agenda had been planned, one that had been formulated especially with him in mind. After a relatively low-key reaction to my candidate's resignation and virtual silence for eight days, this team had assembled a highly coordinated counter-offer that was designed to get my candidate to stay. Truly devious.

They announced that they respected my candidate's desire to leave but were motivated to demonstrate that his career would be best served if he were to stay. They threw everything at him, *including* the kitchen sink. First they told him about his promotion and new title. Then they went on to carefully characterize his new project responsibilities, and the two new project teams that he would lead. Next came the salary increase, followed by the bonus increase, and, of course, they couldn't leave out the obligatory company car. They said that much of this had been in the works prior to my candidate's resignation, and that they regretted not having been able to act sooner. All in all, pretty impressive, right? Impressive, but these guys had just gotten warmed up.

The next day, a steady parade of executives stopped by my candidate's office to reiterate that he should stay; he was, after all, a key member of the team. They continued to reinforce the idea that he would be crazy to walk away from the choice assignments that had just fallen in his lap. This flurry of activity culminated with a phone call from the Sector Vice President who invited my candidate and his wife to dinner at his home that Saturday evening.

Over dinner, the Sector Vice President spent quality time discussing the future of the business unit and repeatedly commented that he absolutely needed key people like my candidate on board to deal with projected growth. The sky was the limit. My candidate was overwhelmed and capitulated to the pressure.

I was devastated for about a week. No big deal closed, after all. No commission check. No happy client and not much in my business pipeline. I resolved, however, that I would never be blindsided again and would make a concerted effort to figure out a way to significantly reduce the likelihood of having my candidates fall prey to counter-offers. Incidentally, I would later go on to recruit another individual out of the employer referenced above, but realized a significantly different outcome – more on that shortly.

The process that I devised enabled me to drastically reduce the possibility of counter-offer situations, and they will hopefully do the same for you. But before we get into specific techniques, it is important to fully understand the candidate mind-set during the resignation process.

Understanding The Candidate's Frame Of Mind

It has long been held that making a job change is among the more stressful things a person can do in life. Sometimes recruiters become numb to the emotional ups and downs that a candidate experiences in those late stages of the recruiting process, because recruiters work in a profession that is defined by chronic and constant change, and must deal with the resulting stress on a daily basis. In certain respects, recruiters are the ultimate change agents.

Logically, a candidate is apt to experience an emotional "high" at the point of accepting an employment offer. After all, accepting a new position is exciting and represents an opportunity for a new beginning and career growth. While not always the case, many candidates are also emotional about the prospect of tendering a resignation.

For most of us the act of resigning is fundamentally uncomfortable. Are there candidates who lay awake at night contemplating how to make the resignation process as excruciatingly painful as possible for their current boss or employer? Yes, but for most candidates giving bad news via a resignation is just not something they regard as being fun.

Giving bad news to a boss and colleagues is understandably difficult. At its essence, a resignation is a statement of rejection that tells an employer, *"I'm no longer satisfied with the company or my role here, and I'm moving on to greener pastures."* In most instances the candidate is not just departing from people with whom they have established very close working relationships, but just as often, close social relationships as well.

In addition to having to deliver what amounts to a fundamentally negative communication (the actual pronouncement of resignation), many candidates are also dealing with "The Fear of The Unknown." In most hiring cycle scenarios (outside of Executive Level Positions), a candidate may meet with a prospective hiring manager and members of the team once or twice over a few hours. They may acquire a positive gut feel for the people in the interview cycle or for the overall quality of the organization, but a candidate can't *truly know* what it will be like to work at the new company until they have been on board for some time.

They can't know what types of relationships they will be able to construct with new team members. They can't really appreciate the degree to which they'll be able to advance in their new job. They can't be entirely comfortable with what they perceive to be the corporate culture until they get on board and get acclimated.

The "Fear of The Unknown" can be a very powerful dynamic and will influence individual candidates differently, based on the candidate's personality and motivations for making a career move, as well as the extent to which external personal issues may be influencing the candidate's life outside of work. I will come back and address offsetting "The Fear of The Unknown" momentarily.

Typical Employer Reaction To A Candidate Resignation

At the point when a candidate hands in his or her resignation, a predictable series of events will take place. The employer's initial reaction is usually one of shock or disbelief. The manager, also being human, is typically going to experience a sequence of negative emotions in response to this untimely news. While I am certain that it has happened somewhere, it's unusual for a manager to respond to a resignation by exclaiming, *"Wow, this is really great news, I was wondering when you would leave!"*

To the contrary, the manager may quickly conclude that the employee's departure is going to impact the manager both personally and professionally. Other people will have to be told of the employee's departure. The appropriate spin will need to be placed on the employee's motivations for wanting to leave. Work will have to be reallocated, which means that key goals or milestones may not be reached. Depending on the employee's rank and influence, much more could be at stake.

This realization leads to the impact phase of the hiring manager's reaction process, where the employee will often be exposed to good, old-fashioned guilt. Upon determining how a group or project is likely to be affected, the manager is likely to conclude that he or she will be tangibly impacted by this departure. Team morale may suffer. The manager may have to personally pick up the slack. Explanations regarding the individual's departure will inevitably have to be presented to staff and possibly customers. None of these are happy events. The manager is apt to say things to deliberately make the departing employee feel guilty, including:

- *"You're leaving us at a really bad time."*

- *"Your departure could really jeopardize the project."*

▪ *"I can't believe you are leaving. The team is already resource constrained – have you thought about how this is going to impact your peers?"*

The third reaction phase is typically an attempt at resolution. Essentially, this phase kicks into gear when the manager realizes the advantages associated with keeping the employee on board and asks, *"What do we need to do to get you to reconsider?"* Or *"How can we modify things so that you would elect to stay?"* In today's job market, where talented people are increasingly difficult to find and the labor pool is already constrained, it's easy to appreciate the business reasons that motivate companies to extend counter-offers to individuals.

Highly specialized professionals may possess specific domain or institutional knowledge that could be difficult, painful, or potentially impossible to replace. Getting a new employee up to speed takes time and resources, with little assurance that the new person will be as good as the one who is exiting. Just as importantly, most managers want to mitigate anything that could potentially impact team morale or existing workflows. Finally, it is often cheaper in the long run to present a counter-offer that compels a departing employee to stay as opposed to training someone new. Indeed, various studies suggest that the total cost of replacing a tenured employee (including lost revenue, opportunity cost, and domain knowledge loss) runs anywhere between 1.5 and 5.0 times the departing individual's salary dependent upon the role of the individual in question.

Deploying Counter-Offer Counter-Measures

What can recruiters do to reduce the chances of a counter-offer being accepted by their candidates? Well, thankfully, a number of steps can be taken to make candidates less susceptible to counter-offer tactics. By talking about the counter-offer process *early* and *often* throughout your relationship with a candidate, you can help the candidate establish a set of expectations that play directly off of the employer's likely reactions and responses to a candidate's resignation.

First, you want to bring up the counter-offer issue very early in the process with your candidates, ideally in the initial stages of a face-to-face meeting or a detailed phone interview. A face-to-face meeting gives you the ability to monitor physical reactions and body language.

After greeting a new candidate, and spending a few moments making small talk, you should look the candidate directly in the eye and make a comment along the following lines:

"Tom, I'm really pleased that we could meet today. As I mentioned when we talked previously, I find your background to be very impressive. You have a really good skill set and have progressed steadily.

We have talked to some degree about your motivations for making a move and will discuss these further momentarily. But I have to be honest. When I look at your background, I have to wonder what is your boss going to say when you resign?"

Then you must remain absolutely <u>SILENT</u>.

The purpose of asking this question is rather straightforward. You are attempting to place the candidate into an admittedly uncomfortable, but highly realistic situation that the candidate will absolutely encounter if they truly intend to make a career change.

Watch the candidate's reaction to this question closely. Pay close attention to their body language and listen to what they say. By doing so, you may be able to gauge the likelihood of a counter-offer issue arising at the back-end of the recruiting process.

When you ask what their boss's reaction is going to be when they tender their resignation, some candidates will look you in the eye and confidently state that their boss isn't going to be happy. Then they will reassure you that they've carefully and thoughtfully decided to make a career change and are determined to proceed.

Perceptive candidates will remark that the recruiter needn't be concerned about the possibility of a counter-offer. They are not "playing the market" and are dedicated to leaving.

Some candidates will even say, *"I believe that when you make a decision to do something, you stick with it. I'm not in this for a counter-offer – if I decide to leave, that's the end of the issue."* These candidates tend to be a bit more seasoned both in life and in their careers. By and large, they are unlikely to "short-circuit" during the resignation process and notice period. Regardless, I strongly advise you to specifically ask these individuals if they have ever previously experienced a counter-offer situation and, if so, how they handled it.

Another contingent of candidates will react quite a bit differently. Upon being asked how their boss will respond to their resignation, they will pause to think before thoughtfully answering, *"Oh, it's not going to be fun. She will be very disappointed."* Sometimes, candidates will surprise you and say, *"That's a really good question. I haven't considered what her reaction will be."*

Here's a great example to help illustrate this point. A recruiting manager attending one of my training programs stated that she had never considered covering counter-offers "up-front" in the process and assumed that the periodic counter-offers that her candidates received and accepted were just an unfortunate aspect of the recruiting landscape.

She later wrote me to say that upon returning to her office from the training program, she asked the very first candidate she interviewed, *"What is your boss going to say when you tender your resignation?"* The candidate's response was exceptionally revealing: *"He is going to say the same thing he has said the past four times I have tried to resign."* Needless to say, the recruiter's eyes nearly popped out of her head as she realized that she was speaking to a candidate who had accepted counter-offers on four previous occasions from the same employer.

When dealing with candidates who haven't given this scenario much thought or who physically demonstrate something akin to a painful epiphany, you must be absolutely certain to help them realize a graphic and detailed sense of exactly what may transpire at the moment they give notice. This point is particularly true for people who are relatively early on in their careers or who have been employed by the same company for a prolonged period of time, because these two categories of candidates are most susceptible to a counter-offer.

Another tool that you might consider utilizing is a Candidate Attitudinal Survey, shown in Figure 11.0 on page 237. The survey can be completed at the onset of your relationship with a candidate. It is designed to provide you with insights about how the candidate regards his or her employer, boss, peers and other issues of significance.

If a candidate assigns high marks to his or her supervisor and peers, for example, you will want to be very thoughtful in addressing the counter-offer issue. A well-regarded and respected boss is someone whose influence on a direct report (your candidate) should not be underestimated. He or she is someone who likely has the ability, capacity, and desire to do whatever is necessary to keep a well-liked and capable employee.

As you can see, the survey is not complicated, nor is it intended to be. The goal of having candidates complete the survey is to gain honest insight about how they regard their current work environment. This information can be very useful in counseling the candidate about what events may unfold relative to a counter-offer.

Figure 11.0

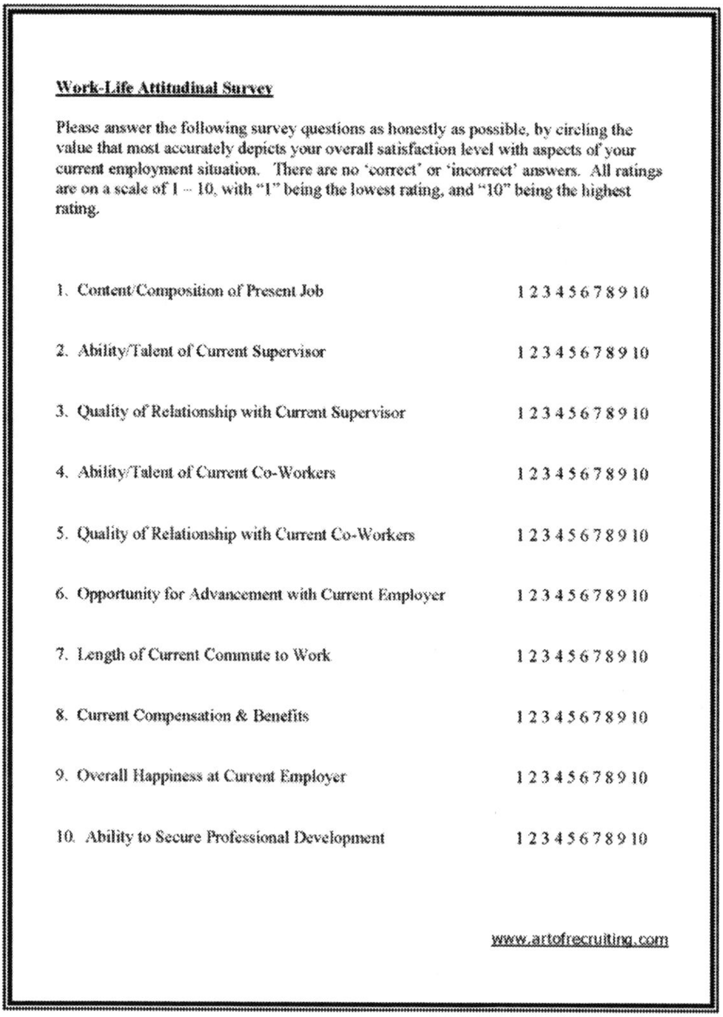

Work-Life Attitudinal Survey

Please answer the following survey questions as honestly as possible, by circling the value that most accurately depicts your overall satisfaction level with aspects of your current employment situation. There are no 'correct' or 'incorrect' answers. All ratings are on a scale of 1 – 10, with "1" being the lowest rating, and "10" being the highest rating.

1. Content/Composition of Present Job   1 2 3 4 5 6 7 8 9 10

2. Ability/Talent of Current Supervisor   1 2 3 4 5 6 7 8 9 10

3. Quality of Relationship with Current Supervisor   1 2 3 4 5 6 7 8 9 10

4. Ability/Talent of Current Co-Workers   1 2 3 4 5 6 7 8 9 10

5. Quality of Relationship with Current Co-Workers   1 2 3 4 5 6 7 8 9 10

6. Opportunity for Advancement with Current Employer   1 2 3 4 5 6 7 8 9 10

7. Length of Current Commute to Work   1 2 3 4 5 6 7 8 9 10

8. Current Compensation & Benefits   1 2 3 4 5 6 7 8 9 10

9. Overall Happiness at Current Employer   1 2 3 4 5 6 7 8 9 10

10. Ability to Secure Professional Development   1 2 3 4 5 6 7 8 9 10

www.artofrecruiting.com

In particular, you want to pay close attention to the ratings that a candidate assigns to his or her current boss, peers, and current employer. If a candidate rates his boss as a "10" and his peers a "9", for example, you need to carefully investigate how this individual is truly going to feel about leaving these co-workers.

When appropriate, I recommend walking candidates through the three reaction phases that their employer/boss is likely to exhibit. Again, these are:

A) The Shock/Disbelief Phase;

B) The Impact Phase; and

C) The Resolution Phase.

Advise the candidate that you are addressing the realities of counter-offers early on in your relationship because the last thing you want to do is waste anyone's time: theirs, yours, or a hiring manager's time. You should additionally explain that while you respect and support the candidate's need to make the best and most informed career decision, your credibility as a recruiter has been built on allowing hiring managers to only extend offers that will really close and that enable candidates to achieve something of consequence in their careers. You should further indicate that the managers for whom you work expect that candidates to whom they extend offers have fully considered the consequences of their actions and are not susceptible to a counter-offer scenario from their present employer.

Some candidates, typically those who are less experienced with respect to making career changes, will actually tell you that they would openly entertain a counter-offer or could be compelled to stay at their current employer for the "right incentives." Your best bet with this type of candidate is to slowly close your interview notebook and explain to them why it may be unproductive to work with them. They need to understand that you are chartered to identify talented and qualified professionals who are looking to upgrade their careers, not ones who are ambiguous about making a job change.

I remember one candidate who turned out to be the consummate "tire kicker." Over the course of qualifying her, I learned that while she had a very marketable background, her motivations for leaving her current employer were relatively weak. She was engaged in quality work, had a great salary, and generally liked her peers.

I asked her why she felt compelled to consider other situations. She finally explained that she was meeting with me *"just to see what else was out there."*

After we talked for a bit, I politely advised her that I thought it would be best for us not to work together. I explained that inasmuch as I was obligated to look out for the well-being of the candidates with whom I worked, I was equally obligated to look out for the well-being of the hiring managers that I supported. I told her that she really needed to consider her motivations for contemplating a move, and that she was welcome to contact me if her situation changed. Interestingly, another recruiter that I know disregarded this candidate's lack of a compelling motivator and secured her an offer from a client, only to see the entire deal come crashing to earth when she accepted a counter-offer and stayed with her original employer.

This anecdote highlights the importance of understanding and testing candidate motivators, because the quality of a candidate's motivations for making a move tend to correlate directly with the probability of dealing with a counter-offer scenario. As was addressed in Chapter Seven, a candidate's motivators for making a career change need to be thoroughly diagnosed and validated.

Discussing the resignation process and potential for counter-offers in the initial interview are just as important as insuring that the candidate has compelling reasons for wanting to consider leaving his or her current employer. At the conclusion of an initial meeting, you should have a reasonable degree of confidence regarding the likelihood of your candidate being susceptible to a counter-offer should one emerge.

I must stress, however, that talking to your candidates about counter-offers shouldn't end during the initial interview. You should engage candidates in additional discussions about counter-offers at various stages throughout the recruiting process. In every subsequent conversation you have with your candidate, you will want to reaffirm that everything is status quo relative to their reasons for wanting to depart his or her current employer. If things have changed, and indeed they sometimes do, you need to take the time to understand whether these new developments have materially impacted the candidate's overall desire to make a move.

Never assume that your candidate will feel compelled to share with you everything that is happening in their professional life. Some candidates may not keep you up to date simply out of naïveté, while others may fear calling you when they decide not to make a move after all.

As your candidate progresses to the client interview stage, you will want to again revisit the counter-offer issue. You should advise your candidate to anticipate being directly asked during the interview whether or not the candidate's current employer can do anything to compel them to stay. Ask them how they intend to respond if this question is put forth during the interview process.

After a candidate has interviewed and positive feedback has been obtained from all parties, you again should reinforce that entertaining a counter-offer is not acceptable. As I explained previously, a written employment offer should not be extended unless you know it will be accepted. You can, however, present the candidate with a general overview of the elements that a potential offer might comprise.

As I advised in Chapter Ten, Salaries, Offers & Closing The Deal, it is pointless to secure a written offer unless you are extremely confident that a candidate is prepared to accept the offer terms that you have outlined. Specifically, you can advise a candidate that out of fairness to everyone involved in the process, you cannot request a written offer without confirmation from the candidate that:

A) The offer, as it has been generally outlined, is acceptable, and

B) The candidate is entirely committed to moving forward and will not accept a counter-offer from their current employer.

If the candidate responds favorably to these requirements for obtaining a written offer, you are getting closer to a non-counter-offer scenario.

After securing the written offer, you must provide some timely advice to your candidate *before* he or she resigns. Specifically, you want to acknowledge that the resignation process is emotional for many people. It represents the termination of one relationship and the beginning of another. Not everyone is going to be understanding of the candidate's desire to leave. Generally speaking, companies don't like to lose good people.

You will want to reiterate that the candidate should expect a multi-stage reaction from their supervisor, with the final stage being aimed at solving an immediate business problem. It may appear that the supervisor is somehow magically motivated to make changes that were previously deemed impractical or even impossible.

At the beginning of this chapter, I recounted a story regarding a painful counter-offer experience that I encountered early on in my recruiting career. I also referenced the fact that years later I recruited another individual out of this same employer, but gratefully was able to realize a very different outcome.

From the moment that I began speaking with this particular candidate, Bob, I knew that he was likely to be a counter-offer recipient. A software project manager, Bob was the kind of employee that any company would want on its team. Grounded, articulate, and personable, Bob was also very accomplished technically and a well-regarded manager.

In our initial meeting I told him, *"You know if you attempt to leave you're going to be the recipient of a counter-offer, don't you?"* *"Yes,"* he replied pragmatically, *"That's probably very likely."* We had a lengthy discussion about counter-offers; but more importantly, I was able to share in detail the likely manner in which the counter-offer would unfold.

Bob interviewed with a long-standing client and subsequently received and accepted an employment offer for a Director level position. I again reminded Bob of the specific steps that his current employer would likely take in order to convince him to stay. We agreed to remain in close contact throughout the resignation process and notice period.

True to his word, Bob called me the day that he tendered his resignation and said, *"Well, Paul, their initial reaction was pretty much in line with what you indicated. My boss told me that he was really disappointed and asked if he could do anything to get me to reconsider. I told him that my decision was firm, but I suppose in the coming days we will see if they elect to do anything or not."*

We talked a few days later, and as anticipated, Bob hadn't heard anything further from his soon to be ex-employer. The following Tuesday, I called Bob again to caution him to, *"Be prepared,"* for a major counter-offer play within the next day or so.

Like clockwork, on Wednesday I received a call from Bob advising me that he had been asked to attend a "special" meeting that day with several executives. I said, *"Here we go,"* and advised Bob that he should expect the executives to outline a master plan that would offer him additional compensation, more responsibility, and greater growth potential. Bob laughed and responded that he would stand firm.

He called me later that afternoon and immediately said, *"They did exactly what you said they would do."* As he characterized the counter-offer meeting, it became abundantly clear that the intended effect of the employer's counter-offer presentation had been greatly diminished. In fact, as Bob candidly put it, *"The entire thing became so predictable that it started to seem really contrived and disingenuous."*

Bob didn't accept the counter-offer. I am completely convinced that by advising him of what to expect in advance and by making him intimately familiar with the employer's motivations for the counter-offer, he truly became turned off. As Mark Twain aptly stated, *"Familiarity breeds contempt."*

The fundamental bottom-line argument against counter-offers is that the candidate shouldn't be forced to "hold a gun to a supervisor's head" to get better compensation, better project work, tangible career progression, or anything else for that matter. Some recruiters like to quote from articles that address the negative aspects of accepting counter-offers. These articles generally report that most individuals who accept counter-offers end up back on the job market within the next six to nine months and the changes that an organization pledges to make in order to retain an employee often end up falling far short of expectations.

In my own experience, candidates who accept counter-offers do often end up back on the job market within a relatively short period of time. In fairness, however, it isn't always this way. Occasionally a candidate's resignation serves as a catalyst for significant organizational change.

To illustrate this point, I can cite an instance when a candidate was compelled to leave his current employer because he saw no way to get into a higher level of responsibility within his company. He regarded his boss as ineffective and felt that the only way to enhance his career prospects would be to join another firm.

A colleague had found a great role for this individual. The client was hiring the candidate to manage an important project that would provide ample visibility and future growth potential. In addition, the offer provided the candidate with a significant salary increase.

Upon tendering his resignation, he was immediately called into his current CEO's office. The CEO asked what was prompting him to leave the firm and indicated that he had no idea that the employee was dissatisfied. The candidate explained his motivations for wanting to leave the firm. In response, the CEO went to great lengths to project his vision for the company, concluding that he had always regarded the employee to be a rising star within the firm.

He told the employee that he would prepare a plan of action. The very next day the CEO met with the employee to explain what he intended to do. First, the employee would be promoted to the VP level and immediately assume his current manager's responsibilities. His current boss would be transferred to another role within the firm.

Next, as a VP, he would report directly to the CEO and work on several new initiatives for the company. Finally, the employee's salary would immediately be raised by $40,000.00. He would be paid a retention bonus of $20,000.00 as well, which would have to be repaid only if the employee left the firm voluntarily within two years. To demonstrate his sincerity, the CEO put everything in writing. The candidate ended up staying at the firm, and everything that had been promised quickly became a reality.

The moral of this story is that you must exercise caution in making sweeping generalizations that counter-offer scenarios never work out, because occasionally they do. If a candidate is utilizing you as a sounding board in characterizing the elements of a counter-offer, it is important that you continue to present yourself in a consultative manner and remain objective. This doesn't mean that you shouldn't ask tough questions or raise important concerns. In the scenario that I just described, the candidate legitimately felt that the prominent issues that had motivated him to look outside his current employer in the first place were effectively being addressed. He had great respect for his CEO and felt entirely comfortable taking this individual at his word. It would have been patronizing, condescending, and inconsistent to suddenly adopt an argument that essentially amounted to: *"Don't believe what someone you have great respect for (the CEO) is telling you. He is a liar."*

You can further help your candidates to avoid counter-offers altogether by assisting them in drafting a letter of resignation. The letter should adopt a complimentary tone to the candidate's current employer. It should then explain that an opportunity more closely aligned with the candidate's goals and objectives has emerged, and after careful and thoughtful consideration, the candidate has elected to accept the new opportunity. The letter should go on to indicate that the candidate is interested in helping to smoothly transition work to colleagues. Finally, the letter should explicitly state that the candidate's decision is irreversible and express the candidate's hope that the company will respect the decision as being final. Below is a sample resignation letter:

Dear John:

It is with mixed emotions that I must advise you of my decision to resign from XYZ Corporation. My final day of employment will be August 17, 2007. Please know that I have very much appreciated my time here. XYZ has provided me with a host of great learning opportunities, and I have the utmost respect for the people with whom I have worked. On a personal note, I have enjoyed working with you very much.

My decision is based on the fact that I have obtained a new opportunity that allows me the chance for significant professional and personal growth. Please know that I have given this decision a tremendous amount of thought and regard it to be irreversible. I truly hope that you will respect my decision, as I perceive it to be in the best interests of my family and my career.

During my remaining time at XYZ, I will do everything possible to assist in a smooth transition of my responsibilities.

Sincerely,

Jane Doe

Stay In Contact Throughout The Notice Period

It is imperative that you keep in touch with the candidate throughout the notice period subsequent to his or her resignation. Earlier, I referenced the "The Fear of The Unknown" that many candidates encounter when they resign. The notice period is a perfect time to project empathy for the candidate who is embarking into what may seem like uncharted waters. Share with the candidate that it is perfectly normal and natural to feel some measure of anxiety; millions of people each year go through the process of making a job change and experience many of the same emotions. You need to reassure them that you are here to help, and while they may feel a bit anxious, everything will be fine.

Interestingly, once you openly acknowledge to your candidate that there is such a thing as "The Fear of The Unknown," you may find that your candidate is clearly relieved that someone appreciates what he or she is going through. Don't hesitate to specifically ask the candidate if they are getting counter-offer pressure. Remind the candidate that while counter-offers are very flattering, they are ultimately nothing more than a business decision designed to achieve a specific business objective, namely to offset the disruption of workflow within the organization.

This particular point cannot be over emphasized, so I will say it again: *A counter-offer is a business decision designed to achieve a specific objective and offset the disruption of workflow within the organization.* It is critical that you communicate this point to all candidates with whom you work.

Many candidates view the decision to leave a current employer from an emotional perspective. You can help your candidates view the resignation process much more objectively by working to strip out the emotional dynamic and reinforcing that the employer is merely doing what is in its best interests. At every opportunity, you also want to remind the candidate of his or her stated objectives for wanting to exit their current employer in the first place and reinforce the things that are attracting them to your company or client company.

If possible, and if geography permits, I recommend taking the candidate out for coffee, lunch or dinner after he or she has tendered a resignation. There are numerous benefits for doing this. First, as I discussed earlier, many individuals who decide to leave their employer are going to experience a state of heightened anxiety and could probably use a friend to counteract any lingering doubts about their decision. They have shared many aspects of their life with you as their recruiter and are likely to appreciate a reassuring and supportive voice.

Second, you are now trying to help the candidate channel the potential sense of loss from leaving a group of friends and colleagues into a sense of gain and excitement that comes with a new beginning. You want to help your candidate focus on the positives of the new opportunity.

As I advised in Chapter Ten, I also recommend getting the candidate together with the hiring manager to whom they will be reporting, if possible. Anything that can foster a connection between the candidate and their new employer is a positive. You can recommend that the hiring manager invite the candidate to lunch or to a staff meeting. Alternatively, the new hire can be invited to stop by prior to his or her actual start date to complete pre-employment paperwork.

Anything that facilitates a positive transition is beneficial and will create a more immediate sense of bonding. It will reaffirm the candidate's decision to join a new company and engender good will.

Finally, I strongly encourage you to keep in touch with the candidate as they formally begin working at their new job. Counter-offers don't always occur immediately after a candidate's resignation. Many shrewd companies will attempt to entice a former employee to come back only weeks after they leave, knowing that an employee's first days on a new job can be awkward and stressful. Sometimes it takes a little while for a new employee to settle into the day-to-day of a new job, a new boss, a new project, and a new culture. Staying in close contact with your candidate will give you a clear sense as to how well your candidate is adapting to their new environment and will allow you to resolve issues or concerns that may emerge.

The bottom line is this: The potential for a counter-offer exists with virtually every deal. Adopting a pro-active approach by speaking with candidates early and often about counter-offers, validating that the candidate has legitimate reasons for wanting to make a career move, and staying in close contact with the candidate throughout the offer, resignation, and transition processes will dramatically reduce the frequency of counter-offer scenarios. I strongly encourage you to implement the various techniques outlined in this chapter. The net result will be that you realize more stable placements and reduce the potential for last minute counter-offer acceptances.

Chapter 12: Planning & Performance Metrics

Virtually all recruiters have found themselves at the end of a business day wondering, *"Where on earth did the day go?"* or *"I don't feel as though I accomplished anything."* As Benjamin Franklin wisely observed, *"By failing to prepare, you are preparing to fail."* For recruiters, this is particularly true. To be an effective recruiter, it is essential that one have the ability to construct and execute a realistic and viable daily plan.

Too often, recruiters allow their work day to be divined for them. They may start the day with an ambitious plan of attack, only to find themselves quickly transitioning into a purely reactive mode. Seemingly, the day spins out of control, and the daily plan that was intended to bring order to chaos becomes nothing more than a well intentioned organizational exercise.

Truthfully, there are no "silver bullet" approaches to formulating and following an effective daily plan that will enable you to maximize your productivity *each and every* day. All recruiters, no matter how seasoned or organized, will inevitably have those days where the proverbial "wheels fall off the bus." A deal blows up; an interview cancels; a requirement goes away; priorities suddenly shift. These are basic examples of things that can and do go wrong, steal time from the day, and threaten a recruiter's ability to execute his or her overall plan.

Because a range of activities require attention in any given day, as is the case with any sales vocation, time is a recruiter's most precious resource. Time spent unproductively, time spent purely in a reactive mode, or time unnecessarily allocated to lower priority activities will absolutely impact overall performance.

In this chapter I explore key considerations that should factor into a recruiter's daily plan. I also outline planning strategies for enhancing time utilization. Finally, I outline some steps that a recruiter can take to evaluate efficiency and assess performance.

Priority Assessment

At the onset of each business week, and for that matter, every business day, some consideration should be given to whether core priorities have changed. Priorities can be strategic or tactical in nature. Strategic priorities are oriented to achieving specific goals that support the business mission and may involve your particular recruitment focus. For example, if you work for a company that is creating a specialized marketing function to support new product initiatives, the strategic priority for a recruiter might be to hire a Marketing Director and four subordinates within the next ninety days.

Whereas strategic priorities represent the overarching goals that you are striving to accomplish, tactical priorities are the defined actions that you will execute to achieve your defined strategic objectives. Tactical priorities are usually task oriented. With respect to the marketing project example referenced earlier, the tactical priorities could include defining the positions within the new marketing function and determining the exact steps that must be taken to identify, engage, and recruit qualified prospective candidates.

Another way to look at the distinction between strategic and tactical priorities is to consider the process of taking a trip. In this scenario, the strategic priority is your ultimate destination; tactical priorities are the manner by which you will get there. If you are taking a trip from New York to Los Angeles, you know where you are going, but you have many options as to how you will get there. Will you fly? Drive? Take a train? Will you stop along the way? How much money will you need? How much time should you allocate to travel? I could go on, but you get the idea.

The principal reason for regularly considering strategic and tactical priorities is simply to validate that the recruiting projects on which you are working, and the activities that you are pursuing in support of these efforts, offer you the greatest opportunity for success.

Discerning your strategic and tactical recruiting priorities will help you to reflect upon what's really important and what's really a priority, particularly if you sense that your present mode of recruitment is more reactive in nature.

Structuring Your Day

At the beginning of this chapter, I referenced the expression, *"Where did the day go – I don't feel as though I've gotten anything done."* Years ago, I found myself asking this very question at the conclusion of a busy day. Frustrated, I resolved that the next day I would attempt to write down everything that I did. The next morning I took out a legal pad and started documenting every phone call (outbound and inbound), every meeting (internal and external), and every other activity that consumed time in my day. By the end of the day, I had several legal sheets filled with notations about what I had done.

As I sat looking over this snapshot of my day, I felt an initial sense of accomplishment. Upon further review, I began to see basic inefficiencies. Activities were disjointed and my day seemed terribly scattered. While I could point to tangible accomplishments, I sensed that I could be more efficient and successful by plotting out my day more thoughtfully.

There is no universal daily planning strategy that will address the needs of every recruiter. A recruiter's daily plan will be driven by the degree to which they are involved in the entire recruitment lifecycle. But whether you only participate in specific portions of the recruiting process or are engaged in the entire lifecycle, the initial step in formulating a solid daily plan is to make a comprehensive list of each recruitment-related activity area in which you are involved.

Your list of activity areas may be lengthy or brief depending on your specific responsibilities. Figure 12.0 below illustrates a sample list.

Figure 12.0

Activity Area	Time Per Day	Days Per Week	Weekly Hours
Sourcing Calls	1 Hour	5	5
Research	1 Hour	5	5
Cold Calls	1.5 Hours	5	7.5
Screening Calls	1 Hour	4	4
Interviews	2 Hours	4	8
Reference Checks	45 Minutes	5	3.75
Internal Meetings	1 Hour	4	4
Administrative	1 Hour	5	5
Maintenance	45 Minutes	5	3.75
Planning	30 Minutes	5	2.5
			48.5

The categories used within the Activity Area column in Figure 12.0 are deliberately broad for the purposes of discussion. Each of the labeled Activity Areas can theoretically be broken into sub-areas that further define activities that should or must be performed. For example, sourcing calls could be broken out to include securing names from targeted employers, contacting individuals for referrals, and so on. Administrative activities could include processing email and other correspondence, performing database related activities, preparing offer letters, or coordinating the interview logistics.

One reality that Figure 12.0 hopefully underscores is that to be effective, a recruiter must have the ability to keep many balls in the air. The job is not one-dimensional.

Another reality characterized in Figure 12.0 is that there are various functional areas within the recruitment process that are competing for your time. In the above example, I have mapped out a very rough breakdown of sample activities that must be performed each week and the corresponding amount of time that these activities will consume. The chart shows that a recruiter needs approximately 48.5 hours to do the job. Many successful recruiters are apt to look at this number and think, *"Boy, would I love a work week that was only 48.5 hours."* Suffice to say that most successful recruiters are putting in far more than a conventional 40 hour work-week.

Again, depending on your organization and the nature of your actual responsibilities, your time allocations may be different. Regardless, if you have never taken the time to truly sort out and understand how much time you are presently allocating to various facets of the recruitment process, it is an exercise well worth doing. At a minimum, you will gain meaningful insight on how you presently utilize time and will likely identify opportunities to optimize your workday.

After determining the activities within the recruitment process for which you are responsible and after giving some consideration to the cumulative amount of time that must be devoted to each activity, you are prepared to map out how each activity factors into your week. Certain activities may take place everyday, and others may occur at specific intervals each week. Again, every individual's situation will be unique to their particular environment.

Planning the workload on a weekly basis will help you to visualize workflows and potentially offset apparent overloads. For example, if you know that every Monday you participate in three hours of internal staff or management meetings, it is unlikely that you will be able to dedicate an appropriate amount of time to performing all of the other facets of your job on that day. Likewise, if you know that you have booked six interviews on a Wednesday, you will likely need to reassign other key tasks to alternative days in the week.

Mapping out your work week at a high level will allow you to drill down on the anticipated workload that corresponds with each day. It's a bit of a logistical puzzle to get everything to fit neatly; but again, doing this organizational exercise of predetermining what you hope to accomplish each day will enable you to realistically plan how you intend to use your most precious resource: time.

One deliberate omission from the chart is what might be best characterized as "buffer time" – the time that is consumed when something goes wrong. An example would be when a candidate calls 20 minutes prior to a scheduled interview to say, *"I'm sorry but an emergency came up at work, and I can't come in today. I would very much like to come in tomorrow or the next day if possible."*

If the caller was scheduled solely to meet with you, this last minute change might not result in a terrible disruption to your plan. You can shuffle activities and reallocate your use of time. If the individual was set to meet with hiring managers, however, then you can anticipate spending time canceling and subsequently resetting these meetings. Unless you can delegate the rescheduling process to someone else, time will have been lost and some aspect of your daily plan will be sacrificed.

No matter how much thought goes into formulating a daily plan, it is impossible to entirely eliminate the reactive dynamic inherent to recruitment. Because recruitment is centered on people and people are dynamic creatures, things are going to happen that are out of your control. As such, it may be wise to incorporate a modest amount of buffer time within your daily plan.

Compartmentalization of Activities

Blocking out dedicated timeframes to execute key components of the recruitment process is a really smart thing to do for two reasons. First, you are afforded the opportunity to place all of your energy and focus into one aspect of the process. This makes terrific sense, particularly when you are performing tasks which require a high degree of concentration such as researching, conducting interviews, or making sourcing calls, cold calls, or reference check calls.

Secondly, grouping your efforts into single activity areas also allows you to get into the appropriate "zone" for the given activity you are executing. It is much more productive to spend 50 minutes making an array of cold calls than it is to make a cold call, then execute a reference check call, followed by a sourcing call, and then some research. You naturally derive a greater degree of overall efficiency by batching and executing like activities.

Figures 12.1 and 12.2 on pages 256 and 257 reflect how a compartmentalized daily plan might look. In addition to mapping out the hours in a typical workday, the plan highlights key activity areas for which the recruiter is responsible. Additionally, this plan provides areas to note whether a given activity was completed.

While there are a variety of ways to set up your daily plan, the specific activity areas reflected in this sample plan include:

- Daily Appointments

- Active Recruiting Assignments

- Candidate Reference Check Calls

- Candidate Interview Status

- Candidate Sourcing & Research

- Candidate Recruiting Calls

- Candidate Action Items

Figure 12.1

Recruiter's Daily Planner

Date: June 16, 2005	Associate Name: Jennifer Garnett

Appointments & Tasks For Today

Time	Task	Time	Task
7:00 AM	Workout W/Tom at Gold's Gym- 6:15 AM	1:00 PM	
7:45 AM	Drycleaners - Drop Off Suits		
8:00 AM	Touch base with John Carter - Finish Job Description	2:00 PM	Sue Armachi - Round II Interview
	Recruiting Calls- Marcomm Role		
9:00 AM	Recruiting Calls	3:00 PM	Sourcing Calls
	Tom Baxter - Candidate Interview	3:30 PM	Reference Checks, Pastor, Young, Armachi
10:00 AM		4:00 PM	
10:30 AM	Recruiting Calls	4:30 PM	Staff Meeting
11:00 AM	Paula Wright - Candidate Interview	5:00 PM	
		5:30 PM	Craig Olsen - Candidate Interview
12:00 PM	Extend Berkman Offer	6:00 PM	
12:30 PM	Lunch with Donna - Sam's Deli	6:45 PM	Happy Hour @ Artie's

Active Recruiting Assignments

Manager	Department	Phone	Position
1. K. Marburg	Finance	703-338-5324	Accounting Analyst - (Job being finalized)
2. P. Phillips	IT	815-571-7397	Oracle DBMS Manager
3. C. Fortuci	Distribution	704-712-1011 x 657	Project Manager - Supply Chain Tools
4. P. King	Marketing	703-596-1144	Sr. MarComm Specialist
5. T. Scott	Finance	703-338-5354	Accounting Analyst II (Share with Marburg)
6.			

Candidate Reference Check Calls

	Candidate Name	Reference Name/Title	Phone
☒Attempted ☒Completed	1. Glen Pastor	Dan Broward/VP ITS	703-315-8881 (M)
☒Attempted ☐Completed	2. Glen Pastor	Kim Sweet/Mgr. BSD - ICMR	703-981-1601 x 2341
☒Attempted ☒Completed	3. Michelle Young	Alan Waters/Director - Parkes, Inc.	813-277-2008 x 1648
☒Attempted ☒Completed	4. Michelle Young	Qu Nguyen/Team Lead - Parkes, Inc.	813-277-2008 x 1424
☒Attempted ☐Completed	5. Sue Armachi	Mike Kohonoski/COO, NGS, Inc.	704-232-6971 (H)

Candidate Interview Status

Candidate Name	Manager	Interview Date	Interview Stage
Sue Armachi	Scott/Phillips	6/24/05	Round II - Offer Expected
Glen Pastor	Scott/Fortuci	6/29/05	Round II - Interview Pending
Patti Corland	King	6/17/05	Round I - Interview Pending
Zoe McCracken	King	6/17/05	Round I - Interview Pending
Karl Sears	Fortuci	6/22/05	Round I - Interview Pending
Mesbi Mohammed	Phillips	6/21/05	Round III - Offer Expected

Candidate Sourcing & Research

Target/Source	Phone	Results: Name/Title	Skills
Dustecco Ind	801-656-0900	Peter Zimmerman - Finance - AP	AP/AR Accounting Analyst
www.dusteccoind.com	Extensions 433, 456	Carla Madison - Finance - Tax??	Accounting Analyst - Tax Focus ??
Teknowlogy	815-238-4242	Cab Calloway - Mgr Dist	Distribution & Fulfillment
www.teknology.net	Fulfillment - X300	Zim Pulney - Dir. Fulfillment	Distribution & Fulfillment
Ingway Corp.	513-871-8700	Candace Rouseau	Director of Marketing
www.ingway.com	Marketing - X444	Jack Perelli	MarComm Coordinator

Figure 12.2

Candidate Recruiting Calls

Name	Phone	Skill/Title	Result	Status
1. Mike Wilson	703-584-8664	Finance Manager	Left Message	☒ Attempted ☐ Completed
2. Janice Mitchels	703-448-2500x305	Financial Consultant	Interested - call tonight 8 PM -443-9077	☒ Attempted ☒ Completed
3. Pamela Waters	919-557-8479	IT Manager	Happy - Ref'd TJ Harmon -405-873-3445	☒ Attempted ☒ Completed
4. John Taylor	919-889-7566	IT Supervisor	Left Message	☒ Attempted ☒ Completed
5. Sandy Baker	703-465-9856	Marketing Manager	On Vacation - Left Message	☒ Attempted ☐ Completed
6. Christy Reistrup	540-759-4488	Marketing Coordinator	Very interested - Sending Info	☒ Attempted ☒ Completed
7. Steven Darling	703-557-8154	Supply Chain Manager	At NY Office - 212-989-8877	☒ Attempted ☐ Completed
8. Kathryn Cornell	703-726-8597	IT Supervisor	Happy - Asked for info - may know someone	☒ Attempted ☒ Completed
9. Paul Seaton	704-548-4498	Finance Manager	Connect - Sending me resume - sounds good	☒ Attempted ☒ Completed
10. Rich Marson	540-449-8264	IT Field / ???	Couldn't Talk - Calling me tomorrow at 10 AM	☒ Attempted ☐ Completed
11. Jason Taylor	703-849-5866	Distribution	Wrong number??	☒ Attempted ☒ Completed
12.				☐ Attempted ☐ Completed
13.				☐ Attempted ☐ Completed
14.				☐ Attempted ☐ Completed
15.				☐ Attempted ☐ Completed

Candidate Action Items

Name	Action Item	Notes	Priority	Status
1. Cindy Huddleston	Background Check	Making an offer as soon as check goes through	High	☐ Attempted ☒ Completed
2. Tim Smith	E-mail Job Description	Possible Candidate for IT Job	Medium	☐ Attempted ☒ Completed
3. Bill Marshall	Set Interview	Also Get References -	High	☐ Attempted ☐ Completed
4. Marsha Billings	Background Check	Making an offer for PR Position	High	☐ Attempted ☒ Completed
5. Jenny Gilford	Follow - Up Call	Send Out Pre-employment package	Medium	☐ Attempted ☐ Completed
6. Christy Reistrup	E-mail Job Description	Spoke with her today .e-mail Mktg. description	Medium	☐ Attempted ☒ Completed
7. Kathryn Cornell	Email - Description	Follow-up on 8/20/05 - knows someone	Medium	☐ Attempted ☒ Completed
8. Bob Tanner	Thank you note	Thank for referral of Sue Painter	Medium	☐ Attempted ☒ Completed
9. Candice Turner	Set-Drug Screen	On Vacation through next week	Low	☐ Attempted ☐ Completed

NOTES

** Really need to get more candidates for the Finance Position!! Been open for too long.
Check into attending local user group meeting with S. Phillips - sounds like we can present our openings
Ping accounting about Ad budget - last month's report seems too high.
Send in company profile to Professor Keating at LU - local campus

Set time to take Dave Driscoll out for celebratory lunch - see if Fortuol wants to join us.

Send Dad Birthday Card!!!
Set Car Appointment
Find out when Sandy's shower is taking place

Activity Metrics

Timeframe	Connected Calls	Initial Interviews	Candidate Submittals	Manager Interviews	Offers	Placements
Weekly Goals	75	8	10	5	2	2
W-T-D Actual	42	6	4	4	2	2
Monthly Goals	300	32	40	20	10	10
M-T-D Actual	162	16	15	13	7	6

Copyright© Advanced Recruiting Trends - 2004

If you look at the bottom of Figure 12.2, you will see that it contains an area for Activity Metrics. Metrics are essentially the quantitative analysis of specific activities within the recruiting process. The axiom that "the past is the key to the future" has great relevance to recruiting, particularly with respect to optimizing how you utilize time. As will become apparent, documenting and tracking your activities will not only provide you with a tremendous opportunity to understand how you utilize time, but will enable you to evaluate your overall efficiency as well.

Performance ratios enable us to evaluate the relative efficiency of different aspects of the recruiting process. They are essentially a statistical means of characterizing and drawing conclusions about the relationship that exists between distinct activity areas within the recruiting lifecycle. Figure 12.3 on page 259 depicts a chart that characterizes the relationship between various components of the recruiting process.

In the Activity Metrics section of Figure 12.2, the specific activities being tracked include: Connected Calls, Initial Interviews, Candidate Submittals, Manager Interviews, Offers Extended, and Placements. These areas are by no means the only activities that can or necessarily should be tracked, but will be utilized here for discussion purposes.

Tracking these activities will provide an immediate sense of how much work you are performing in key areas of the recruitment lifecycle. For example, if I only have three connected outbound calls to prospective candidates in a given week, I probably shouldn't expect to be particularly successful in staffing existing openings. I simply haven't generated enough activity to have a realistic expectation for success. Measuring the total volume of work output in a given activity area provides a recruiter with a tangible appreciation for what has actually been accomplished and gives a baseline for understanding how time is utilized. Furthermore, once this data has been compiled, a recruiter is capable of looking at the overall efficiency of his or her efforts via performance ratios.

Figure 12.3

Ratio Analysis Example						
Monthly Activities		**Calls**	**Connects**	**Interviews**	**Submittals**	**Hiring Mgr. Int.**
		200	150	30	15	7
Calls	200		1.33:1	6.6:1	13.3:1	28.6:1
Connects	150	1.33:1		5:1	10:1	21.4:1
Interviews	30	6.6:1	5:1		2:1	4.28:1
Submittals	15	13.3:1	10:1	2:1		2.14:1
Hiring Mgr. Int.	7	28.6:1	21.4:1	4.28:1	2.14:1	
Placements	3	66.6:1	50:1	10:1	5:1	2.3:1

Figure 12.3 presents us with hypothetical monthly summary data for Attempted and Connected Calls, Interviews, Submittals, Hiring Authority Interviews, and Placements. All of the activity numbers reflected within the grid are for discussion purposes and are not indicative of acceptable activity levels. With the exception of Placements, each activity area is labeled on both the X and Y axis of the grid.

In this sample, 200 calls to prospects were attempted with 150 calls being connected. The grid further reflects that 30 initial interviews (either face-to-face or on the phone) were conducted and that 15 individuals were submitted for hiring authority consideration. This resulted in seven candidate interviews with hiring authorities which led to three hires.

The ratios highlighted throughout the grid reflect the degree of efficiency between various activity areas. If you attempt 200 phone calls in a month and have 150 connected calls (where you speak to a prospective candidate), you can determine the efficiency of your calling process by dividing 200 by 150 (200/150 = 1.33). So, you can conclude that for every 1.33 calls that you attempt, you will get a connected call, a 1.33:1 ratio. Similarly, if you divide your 150 connected calls by the 30 interviews that you have conducted (150/30 = 5), you can conclude that for every five connected calls, you are likely to schedule one interview, thus producing a 5:1 ratio between connected calls and interviews.

The lower the ratio is between two activity areas, the more efficient your process and theoretically your utilization of time. In examining the interview to submittal ratio, for example, you can conclude that for every two interviews conducted, you are likely to make one candidate submittal to a hiring authority. In terms of relative efficiency, a 2:1 ratio is pretty good, particularly when considering that the optimal ratio between two activity areas is 1:1.

The greatest value in evaluating performance ratios comes from the insight that they can provide into aspects of your recruiting process that can potentially be improved. If you know that your connected call to interview ratio is 5:1, you may want to look at whether you are communicating with the right prospective candidate audience. If you can find a way to make the same number of connected calls, but increase interviews from 30 to 37, you will end up with a connected call to interview ratio of 4:1, which represents a 20 percent increase in efficiency between these two activity areas.

Ratio analysis enables you to ask yourself thoughtful questions about specific aspects of your process. I distinctly recall working with a recruiter who had terrific interview and submittal numbers, but suffered a significant drop-off in the areas of hiring authority interviews and placements over a three month timeframe.

The drop-off was so significant that we knew something must be amiss within the front-end of her process. We sat down to talk about aspects of her recruiting process, and our discussion turned to the candidate interview phase. She had been conducting far more candidate interviews than anyone else in the department, but had little to show for her efforts. I had her walk me through her typical candidate interview process, which seemed fine at a high level. As I probed on the amount of time that she was spending with each prospect, however, I discovered why the quantity of her initial interviews was higher than the norm. She was completing these meetings in less than 30 minutes, which is not enough time to really learn about a candidate and what they were seeking, let alone establish any meaningful rapport.

Because the initial interviews were so brief, she had failed to capture key information about her prospects. She would submit candidates to interested hiring authorities, but without adequately qualifying candidate interest in the opportunities at hand. The net result was that candidates were regularly opting out of the process.

This recruiter accepted my recommendation to invest more time with each candidate and to delve deeper into understanding candidate motivators and how the opportunities that she was working correlated with each candidate's goals and objectives. The results were readily apparent. Over the next three months, the total number of candidate interviews dropped, but the ratio between submittals and hiring authority interviews improved dramatically, and placements began to occur almost immediately.

While we may have uncovered the deficiency in this recruiter's interview process without performing ratio analysis, having the ability to utilize tangible data unquestionably helped to pinpoint the problem. Ratio analysis is simply another way to evaluate performance and identify opportunities for potential improvement.

Staying Out of Reactive Mode

Recruiters have the ability to establish a proactive tone to the business day and to reduce the amount of time that is spent in "reactive mode." Earlier, I discussed the importance of breaking out the individual components of the recruitment lifecycle to better appreciate the actual scope of activities that must be performed.

While this exercise is very productive, it is of little use if a recruiter is typically in a reactive posture.

For example, voicemail and email enable you to quickly reach out and communicate with a spectrum of prospects; but the manner in which you react to voicemail and email may be significantly disrupting your work day. Immediately upon getting an audible or visual cue that they have received a new email or voicemail message, many people react like Pavlov's Dog and can't resist the urge to quickly check the message. I am not referring to times when a recruiter anticipates getting a critical email or voicemail message. I am talking about the compulsive habit of checking messages for the sake of checking messages.

If you are compulsive in checking messages, you are placing yourself into a reactive posture. Voluntarily responding to every email and voicemail message as it arrives throughout the day impacts how you utilize time. Chronic disruptions inevitably affect one's ability to pursue work with any significant degree of continuity. In many sports, athletes express the need to "get in the flow of the game." What they are really saying is that to be effective they need to optimize the degree to which they can focus or concentrate on the task at hand. With rare exception, both the quality of your work day and the quantity of work output will suffer if you allow regular disruptions to occur.

The easiest way to reduce being placed in reactive mode by email and voicemail is to ignore them. Close your email inbox when you are set to make outbound recruiting calls. Check email at defined intervals during the day, rather than every time a new message appears. You should check voicemail periodically, but try to differentiate between those calls that must be addressed right away and those that can wait until later. If you have administrative support, instruct them to filter the really important calls from those that are a lower priority.

There are other ways that you can protect your time and stay out of reactive mode. If you are an in-house recruiter and support specific hiring authorities with whom you regularly communicate, it may be productive to condition them to contact you during specific timeframes. Providing good customer service doesn't have to mean that you must always deviate from your daily plan to make yourself available at the discretion of a hiring authority.

Below are several examples of the kinds of messages you might receive from a hiring authority that could significantly impact your daily plan:

"Hi Sue, this is Tom in Accounting. I need you to swing by my office as soon as possible so that we can discuss several positions I have in the works. It's 10:00 AM right now – if you can stop by in the next 45 minutes, I can give you the details."

"Hi Steve, this is Ellen in Marketing. I have set a meeting up for tomorrow at 3:00 PM to discuss departmental staffing requirements. See you then."

"Hi Sue, this is Dan in Sales. As you know, Bill Johnson will be joining us next week. Bill called with a couple of quick questions about benefits. I know that technically this isn't your area, but Teresa in Benefits is at an offsite meeting until mid-afternoon, and I thought you could speak to Bill's questions. He can be reached at 867-5309. Thanks for handling this for me."

Again, hiring managers are your ultimate customers, but you cannot expect them to have any intuition or appreciation for the activities that consume a recruiter's day. It's not their job to understand recruiting. It's not their job to understand how a recruiter has structured his or her day. Recruiters who wish to protect their daily plan must talk with their hiring managers and establish clear parameters regarding their availability.

You can accomplish this objective by meeting with managers early on to explain that you have allocated specific times during the week expressly for meeting or communicating with them. Let them know that you will certainly drop what you are doing to assist them in emergency or high priority situations, but that you would be extremely appreciative and will ultimately be able to better serve their needs if they try to accommodate your schedule.

This same approach can be utilized with active candidates who are in various phases of the recruitment process. Establishing clear expectations up front about when you can be reached will dramatically reduce the number of "follow-up" or maintenance calls that will otherwise randomly come in throughout your day. Again, candidates can't be expected to appreciate the composition of a recruiter's workday, so you have to let them know when they can reach you.

Because recruiting is such a dynamic sales process with an array of moving parts, it is imperative that recruiters place considerable thought into optimizing their fundamental use of time. Evaluating your recruiting process and prioritizing strategic and tactical activities will better enable you to map out what needs to get done and to determine optimal workflows. Furthermore, you will save time as well as identify potential opportunities for improving your overall process and productivity by taking steps to stay out of a reactive posture and by regularly evaluating the efficiency of your efforts.

Afterword

My core motivation for writing this book was to address key aspects of the talent acquisition and recruitment sales lifecycles that I regard to be integral to successfully identifying and engaging passive candidates.

There is little doubt that the employment landscape is undergoing a significant evolution. Gaps are emerging in various market niches where the demand for talent outstrips the available supply of skilled workers. This reality means that effective talent acquisition will increasingly require that organizations and recruiters possess the ability and wherewithal to proactively navigate within the passive candidate marketplace.

Legacy recruitment channels such as job boards and newspaper ads will always have their place. As our economy continues to expand and the demand for talent accelerates, however, the relative effectiveness of these channels will diminish and organizations that are largely or entirely reliant upon these recruitment modes will suffer.

In this initial edition of Proactive Recruiting in a War For Talent Economy, I concentrated on the topics that struck me as being of greatest relevance to today's recruiting professional. Where applicable, I have attempted to address subject matter from both a strategic and a tactical perspective.

I have always regarded recruiting as a complex sales cycle. I believe that in the near future corporate leaders will become profoundly aware of the fact that recruiting is not only a front-line sales vocation, but is as pivotal to the success of an organization as traditional revenue generating functions. Talent can no longer be regarded as a commodity. Organizations that recognize this reality sooner, as opposed to later have a distinct opportunity to acquire a competitive advantage in their respective market sectors.

Implementing the recruiting techniques and strategies that I have addressed will not only enable you to add breadth to your recruiting arsenal, but will also enable you to recruit more effectively, more efficiently, and more holistically.

While I am a devout believer in the power and applicability of proactive recruiting techniques, implementation of the methodologies and approaches that I advocate are not a recruiting panacea. In recruiting, there are no silver bullets or magic cure-alls. Rome wasn't built in a day, and the process of proactively engaging passive candidates is something that progressively yields the greatest dividends over time.

I wish you sustained success in all of your recruiting endeavors. *Carpe Diem!*

Paul Siker

About The Author

Embarking on his recruiting career in 1987, Paul Siker is the Founder and CEO of Advanced Recruiting Trends, a recruitment training and consulting firm. He is also Managing Partner of The Artisan Group, an executive search firm.

Previously, Paul served as an Officer, Partner, and Senior Executive Search Consultant at The Guild Corporation, an undisputed leader in the Washington, D.C. recruitment marketplace. Over the last decade, The Guild Corporation experienced extensive growth by building a staff of 18 tenured recruiters and by achieving a client repeat business ratio in excess of 95 percent.

Following the sale of The Guild Corporation to SystemOne Technical Services (later acquired by TMP Worldwide), Paul continued to perform in managerial, leadership, and recruiting roles, and was instrumental in the creation and roll out of a comprehensive, division-wide recruitment training program.

Concurrent to his managerial responsibilities at Guild, SystemOne, and TMP Worldwide, Paul successfully executed assignments on a contingent, retained, and contract placement basis. In his career, he has placed hundreds of professionals into individual contributor, managerial, and executive officer level positions.

Paul has been a featured speaker at the American Staffing Association (ASA) World Expo and Convention, the New England Association of Personnel Services (NEAPS) Conference, and at the National Association of Personnel Services (NAPS) Annual Conference. Paul is a frequent presenter to firms seeking to implement recruiting and selling "best practices," and has regularly been cited in recruiting and employment articles by "The Washington Post," "National Business Employment Weekly," "Virginia Human Resources Today," and other trade publications.

Paul obtained a B.A. in Political Science from Wittenberg University and has also obtained the National Association of Personnel Services (NAPS) CPC (Certified Personnel Consultant) designation. He resides in Northern Virginia with his wife, Joni, and his sons, Steven and Scott.

Index